RACISM

Racism is as pertinent an issue today as it was twenty years ago. This fully updated new edition of *Racism* provides a thought-provoking account of the history and debate about the concept. Combining historical and theoretical analysis, it surveys the history of the ways in which European peoples have described and experienced non-Europeans, and summarizes the emergence and evolution of the concept of racism within the Western sociological tradition.

This edition brings the book up to date by reviewing recent developments in the debate and by looking at examples such as the war in the former Yugoslavia and the cases of Stephen Lawrence and Rodney King, as well as considering Islamophobia in Western societies. This book will be essential reading for students studying racism or ethnicity in sociology, anthropology and politics.

Robert Miles is Director of Study Abroad and Professor of Sociology and International Studies at the University of North Carolina, Chapel Hill. **Malcolm Brown** is Lecturer in Sociology at the University of Exeter.

KEY IDEAS

Series Editor: PETER HAMILTON, The Open University, Milton Keynes

Designed to complement the successful *Key Sociologists*, this series covers the main concepts, issues, debates, and controversies in sociology and the social sciences. The series aims to provide authoritative essays on central topics of social science, such as community, power, work, sexuality, inequality, benefits and ideology, class, family, etc. Books adopt a strong individual 'line' constituting original essays rather than literary surveys, and form lively and original treatments of their subject matter. The books will be useful to students and teachers of sociology, political science, economics, psychology, philosophy and geography.

Citizenship
KEITH FAULKS

Class
STEPHEN EDGELL

Community
GERARD DELANTY

Consumption
ROBERT BOCOCK

Culture
CHRIS JENKS

Globalization – second edition
MALCOLM WATERS

Lifestyle
DAVID CHANEY

Mass Media
PIERRE SORLIN

Moral Panics
KENNETH THOMPSON

Old Age
JOHN VINCENT

Postmodernity
BARRY SMART

Racism – second edition
ROBERT MILES AND MALCOLM BROWN

Risk
DEBORAH LUPTON

Sexuality
JEFFREY WEEKS

Social Capital
JOHN FIELD

Transgression
CHRIS JENKS

The Virtual
ROB SHIELDS

RACISM

SECOND EDITION

Robert Miles and Malcolm Brown

Routledge
Taylor & Francis Group

LONDON AND NEW YORK

First edition published 1989 by Routledge
2 Park Square, Milton Park, Abingdon, Oxon, OX14 4RN

Simultaneously published in the USA and Canada
by Routledge
270 Madison Ave, New York, NY 10016

Second edition 2003

Reprinted 2004

Transferred to Digital Printing 2006

Routledge is an imprint of the Taylor & Francis Group, an informa business

© 1989, 2003 Robert Miles and Malcolm Brown

Typeset in Garamond and Scala Sans by Keystroke,
Jacaranda Lodge, Wolverhampton
Printed and bound in Great Britain by
TJI Digital, Padstow, Cornwall

British Library Cataloguing in Publication Data
A catalogue record for this book is available from the British Library

Library of Congress Cataloging in Publication Data
A catalog record for this book has been requested

ISBN 10: 0-415-29676-5 (hbk)   ISBN 13: 978-0-415-29676-2 (hbk)
ISBN 13: 0-415-29677-3 (pbk)   ISBN 13: 978-0-415-29677-9 (pbk)

For Sara and Becca

When I was a boy, I used to wonder where my mother came from, how she got on this earth. When I asked her where she was from, she would say, 'God made me', and change the subject. When I asked her if she was white, she'd say, 'No. I'm light-skinned', and change the subject again. Answering questions about her personal history did not jibe with Mommy's view of parenting twelve curious, wild, brown-skinned children. . . . She never spoke about Jewish people as white. She spoke about them as Jews, which made them somehow different.

(McBride 1998: 15, 66–7)

The discourse promoting resistance to racism must not prompt identification with and in terms of categories fundamental to the discourse of oppression. Resistance must break not only with *practices* of oppression, although its first task is to do that. Resistance must oppose also the *language* of oppression, including the categories in terms of which the oppressor (or racist) represents the form in which resistance is expressed.

(Goldberg 1990: 313–14)

It is one of the penalties of toying with the race-notion that even a strong mind trying to repudiate it will find himself making assumptions and passing judgments on the basis of the theory he disclaims.

(Barzun 1965: 29–30)

Contents

Acknowledgements

It is ironic that the authors of a book which, at least partially, situates racism within a context of international migration should themselves have joined the internal and international migration flows since they started collaborating on this subject. Therefore, it is particularly important that we repeat the thanks expressed in the first edition to former colleagues at the University of Glasgow, especially Bruce Armstrong, Paula Cleary, Anne Dunlop, Jackie Lamont, Diana Kay, Nello Paoletti, Vic Satzewich and Edelweisse Thornley. In the same institution, we would particularly single out Dave Frisby for thanks. Elsewhere in Europe and the world, we wish to reiterate thanks to Frank Bovenkerk, Kristen Couper, Moustapha Diop, Han Enzinger, Marjan van Hunnik, Francien Keers, Marie de Lepervanche, Marel Rietman, Daniel Singer, Jeanne Singer-Kerel and Gilles Verbunt. We also restate the acknowledgement of financial support from the British Council, the Carnegie Trust for the Universities of Scotland, the EEC (as it then was) and the University of Glasgow.

There are others whose contribution to this second edition is also deserving of recognition. We would like to thank our colleagues at the University of Exeter and the University of North Carolina at Chapel Hill, and make particular mention of Tia De Nora, Charlie Kurzman, Nigel Pleasants, Dick Soloway, Katharine Tyler and Bob Witkin. The aforementioned universities also provided financial support, which made possible the completion of this work. We would also like to thank Mari Shullaw and James McNally at Routledge, and wish Mari the very best for her future life away from publishing.

For others who have contributed, we hope that our verbal thanks or grateful thoughts will count for as much as a written acknowledgement. Responsibility, of course, rests with ourselves.

This book is dedicated to our respective partners, whose support has been more than just academic.

Robert Miles and Malcolm Brown

I

SITUATING RACISM

INTRODUCTION

... even in the very midst of a battle in which one is unmistakably on one side against another, there should be criticism, because there must be critical consciousness if there are to be issues, problems, values, even lives to be fought for.

(Said 1983: 28)

Like many sociological concepts, racism has an everyday use and many everyday meanings. During the last fifty years or so, it has become a key idea in daily discourse as well as in sociological theory. Like other elements of 'common sense' discourse (Gramsci 1971: 323–33), much of the everyday language is uncritical, taken-for-granted. The concept of racism is also heavily negatively loaded, morally and politically. Thus, to claim that someone has expressed a racist opinion is to denounce them as immoral and unworthy. In sum, racism has become a term of political abuse. This presents special difficulties for the social scientist who defends the use of the concept. Whatever definition is offered has significance for not only academic work, but also political and moral debate.

While the principal objective of this book is to set out a case for the continued use of the concept of racism in sociological analysis, its first edition became known for two other arguments: its definition of racism; and its critique of the 'race relations paradigm'. While defining racism may seem pedantic and outmoded, it is *concretely* connected with political and moral debate. There is a strong argument, made by Goldberg (1993), for example, that a definition of racism needs to be 'grounded', based on empirical observation of racism, not a priori theorising. Such an argument is persuasive, and in tune with the Wittgenstinian sensibilities of twentieth-century philosophy, but it needs to be counterbalanced with the following *political* imperative. *If racism is defined as politically or morally unacceptable, there must be a reasonable consensus about what it is*. A definition of racism cannot establish simple criteria for deciding whether or not a given discourse is racist (though cf. Wetherell and Potter 1992: 15–16, 69–71), but in the absence of any definition, the concept becomes meaningless, and opposition to racism is hindered. If racism is defined too broadly – 'all white people are racists', for example, or even 'everyone is racist' – the concept again becomes meaningless, and racism escapes censure, for it becomes nothing worse than a product of cultural determinism or an expression of human nature. If racism is defined too narrowly – as an explicit belief in 'racial' hierarchy, for example – then discourses that would otherwise be regarded as racist may attain a degree of legitimacy. This acquires political urgency when we remember that extreme right-wing parties have tended (since the 1950s) to refer to themselves as nationalist, not racist. For example, the British National Party is not the British Racial Party, the French *Front National* is not the *Front Racial*, and its leader, Jean-Marie Le Pen, denounced his former deputy, Bruno Mégret, who had formed a rival 'nationalist' party, as 'racist'.

THE RACISM PARADIGM

If the first edition of this book was noted for its critique of the 'race relations paradigm' (see also Miles 1993), it has been argued that it created a 'racism paradigm' with its own shortcomings. Banton (2001) suggests that this paradigm is characterised by rejection of everyday language, one end of an acceptance–rejection continuum, and he proposes a middle way that separates the two. He argues: 'Some elements of the racial idiom are still needed in law' because 'the concept of a *racial group* is the price to be paid for a law against indirect discrimination'. Similarly: 'They are needed in social policy for combating discrimination and prejudice', while other elements 'are useful to the victim groups'. Consequently, social scientists talk in terms of 'race' when discussing policy issues, but 'they should seek ways of eliminating the racial idiom from their theoretical language' (2001: 184).

Banton's argument demands careful attention because of its reference to policy and political action, but it is appropriate to examine its presuppositions. While he sees social scientists as contributors to politico-legal debate, Banton's argument has the effect of separating social-scientific analysis from the everyday world of social interaction and language production. An acceptance of everyday language within social-scientific analysis has the virtue of recognising that such analysis takes place within the everyday world, that social scientists are social beings, and that our interactions are social interactions (which the social sciences purport to study). Nevertheless, such an approach subsumes social-scientific analysis under everyday interaction, whereas our approach utilises social-scientific analysis in a *critique* of everyday interaction, language production, the uses of everyday language within the social sciences, and of society itself.

Earlier, Banton argued in more general terms: 'Miles' claim that the sociology of race relations necessarily reifies race has not been substantiated, and the racism problematic has difficulties of its own' (1991: 129). In defence of the 'race relations' problematic, Banton points out that the use of the concept of 'race' in law has the effect of stigmatising, not legitimating, the false ideas inherent in racism. Against the racism problematic, he argues that it 'tended to neglect interpersonal relations, to aggregate aspects of behaviour that were best examined separately, and to represent racism as something with a life of its own that changed form as circumstances changed' (1991: 118). Elsewhere (1996b: 29), he claims that racism is an ideological notion which is 'used to construct and negotiate social relations', and that the concept of 'race relations' is only rhetorically linked to that of 'race'. In other words, racism is reified by the 'racism paradigm', not 'race' by the 'race relations paradigm'. Additionally, Banton implies that the racism paradigm reduces essential social relations to class (although he recognises that Marxism can represent a method rather than a doctrine), is doctrinaire in its wholesale rejection of the 'race relations paradigm', and ignores racial consciousness among oppressed racialised groups. Furthermore, the racism problematic 'reinforce[s]' notions of biological difference' when racism is conceived as 'directed only against physically distinctive categories of people' (1991: 129, 1996b: 24).

We deal with a number of these issues. First, Miles (1993: 5–7) has responded elsewhere to Banton's discussion of the legal issue. We add here that, although the term 'race' may be articulated with the *intention* of stigmatising racism, the extent to which this is *achieved* is questionable. For example, Banton's own research (1996a) has shown that the bureaucratic language of international law enables nation states to adopt different definitions of racial discrimination and different understandings of their legal obligations to further their foreign policy objectives and avoid taking action against racism 'at home', and has explicitly excluded any consideration of discrimination against 'non-citizens' (article 1.2 of the International Convention on the Elimination of All Forms of Racial Discrimination; see Banton 1996a: 321). Basing analysis or praxis on legal fiction is probably doomed to be counterproductive. This is probably why Gilroy (2000: 52) argues that we 'must step away from the pious ritual in which we always agree that "race" is invented but are then required to defer to its embeddedness in the world and to accept that the demand for justice requires us nevertheless innocently to enter the political arenas it helps to mark out'.

Second, Banton observes correctly that our approach represents racism as changing form according to circumstances. This emphasis on shifting meanings is taken up by other writers (e.g. Mac an Ghaill 1999; Wetherell and Potter 1992), and we continue to argue for its validity in this book. Banton himself summarises the reason for this approach, when he observes that most exponents of a racism problematic choose not to define racism 'because they do not conceive it as something independent of other social features' and it is 'not a static phenomenon' (Banton 1996b: 24–5). We do define racism, but we assert that it does interact with other social phenomena and that it is not static. Such a hypothesis is at least heuristic, because it enables us to 'ground' our definitions, as Goldberg advocates. Racism cannot be reduced to relations of class, agreed, but any analysis of racism that ignores class relations, especially those inherent in the political economy of migration, is in our view deficient. Mac an Ghaill (1999: 6) argues that 'recent cultural theorising' (for example that inspired by postmodernism, with its near-obsession with shifting meanings) 'needs to recover the history of earlier class-based accounts and in the process re-read "old times" texts as providing innovative understandings of racial conflict and social change'. So we must hold on to both ends of the chain, conceptualising racism as a continuous, yet fluid, phenomenon.

Third, there is racialised consciousness among oppressed racialised groups, but they are groups by virtue of being racialised (socially defined as a 'race'), not vice versa. They are defined as a 'race' by others, acquire a group identity and become oppressed, and then use the idiom of 'race' in relation to themselves, their identities and grievances. This is borne out by African-American history, from pre-colonial Africa to slavery to an African-American 'racial' consciousness. None of this is denied by our critique of the 'race relations' paradigm.

Fourth, if racism has been conceived in terms of the physical distinctiveness of its victims, academic and political developments throughout the 1990s have shown the poverty of this conceptualisation. It is impossible to describe how Bosnian Muslims are physically distinguishable from Bosnian Serbs, or Rwandan Hutus from Tutsis, yet imagined distinctions between these groups produced discourses of racism and some of the worst genocides of the second half of the twentieth century. In reality, the poverty of conceptualising racism in terms of the physical distinctiveness of its victims should have been clear much earlier. The development of racism went hand in hand with the development of the nation state and nationalist ideology. Although racism and nationalism are not the same ideology, they have much in common, and, as Balibar (1991) has demonstrated, they depend on each other, as it were, for existence-as-such.

RACISM AS IDEOLOGY

We have already observed that the first edition of this book was noted for its definition of racism, and this included defining racism as ideology. Mac an Ghaill (1999: 28) points to the definition of racism as ideology as a central issue in the ensuing debate, and identifies Gilroy, and Anthias and Yuval-Davis, as offering the most important criticisms.

For Gilroy (1987: 22ff.), the initial criticism is not so much of the notion of racism-as-ideology *per se*, but of the identification of 'race' as 'nothing more than an ideological effect', in contrast to the 'radical' or 'black' writers who 'use "race", in spite of its illusory status, to "encourage the formation of a particular political force"'. The problem, then, with conceiving of racism as ideology is the implication that racism distortedly represents human beings, and the social relations between human beings, specifically in terms of 'race', and this undermines attempts to create a 'race' consciousness among the *victims* of racism. That, in turn, undermines their 'racial' solidarity and an anti-racist praxis of 'black protest and self-organisation'.

Philosophically, it is possible to believe the wrong thing for the right reason. The matter of whether 'races' exist, or whether the concept of 'race' represents human beings and social relations in a distorted manner, are epistemological and ontological questions, to which the answer is unambiguously that they do not exist, and that the concept does create such a distorted representation. It is indeed possible to use the idea of 'race' to generate anti-racist mobilisation or legislation against indirect racism, but this does not alter its epistemological and ontological status.

However, Gilroy's concept of 'race' is not necessarily biological or somatic; it is more a concept that delineates a certain form of social stratification – like class stratification, but not identical to it, and certainly not subsumable under it. In contrast, when we define racism as ideology, and the concept of 'race' as central to that ideology, we refer to the pseudo-biological concept of 'race', and do not deny that the structure of social stratification can be and is racialised. Moreover, Gilroy's later work (2000) represents a significant shift in perspective and highlights the illusory status of 'race'. This represents a theoretical convergence between two intellectual traditions that have perhaps been too simply identified as antagonistic.

Anthias and Yuval-Davis (1993: 1–2) (like Banton) criticise the rejection of everyday language, and (perhaps paradoxically) the *definition* of ideology that is offered in the first edition of this book ('any discourse which, as a whole (but not necessarily in terms of all its component parts) represents human beings, and the social relations between human beings, in a distorted manner'). They write:

> This is a very narrow and in fact old polarisation between ideological and true statements. Even as a Marxist notion, it has now been largely supplanted by the development of Marx's other definition, which regards ideology as embedded in the historic *Weltanschauung* or world-view. The contributions by Althusserian . . . and post-structuralist writers as well as the development of Gramsci's approach . . . are now widely disseminated. Miles's retention of the notion of ideology as 'false' is therefore somewhat surprising . . .
>
> (1993: 13)

Apart from the implication that an older approach is necessarily worse than a contemporary one, and the assumption that Marx's two definitions of ideology are necessarily incompatible (whereas 'falsity' is embedded in the *Weltanschauung*, and hegemonic discourse, by its very nature, represents human beings and social relations in a distorted, that is, unequal and anti-creative, manner), the precise definition of ideology is not important. Rather, it is the *content* of this ideology that is important. Is the notion that humanity is divided into biologically or somatically-determined 'races' false? Does racism represent human beings in a distorted manner? Does it represent the relations between human beings in a distorted manner? Is it part of the historic and hegemonic *Weltanschauung*? The answer to all these questions is affirmative. Racism is an ideology in all these senses.

Racism postulates the existence of discrete 'races', and attributes a negative evaluation to one or some of these putative 'races' (usually, though not always, the 'race' or 'races' to which the person articulating the racist ideology does not regard himself or herself as belonging). In this sense, as Mac an Ghaill (1999: 28) points out, racism is produced ideologically and discursively. He writes that 'with the ascendancy of cultural analysis,

Miles' work on ideology is an essential reminder that racism is the object of ideological and discursive labouring'. The argument that racism is a form of ideology still holds, and is essential background to other work on racism produced since the first edition of this book. Although Wieviorka (1995: 37) identifies three different 'types' of racism – a set of prejudices, opinions and attitudes that may be held by individuals or groups; a set of exclusionary practices, including exclusion from the labour market and subjection to violence; and a political programme or ideology – there is a potential consensus that racism is *primarily* an ideology (see Brown 2000), but *manifested* in different ways, such as those identified by Wieviorka, or in terms of the different discourses identified by Taguieff (1987, 1995, 2001). We therefore retain tenaciously the conception of racism as an ideology because it represents human beings, and social relations, in a distorted manner while never denying that, qua ideology, racism can be simultaneously deeply embedded in the contemporary *Weltanschauung* and the focus of struggle on the part of those who challenge its hegemony.

Racism is best conceived primarily as an ideology for at least one other reason. Racism, qua ideology, was created historically and became interdependent with the ideology of nationalism. The origins of racism are discussed in Chapter 1, and the interdependence of racism and nationalism is a complex issue, discussed in Chapter 6. We simply note here that racism and nationalism arose together, are often articulated together, and have an influence on each other. Kedourie (1993: 1) argues, somewhat simplistically, that: 'Nationalism is a doctrine invented in Europe at the beginning of the nineteenth century'; while Hobsbawm (1962: 132–45, 1990: 14ff.) argues, in a more sophisticated manner, that nationalism was a creation of the 'dual revolution' (that is, the French Revolution and Industrial Revolution). Nationalism developed throughout the nineteenth century, reaching an initial apogée in the 1848 'springtime of nations', and a historical climax in the fascist period of 1930s Europe (see Nairn 1981: 337, 345–8), a period noted for the intensity and consequences of racism. Racism's birth (like nationalism, after a long gestation) was also in the aftermath of the dual revolution (though influenced by other factors), it became hegemonic in the nineteenth century, and survives even while now being subject to widespread challenge. In present-day Europe, anti-immigrant sentiment and opposition to asylum seekers combine racist language with a language of defending the nation state (see, for example, Wetherell and Potter 1992; van Dijk 2000).

On the mutual influence of the ideologies of nationalism and racism, Balibar writes:

> The excess that racism represents with respect to nationalism, and therefore what it adds to nationalism, tends at one and the same time to universalise it, correcting in sum its lack of universality, and to particularise it, correcting its lack of specificity. In other words, racism simply adds to the ambiguity of nationalism, not only on the theoretical plane – in many respects, racism has supplied nationalism with the only theories it has – but also on the practical plane, which means that through racism, nationalism engages in a 'blind pursuit', a metamorphosis of its ideal contradictions into material ones.
>
> (1991: 54)

In other words, the 'nation' will inevitably identify itself with the 'race', because historical, cultural, political and other distinguishing factors of a 'nation' are ultimately subsumed under the idea of 'race'. This inevitably leads to a nationalistic purism, an ideology that 'we' must not be contaminated by 'them' (whether 'they' are German Jews in the 1930s, Bosnian Muslims in the 1990s, or asylum seekers in early twenty-first century Europe), but this is contradicted by the supernationalistic ethos of racism – hence Balibar's 'blind pursuit'. At the same time, the ideology of nationalism, under the influence of racism, develops into an ethnocentric conception of humanity and, where the national unit is powerful enough, a programme of cultural imperialism. Importantly, racism is implicitly defined as an excess of nationalism, therefore dependent on nationalism for existence-as-such, while it also exerts influence on the ideology of nationalism, as we have seen.

For these reasons, and in these ways, the argument that racism is a form of ideology, if unfashionable for some, is important and worth repeating, like a Socratic gadfly that repeatedly pesters the Athenian cultural theories of racisms, ethnicities, identities and difference that all too often show little interest in exploring the material context of the capitalist world economy.

RACISM AS A MORAL QUESTION

Racism distorts human beings and social relations, brutalises and dehumanises its object, and in so doing also brutalises and dehumanises those who articulate it. Racism is a denial of humanity (substituting, as it does, 'races' for 'the human race') and a means of legitimating inequality (particularly inequality explicit in class structures). It is therefore a problem for all in a social context where it is articulated and sustains exclusionary practices. As a phenomenon of social interaction, all who potentially witness it have a role in its identification, explanation, condemnation and elimination. This role is sometimes specific, sometimes complex. Were we to adapt Habermas's view (see Historikerstreit 1987: 62–76, 95–7, 243–55, 383–6), we would conclude that an empathic understanding (*Verstehen*) of racism is undesirable. This must be considered and respected, and some may conclude that it is correct, even to the extent that any attempt to understand racism is undesirable because of the danger of empathy with a brutal and dehumanising ideology.

Even though attempting to understand racism may be accompanied by certain hazards, we submit that the alternative is more problematic. An absence of *Verstehen* can translate into a lack of awareness, an 'affected ignorance' (see Moody-Adams 1994, 1997: 101–5) of the brutality and dehumanisation inherent in racism, a belief (frequently articulated) that there is 'no problem here' or that racism 'is not an issue any more'. However, the moral question is not simple, and the moralistic tone of much anti-racist discourse is criticised by Taguieff (1995) as exemplifying a 'good-and-evil' approach that has more to do with the categories of vulgar medieval Christian theology than social-scientific analysis. If a *simple* condemnation of racism is inadequate, where are we left?

This question is particularly difficult to answer because, surprisingly, the moral question of racism is not often discussed in academic literature. When it is discussed, the point is sometimes to establish the superiority of one moral philosophy over another (see, for example, Hare's article 'What is wrong with slavery?' (1986), which is really a defence of utilitarianism on the grounds that it shows *why* slavery is wrong). There are notable exceptions, such as the American collection edited by Babbitt and Campbell (1999), and it is implicit in works on anti-racism (e.g. Lloyd 1998; Bonnett 2000). It is also *implicit* in most social-scientific works on racism, but does not dominate the discussion to the same degree.

Essays collected by Babbitt and Campbell (1999) relate the moral question to issues concerning the definition of racism. Blum (1999: 79–97) draws our attention to the conflicting beliefs that only 'white' people can be racist, and that all racism is equally uncondonable. Here, a definition of racism (essentially, what 'whites' do to 'blacks') is juxtaposed with a moral claim (racism is always bad, whoever the victim). Blum argues for a position of 'moral asymmetry', according to which 'no ethnic or racial group is immune from racism' (1999: 79) – correctly, since ethnic and racial groups are imagined, or constructed, but not real – but that some articulations of racism are morally worse than others, sometimes, but not necessarily, because the perpetrator is 'white'. Once more, we see that the definition of racism is inseparable from the moral and political questions.

Bonnett (2000: 4–7) identifies seven 'commonly expressed reasons why racism is opposed': (i) that racism is socially disruptive; (ii) it is foreign; (iii) it sustains the ruling class; (iv) it hinders the progress of 'our community'; (v) it is an intellectual error; (vi) it distorts and erases people's identities; (vii) it is anti-egalitarian and socially unjust. More prescriptively, Martin Luther King, in his 'Letter from the Birmingham Jail' written in 1963 (King 2000: 64–84), enables us to identify seven reasons why racism is wrong. King does not discuss racism so much as segregation, but we can extract an implicit conception of racism, defined by its concrete manifestations (in line with Goldberg's approach).

First, King states that segregation (and implies that racism) is wrong because it is damaging to its victims, causing them, for example, to suffer violence and poverty (e.g. 2000: 69). Second, segregation (and racism) is wrong because it leads to 'reverse racism' – for example the black-nationalist ideology of Elijah Muhammad's movement, with its belief that white people are devils (2000: 75) – which in turn creates wider social conflict. There is a link here with the question of moral asymmetry. No reasonable person argues that 'black' hatred of 'white' people is a good thing: at best, it is an unfortunate consequence of 'white' racism directed against 'black' people. This consequence exacerbates the wrongness of the ideology of racism.

Third, King argues that segregation (racism) is wrong because it is damaging, not only to its victims, but to a whole society and even to the whole of humanity: 'Injustice anywhere is a threat to justice everywhere. We are caught in an inescapable network of mutuality, tied in a single garment of destiny. Whatever affects one directly, affects all indirectly' (2000: 65). The simplicity of this point may lead some to regard it as excessively idealistic, even naïve. This would be a mistake. Enlightenment and post-Enlightenment thinkers like Adam Smith and Karl Marx asserted the economic interdependence of nations, and the early sociologists showed that societies do not exist as discrete and isolated entities, identifiable with a nation state or a local community. Rather, they thought in terms of human society, or at least modern society, and recognised the diffusion of ideas, cultural practices and social norms across artificial boundaries.

Fourth, for King, racism is wrong because it substitutes prejudice, myths and half-truths for creative analysis, objective appraisal, higher understanding and brotherhood. King identifies racism with ignorance, and non-violent struggle against racism with the advancement of human understanding (2000: 67–8). One of the arguments identified by Bonnett, listed above, is that racism is wrong because it is an intellectual error. This poses a risk of confusing two senses of the word 'wrong' (namely the moral sense and the positive sense). Nevertheless, if the search for truth, or commitment to truth, is a moral commitment, and racism entails propositions that are contrary to the truth, then a commitment to oppose racism is a moral commitment, and racism is morally wrong. This may be difficult to sustain with a relativist notion of truth, or in the context of a moral commitment to a plurality of truths. However, a moral relativist is unlikely to contradict the principle that racism is wrong, because racism undermines the basis of relativism: the equality of different cultural values, and the benefits of cultures exchanging moral ideas to produce a still greater plurality of values and truths.

King's fifth point is that racism is wrong because it reverses moral developments and advances that have been accomplished historically, for example the 'most sacred values' of the Judeo-Christian tradition, or the elevation of freedom and democracy in the American Constitution and Declaration of Independence (2000: 83). This entails an appeal to progress, one that is compatible with a range of sociological traditions, including the Marxist one, and that has not been entirely eradicated by postmodern critiques of progress.

Sixth, racism is wrong because oppressed people have a birthright of freedom that racism denies them. This argument presupposes an essential human nature which seems difficult, if not impossible, to identify or even justify from a sociological or anthropological perspective. It is not yet a moral-law argument – rather, it is a discourse of rights qua an attribute of human beings. Human beings, by virtue of the way we are, have certain rights (2000: 76). However out of step with social-scientific theory since Foucault, the concept of human nature is essential to the theories of Chomsky, Lévi-Strauss and others. The human nature, according to King, has reminded the African-American of the birthright of freedom, while surrounding discourses, and social-cultural events, have transformed an inner yearning into an achievable political project.

Finally, racism is wrong because it is unjust, out of harmony with the moral law. Without doubt, this is the most normative statement in King's letter. In response to criticisms that participants in the civil rights movement had broken the law (as a result of which King was himself in the Birmingham Jail), King (2000: 70) argues that there are two types of laws, just and unjust, and that an unjust law should not be considered to be a law. How does one distinguish between them? He responds with the following argument:

> An unjust law is a code that a numerical or power majority group compels a minority to obey but does not make binding on itself. This is *difference* made legal. By the same token, a just law is a code that a majority compels a minority to follow and that it is willing to follow itself. This is *sameness* made legal.
>
> (2000: 71)

For example, the 'Jim Crow' laws were enacted by legislatures that represented the majority, but by denying the minority the right to vote, they lost democratic legitimacy. The increasingly draconian laws on political asylum and the rights of refugees in Western Europe constitute a comparable case (cf. Zolberg *et al.* 1989: 3–33, 258–82; Lambert 1995; Joly 1996). Legislation is enacted against a minority, making impossible demands upon them (such as the requirement to obtain a visa before fleeing persecution) that are not applicable to the majority whose demands are supposedly expressed in such laws. Where the law – the positive-judicial law, not the moral law – is racist, King argues, racism becomes damaging to the legitimacy of law, including the moral law (2000: 72).

While Bonnett's account offers sociological descriptions of why racism is opposed, King's analysis is firmly grounded on moral terrain. We cite this to suggest that racism is wrong within a range of ethical and political frameworks. Some of King's arguments have a particular resonance within particular political traditions: for example, the historical argument is comparable with analyses of racism in the Marxist tradition; the consequentialist arguments are likely to appeal to a communitarian consciousness; and the argument based on the birthright of freedom resonates within a liberal context. The same can be said of Bonnett's points, for example the third reason has a strongly Marxist flavour, while the first and second appeal to a centre-right consciousness, and the seventh is significant in moderate socialist and social-democratic discourses.

RACISM AS A POLITICAL QUESTION

These moral arguments assist us to understand (although do not explain in full) why, in the early twenty-first century, only small minorities of people voluntarily and positively describe themselves as racists. There is an official and unofficial consensus that those who express racist beliefs and/or act in accordance with such beliefs should be condemned, although the rationale varies. Furthermore, the consensus is grounded in the knowledge that racist beliefs are discredited scientifically and in widespread public knowledge of a number of historical events. Examples include the slave trade, the Nazi Holocaust, segregation in the southern United States, and apartheid in South Africa. All of these events led to the deaths of large numbers of people, and all were legitimated to various degrees by racism. Comparable, albeit less well-known, examples persist in the present day.

This consensus may have begun to break down in Western Europe (and elsewhere) since the 1970s. In the 1980s, political parties expressing demands and policies not unlike those of Fascist groups in the 1930s gained political representation in national and supranational parliaments. In the 1990s, some have gained a share of executive power (for example in Austria and Italy), and they may have become regarded as a normal, even if peripheral, feature of the political landscape. During this period, there has been a growth of violence against certain populations within Western Europe, often legitimated by claims that the victims are in some way or another inferior (Castles *et al.* 1984; EEC 1986), or that they are 'illegal immigrants' and 'bogus asylum seekers' who have 'invaded' Western countries where they have no right to be (e.g. UNHCR 2000; Harding 2000). These explicit expressions of racism have not occurred in a vacuum. Despite protestations of opposition to racism, a wider range of organisations and institutions, including the state itself, have actively and passively discriminated against minority populations. These populations are disproportionately represented in low-paid manual work and poor-quality housing, and are more likely to be unemployed. Refugees who are categorised as 'illegal immigrants' are in a particularly precarious position.

Furthermore, minority populations have been subject to incidents of arbitrary violence, to which the authorities have apparently turned a blind eye. In Britain, the murder of Stephen Lawrence in London rightly became a cause célèbre, particularly as nobody was convicted, and the subsequent official inquiry (Macpherson 1999) showed that 'institutional racism' had hampered the police investigation. There was a consensus that something had to be done to ensure that such a situation could never reoccur, but within months police and politicians were complaining that 'political correctness' was hampering their 'operational effectiveness', while Stephen Lawrence's father and a member of the inquiry complained about arbitrary police harassment. The suspicion, if not the claim, is that widespread practices of exclusion are motivated or legitimated by racism, as is the blind eye turned by agents of the state.

Simultaneously, during these three decades, there have emerged groups committed to action to highlight and resist the consequences of racism, some of which have been from within the populations who have been the objects of racist agitation, exclusion and violence (see, for example, ALTARF 1984; Lloyd 1998; Bonnett 2000). They have exposed the contradiction between the official consensus and the actual practice, and have played a major role in retaining the issue of racism on the political agenda. They have been joined by other sections of the population in Western Europe concerned about the rise of Fascist parties and the increase in racist violence, but also about other, less obvious manifestations of racism. Together, they constitute in a broad sense an anti-racist movement, though often disagreeing about means and objectives. Thus, the historical legacy and contemporary political practice interact to focus public attention on the unfavourable treatment and position of certain groups of people. Both in order to ensure that such events as the Holocaust are never repeated and to relieve economic and political disadvantages, a moral and political appeal is made for an active commitment to anti-racism.

Within this arena of political activism, the concept of racism is also the object of political and ideological struggle. Some might argue that the writing of another academic book is the least important task when there are many other, more practical, objectives to be achieved. But the academic project cannot so easily be dismissed. Not only are there people wishing to learn about the nature and origin of racism, but the claims and objectives of the somewhat amorphous anti-racist movement cannot themselves go unquestioned when unwarranted assertions are made about the beast that is to be vanquished. As has been said on countless occasions concerning the unity of theory and practice, if the analysis is wrong, then it is likely that the political strategy will not achieve the intended objectives. Hence, we make no apology for this product of 'armchair reflection' and ethnographic observation. We are not ignorant of the nature and course of the struggles that have occurred, nor unaware that academics are participant members of various social collectivities, with the consequent responsibilities that follow. We offer this book as an expression of our own committed opposition to racism, without apology or reservation.

CONCLUSION

The approach taken in this book, sometimes labelled the 'racism paradigm' or 'problematic', has certain features. First, we offer a limited definition of racism-as-ideology, attempting to walk the tightrope between a deflated concept of racism and an over-inflated one. If the racism paradigm is regarded as an extreme approach to the subject, we are situating it in the *via media*. Second, we utilise a social-scientific analysis of racism for a critique of everyday-language concepts of 'race' and 'racism' (cf. Miles 1993; Miles and Torres 1999). Third, we emphasise the shifting meanings of racism, on the one hand, and the constant importance of class and the political economy of migration, on the other. To put this differently, we define racism a priori, but flexibly, recognising that the nature of racism can and does change, and prepared to ground the (a priori or revised) definition in empirical observation. Fourth, we reject an analysis of racism in terms of a phenotypically identifiable victim, proposing instead an analysis in terms of the historical development of racism and nationalism (in the context of capitalism) which has made both ideologies interdependent. Fifth, we recognise that racism is a political and moral issue as well as a social-scientific one, and this intersection of issues makes the concept of racism politically, morally and sociologically complex.

So, the argument of this book is not that racism and related exclusionary practices are a minor, even insignificant, determinant of the structural position and experience of racialised populations. Rather, it is that the influence of racism and exclusionary practices is always a component part of a wider structure of multiple disadvantage and exclusion (including class); the major challenge is to contextualise the impact of racism and related exclusionary practices, partly to highlight the specificity of that impact, and partly to demonstrate the simultaneous continuities in the class positions and experiences of, for example (in the case of Britain), people of Asian and Caribbean origin and people of indigenous origin. In other words, in the light of the extensive evidence of the existence and impact of racism and related exclusionary practices, the task is to unravel the different forms and levels of determination, the interaction between racism, sexism, nationalism and the exclusionary practices derived from these ideologies, in the context of the reproduction of the capitalist mode of production.

1

REPRESENTATIONS OF THE OTHER

INTRODUCTION

Migration, determined by the interrelation of production, trade and warfare, has been a precondition for the meeting of human individuals and groups over thousands of years. In the course of this interaction, imagery, beliefs and evaluations about the Other have been generated and reproduced in order to explain the appearance and behaviour of those with whom contact has been established, and to formulate a strategy for interaction and reaction. The consequence has been the production of 'representations' (cf. Moscovici 1981, 1982, 1984) of the Other, images and beliefs which categorise people in terms of real or attributed differences when compared with Self ('Us'). There is, therefore, a dialectic of Self and Other in which the attributed characteristics of Other refract contrasting characteristics of Self, and vice versa. This is frequently a theme of cultural analyses of 'identity' or 'identities', which are not simply 'biographical' or 'reflexive projects' (cf. Giddens 1991), because our representations of the Other are important ingredients of our own identities. This is not a new insight, for postmodern (and post-postmodern) thinking on the subject reflects earlier concerns of existentialist writers (e.g. Sartre 1943, 1960). In any case, representations of the Other have a much deeper history, which this chapter traces historically (from the Greco-Roman period) and geographically (from inside and outside Europe).

The first intention of this chapter is to describe the content of the aforementioned images, beliefs and evaluations concerning the Other. Our focus is on representations generated within the Western world about populations elsewhere. However, other such representations have been refracted through European discourses and literatures, so they constitute, paradoxically, *Western* representations of the Other, not vice versa. Apparently, the Muslim world represented the populations beyond its boundaries specifically in terms of religion (Lewis 1982: 64). Also, those populations with whom contact was established by European merchant capitalists, some of whom were later colonised, represented the European merchants, soldiers and administrators in drawings, paintings and carvings, as well as in the written word, and on a variety of artefacts. These images were allegedly often stereotypical, or represented the Other in terms of their own physical and cultural norms (Volkenkundig Museum Nusantara 1986). Finally, European explorers and missionaries report the fascination and, often, fear expressed by certain groups in Africa on their first contact with a person of European origin. One particular feature of Europeans that was reported as exciting interest was their skin colour (Cole 1972: 64; Hibbert 1984: 48, 62, 89, 101, 146).

Certainly, the consequences of the European presence were articulated by those who were its object, and in a manner that reflected the different experience and mode of existence of the colonised. In this literary example, André Brink constructs the following evaluation 'thought' by a descendant of the African population enslaved by the Dutch settlers:

> We of the Khoin, we never thought of these mountains and plains, these long grasslands and marshes as a wild place to be tamed. It was the Whites who called it wild and saw it filled with wild animals and wild people. To us it has always been friendly and tame. It has given us food and drink and shelter, even in the worst of droughts. It was only when the Whites moved in and started digging and breaking and shooting, and driving off the animals, that it really became wild.
>
> (Brink 1983: 21)

Such literary discourse, like the examples mentioned previously, raises the following question. Does this example reflect the thoughts of the Khoin people themselves, or does it reflect a European representation of the Khoin as 'noble savages'? Similarly, does Lewis's portrayal of Muslim representations of the (religious) Other reflect the 'real' thoughts of Muslim people, or a current Western perception of Muslims as unhealthily obsessed with religion?

It is probably impossible to answer this question on a case by case basis. However, the principle is pertinent: apparent representations of the Western Other are frequently interpreted in such a way as to constitute Western representations of the 'non-Western' Other. Arens (1979: 11–13) recounts a number of cases from East Africa where the local people believed that Europeans were cannibals. In Tanzania, where Arens did his own fieldwork, he was referred to as a '*mchinja-chinja*', which is translated as 'blood-sucker'. Locally, it was believed that:

> . . . a victim would be rendered unconscious and then hung head down in order to let the blood from the slit jugular drain into a bucket. The fluid was then transported by a fire engine to an urban hospital, where it was converted into red capsules. This pills were taken on a regular basis by Europeans who, I was informed, needed these potations to stay alive in Africa.
>
> (1979: 12)

This belief was not, however, arbitrary. Evidence was cited to justify it:

> . . . the British had tried unsuccessfully to mount a blood drive during World War II in their former colony for the African troops fighting overseas, and there was indeed a fire engine stationed not far away at a small airstrip, even though there had never been a fire. To some Africans, this apparently constituted enough circumstantial evidence to substantiate a European conspiracy to drink African blood. Upon reflection, similar beliefs about Africans on our part no longer seemed so reasonable.
>
> (1979: 13)

Of course, when this is recounted to a European audience, it can be seen as illustrative of the backwardness and ignorance of the Africans, since cannibalism is not normally practised in Europe. On the other hand, European travellers' tales of cannibalism in Africa, the Americas and the Pacific Islands are not seen as illustrative of European credulity, but, also, of 'native' backwardness – either they really were cannibals, or there was good reason, based on their backwardness, to believe that they were. So, Western representations of the Other, and Western refractions of the

Other's representation of the West, both create a particular Western image of the Other.

That said, our focus is on more directly *Western* representations of the Other. With this focus, our second intention is to demonstrate a shifting content and evaluation of the Other. Not all elements of representation change over time, but the *combination* of elements do. Furthermore, although certain representations may be dominant in any one period, they do not necessarily remain unchallenged. Hence, because imagery and belief change over time, it is possible to chart a history of representations. The recognition of this dynamic element in Western representations of the Other is the prelude to understanding a significant transformation in the method of European representation. Thus, and third, we demonstrate the emergence of 'scientific' criteria to evaluate the Other. This epistemological break introduced new, universalistic criteria of measurement and assessment, and a measure of truth that led to a new status being attributed to Western representations. It is now clear that these 'scientific' assessments of the Other were mistaken. However, many of the ideas to which they give rise have not been eradicated, but continue to structure common-sense and scientific discourses about the Other.

BEFORE EUROPEAN EXPANSION

European explorers and traders of the sixteenth and seventeenth centuries did not set out without expectations of the characteristics of the peoples they would meet. They occupied class positions in feudal societies that had a long tradition of imagining the Other, partly as a consequence of the experience of direct contact. Thus, for example, the African was represented in European thought long before European involvement in the slave trade (Jordan 1968: 6; Walvin 1973: 2–7, 1986: 69–72). These earlier representations were created and reproduced in a politico-spatial context in which Europe was not imagined, and, therefore, to all intents and purposes, did not exist. The economic and political domination of northwest Europe is historically specific and, prior to the fifteenth century, the geographical region that is now Europe had been subject to invasions from Asia, and the 'old continuous nations' of Europe were haltingly emergent rather than extant (Seton-Watson 1977: 21–87).

The European regions that achieved economic and politico-military significance prior to the fifteenth century were around the Mediterranean. Before then, the regions that are now Italy and Greece established and maintained a dominant economic and cultural position, sustained partly militarily. These societies were built largely upon the use of slave labour, and the imperialistic activities of their ruling classes brought them into contact with other populations in Europe and northern Africa. Contact and interaction occurred in different arenas. The most important were travel, trade and military activity. Travellers' accounts supplied information about populations that were identified as culturally and physically different, while trade and military activity ensured more extensive and direct forms of contact.

In the context of a growing knowledge of the geographical extent of human existence, there developed in Greco-Roman thought an idea of the unity of the human species. A conception of human diversity, spatially dispersed, but bound together by characteristics that distinguished human beings from both gods and animals, existed and was transformed in various ways over five centuries, although it did not seriously challenge the continuity of class and sexual divisions within Greco-Roman society (Baldry 1965: 24–5, 122, 198–203). Moreover, it did not eliminate the perception of 'barbarians' beyond the borders of Greco-Roman society. The barbarian as Other was seen to lack the capacities of intelligible speech and reason, capacities that were considered to be the quintessence of Greco-Roman culture, even though they were recognised as human beings (Baldry 1965: 21–2, 143).

With the military expansion of the Greco-Roman empire into Africa, captured Africans were enslaved like other prisoners of war, while others became, in effect, mercenaries. Additionally, Africans travelled to and were resident in the Greco-Roman world for educational, diplomatic and commercial purposes (Snowden 1970: 121–2, 186, 1983: 33). How were Africans represented in light of this interaction?

First, Africans were identified using certain physical features, notably skin colour but also hair type and nose shape (Snowden 1970: 2–5, 1983: 7). There was a definitive colour symbolism within Greco-Roman culture, by which whiteness was positively evaluated and blackness negatively evaluated, associated with death and a conception of an underworld (Snowden 1983: 82–3). However, the characterisation of Africans as black-skinned did not sustain a negative stereotype or constitute a legitimation of slavery (Davis 1984: 33). Rather, and second, Africans were identified as human beings with the capacity for freedom and justice, piety and wisdom (although some conceptions included elements of idealisation and unreality). They were respected as warriors and soldiers (Snowden 1970:

181, 1983: 55–9, 68), and, although some writers associated beauty with whiteness, there was a widely held assumption that the criteria of beauty were subjective. Indeed, other writers extolled blackness as beautiful (Snowden 1983: 63, 76).

Third, there was speculation about the origin of phenotypical and cultural differences. The dominant explanation in the Greco-Roman world was environmental in nature, the argument being that human physical appearance and cultural variation were determined by climate, topography and hydrography (Baldry 1965: 50). This argument was used to explain the full range of phenotypical diversity that was known at that time. For example, concerning Africans, it was suggested that skin colour and hair type were the product of constant exposure to the hot sun, while the opposite was believed of northern peoples (e.g. Snowden 1970: 172–3, 1983: 85–7).

In addition to the representations of the African as an *experienced* Other (in the sense that there was direct contact and interaction with certain African populations) there were also representations of an *imagined* Other (in the sense that the representations had no empirical reality, although that was not how they were experienced at the time). That the boundary between the experienced and the imagined Other is an artificial one in the Greco-Roman frame of reference is made evident in the *Natural History* of Pliny the Elder; this text included a primarily (though not exclusively) phenotypical typology of populations, many of which were given a particular spatial location in the world, mainly in Africa, India and the Caucasus. This typology included Ethiopians, although their spatial location was imprecise, and also *Cynocephali, Blemmyae, Anthropophagi*, and *Sciopods*. These populations were attributed with various physiological and cultural characteristics: the *Cynocephali* were dog-headed humans and the *Sciopods* had a single, very large foot, while the *Anthropophagi* were represented as eaters of human flesh (Friedman 1981: 8–21).

This typology, and associated representations and explanations, was expanded and modified by other writers and passed into medieval European literary tradition. Within this tradition, a causal relationship between physical appearance, moral character and spatial location was asserted and, as in Greco-Roman thought, climate was considered to be a major determinant, but the threefold climatic division of Greek thought was expanded (Friedman 1981: 52). Additional transformations occurred, the most significant being the popular religious meanings attributed to these representations. Within the Greco-Roman world, natural events considered to be indicators of God's intentions towards human beings were defined as *portenta* or *monstra*. Initially, *monstra* defined unusual individual or anomalous births, but its meaning was extended through the Middle Ages to include whole populations of people supposedly characterised by anomalous phenotypical characteristics, although the sense of divine warning remained (Friedman 1981: 108–16).

This premonitory meaning was subsequently transformed into one of punishment as Christianity became the prism through which knowledge about the world was refracted, as a result of which a Biblically inspired explanation for the material world predominated. Consequently, the nature and origin of these *monstra* had to be explained consistently with the Biblical representation of history as interpreted by the Church. Concerning their nature, the issue was whether or not they were human, a crucial matter which determined whether or not they could be the object of missionary activity and conversion (Friedman 1981: 178–80). It was also necessary to explain the origin of these *monstra*. One explanation advanced by medieval European writers was that they were part of God's creation plan, the purpose of which had yet to be revealed. Others argued that one or a group of Adam's descendants had induced God's wrath; as a result, their descendants had been physically disfigured and exiled to the periphery of the world. This explanation accepted a single origin of humanity as set out in the Bible but accounted for the subsequent diversity in human form. While the latter remained a subordinate explanation for a long period, it received increasing expression and support during the medieval period (1981: 88–103) and came to play a major ideological role in European expansion. The consequence was an association between the Other qua *monstrum* and sin.

We have seen that various human physical features (some imaginary) were signified as monstrous, one of which was skin colour. Western Christian culture associated certain colours with additional meanings, with the result that it embodied a colour symbolism mirroring that of the classical world. A white/black contrast expressed a complex of additional meanings, similarly dichotomous, such as good/evil, pure/diabolical, spiritual/carnal and Christ/Satan (Bastide 1968: 36), even though Manichean dualism was officially regarded as heresy. Colour expressed a hierarchical, popular religious evaluation, which influenced secular Western culture (Gergen 1968: 119). Where distinctions between human beings were designated by reference to skin colour, this symbolism had a powerful evaluative implication. Monstrousness, sin and blackness constituted a rather different form of Trinity in the European Christian culture of this period.

Thus, in medieval Europe, there was a discourse of the Other as a phenotypical and cultural deviant. This Other took a plurality of monstrous forms, some of which were purely imaginary while others were derived, in part, from empirical observations of non-European peoples. Within late medieval European literature, a representation of the wild man emerged:

> This creature possesses many of the features of earlier monstrous peoples – hairiness, nudity, the club or the branch – features that imply violence, lack of civilised arts, and want of a moral sense. The wild man is usually shown in a wooded setting, far from the abode of normal men.
> (Friedman 1981: 200; see also Dickason 1984: 70–80, Taussig 1987: 209–20)

The wild man was attributed with an aggressive and untamed sexuality, the female as a seductress of ordinary men (White 1972: 21–2). The wild man represented the opposite of the ideal Christian life, which was comparable with the Greco-Roman ideal Stoic life: 'He is desire incarnate, possessing the strength, wit and cunning to give full expression to all his lusts' (1972: 21). His condition was thought to be the result of the abolition of social convention and control, and an inevitable punishment for anyone who submitted to desire (1972: 30).

As far as the European feudal ruling classes were concerned, this image masked the boundary of the known and 'civilised' world, a boundary that in the medieval period encompassed Europe and parts of Africa and Asia. The arena within which this image circulated was later expanded by the search of several European feudal ruling classes for new trade routes and, thereby, the 'discovery' of the 'new world'. As a result, the content of the Plinian typology was increasingly challenged by the accumulation of observations arising from travellers' accounts of the populations that they had met. Neither merchants nor pilgrims reported the presence of *Sciopods* or *Cynocephali*, but a representation of the Other remained.

EUROPE AND THE MUSLIM WORLD

Before the interests of the feudal monarchies and merchant capital of Western Europe combined in order to colonise the Americas, the main focus of external interest (and concern) was the Middle East, North Africa and India, collectively known as the Orient. Daniel has observed that 'Europe's idea of the "foreigner" was based for many formative centuries exclusively on the Arab world' (1975: 322). Thus, not only did Europeans create a discourse of an imagined Other at the edge of European civilisation, but they created a discourse of a real Other represented as a result of conflicting material and political interests with a population which came to mark the boundary of Europe, spatially and in consciousness.

In an emergent, feudal Europe, where class domination was legitimated partly by appeal to Christianity, there was a heightened consciousness of the existence of Islam as a theology, and of its dominance in lands within and close to Europe. The consequence was a perception of Islam and the Muslim world as the source of theological and political difficulties for Europe (Southern 1962: 3, 13). Spatially, the sustained point of contact was the Mediterranean region, notably Spain, but commercial contact occurred elsewhere in the Mediterranean and beyond (Daniel 1975: 109, 220, 229). During the early part of this period, the primary contact was with the Arab world, but by the fourteenth century the Islamic 'threat' was increasingly thought to lie with the rise of the Ottoman Turks, although representations of the Muslim Other did not change form substantially (1975: 314–17). The image of the wild Saracen was replaced by that of the wild Turk, but within Europe both groups were seen as Muslims, and the discourse of Other that was constructed took this as the central focus.

The European image of Islam and Muslims achieved a significant degree of coherence in the twelfth and thirteenth centuries, although a number of key themes which recur through the centuries were evident much earlier (Daniel 1960: 275, 1975: 31–9). The Muslim Other was portrayed as barbaric, degenerate and tyrannical, characteristics that were thought to be rooted in the character of Islam as a supposedly false and heretical theology. The object of much of the attack was the Prophet of Islam, Muhammad, who was represented as an impostor, his life as exemplifying violence and sexuality (Daniel 1960: 78, 107; Ruthven 1997: 101). These were not portrayed as purely personal failings. It was argued that the theology Muhammad created for his own ends embodied violence and sexuality, with the consequence that Muslims inevitably behaved in similar ways. Thus Islam was portrayed as founded on aggression and war, as spreading itself by the same means, and as permitting and encouraging polygamy, sodomy and general sexual laxity. It was argued that Islam reproduced the idea of the 'holy war' against all non-Muslims, in the course of which the latter would be either brutally murdered or enslaved, and a notion of Paradise as a garden of sexual delights and passions (e.g. Daniel 1960: 123–5, 136–54, 1966: 5, 1975: 234, 243).

The equation of Islam with violence was sustained by a clerical agitation that culminated in the Crusades. Muslim occupation of the Holy Land was considered illegitimate, and, therefore, as evidence of aggression (Lewis 1982: 22). War against the Saracen to regain the Holy Land was justified theologically in the name of God, and as a means to recover the unity of Christendom. Muslim resistance to the European armies was interpreted as further evidence of an inherent tendency towards violence and cruelty, while identical acts of war by Christians were seen as entirely legitimate, even as means to glorify God (e.g. Daniel 1960: 109–13, 1975: 111–39). It was not until the late seventeenth century that the Muslim world ceased to be perceived within Europe as an external threat (Harbsmeier 1985: 73), after which the stereotype of unrestrained Muslim sexuality – symbolised by belly dancers, harems, snake charmers and degenerate sultans – predominated (Turner 1994: 98; Said 1995: 40, 182, 188 *et passim*). The perception of Islam as violent and threatening was revived towards the end of the twentieth century (Halliday 1996; Said 1997; Commission on British Muslims and Islamophobia 1997; Brown 2000), particularly after four aircraft were hijacked and crashed in the USA on 11 September 2001.

In a context where the nature of the material world, and relations between people, were explained and structured through religion, European representations of the populations of other regions were organised necessarily in terms of religion. Thus, the representation of the Other was a consistent distortion of Islam, grounded in an alternative theology, Christianity. Christian literature about Islam set out to:

> . . . establish that Muslim Arabs were different from Christian Europeans. This was expressed primarily in theological terms, because that is how the conformity of Europe was expressed. In a period when Europe was in a mood of aggression and expansion, its surplus energy created an attitude to its Arab and Arabic-speaking neighbours which was based, not on what the Arabs were like, but on what, for theological reasons, they ought to be like.
>
> (Daniel 1975: 248)

The theological character of this representation of the Other was evident in the characterisation of Islam as the collective embodiment of, and ultimate expression of, heresy. So: 'Islam was seen as the negation of Christianity; Muhammad as an imposter, an evil sensualist, an Antichrist in alliance with the Devil'; and, by extension: 'The Islamic world was seen as Anti-Europe, and was held in suspicion as such' (Kabbani 1986: 5).

However, the structural opposition between Europe and the Muslim world was not perceived as *solely* religious. The perception was based on religion, but was also somatic in character. The 'enemy' of Christendom was represented not only as Muslim, 'heretic' or 'infidel', but also as 'Arab', 'Moor', 'Turk', 'Saracen' and 'foreigner'. In 1059, the Norman feudal lord Robert Guiscard referred to 'the wickedness of the Saracens and . . . the insolence of the foreigners' (cited in Williams 1990: 21), from whom (with the retrospective legitimation of Pope Nicholas II) he had seized land. In his proclamation of the First Crusade in 1095, Pope Urban II was attributed with the following words:

> Distressing news has come to me . . . from the region of Jerusalem . . . news that the people of the Persian kingdom, an *alien* people, a *race* completely *foreign* to God, 'a generation of false aims, of a spirit that broke faith with God', has invaded Christian territory and has devastated this territory with pillage, fire, and the sword. . . . [R]ise up and remember the manly deeds of your ancestors, the prowess and greatness of Charlemagne . . . who destroyed pagan kingdoms and planted the holy church in their territories. You should be especially aroused by the fact that the Holy Sepulcher of the Lord our Saviour is in the hands of these *unclean* people, who shamelessly mistreat and sacrilegiously defile the Holy Places with their *filth*.
>
> (Cited in Williams 1990: 35; added emphasis)

It is unlikely that this 'filth' was conceived in terms of religious ceremonial impurity, not least because that concept has been, at most, peripheral to Western Christianity. Rather, it is attributed to a 'foreign' Other, represented within a primarily religious discourse in quasi-'racial' terms. The Crusaders often made no distinction between Muslims, Jews, pagans and Eastern Christians in the territories where they fought (Jones and Ereira 1996: 17–19, 24–6, 54–6; see also Runciman 1951: 287). Although an important purpose of the Crusades, it was claimed, was the *defence* of Eastern Christians, cultural, somatic and linguistic differences took precedence, at least on occasion, over religious similarities. Ironically, the medieval image of the Muslim 'Saracen', 'Moor' or 'Turk' has largely given way, at the present time, to a perception of the Muslim as a religious Other, a bearded fundamentalist who uses terrorism in support of his objectives (to establish Islamic law on Earth and himself in Paradise), and eroto-phobically confines women to *purdah* (however this term is understood).

In more general terms, however, the medieval European representation of the Muslim Other was of someone intrinsically different, a conception simultaneously expressive and a reinforcement of a 'Self/Other' duality.

FROM ANTI-JUDAISM TO ANTISEMITISM

Negative stereotypes about, and discrimination against, Jewish people have also been central to constructing the Other in Europe and North America during the late eighteenth and early nineteenth centuries. We return to the Greco-Roman period, and the Roman occupation of Palestine, Judea and Jerusalem in the 60s BCE, though we could go back further (see Bauman 1989: 33–4). Within this political system, Jewish people were regarded as a threat to the stability of the Roman Empire because, *inter alia*, their religion was monotheistic: they did not worship the Roman gods, nor, crucially, did they accept the divinity of the Emperor, a doctrine central to the state religion. With the Christianisation of the Empire under Constantine, one might have expected the situation of Christianity's parent religion to improve. However, the same stereotypes and discrimination remained, only with a different rationale – the Jews were regarded as responsible for the death of Jesus Christ, as well as outside and antipathetic towards the established religion, now Christianity (cf. Poliakov 1974).

So, antisemitism, or something like antisemitism, has existed in Europe for centuries. Jewish people were subject to economic exclusion and violence in medieval and Reformation Europe, particularly during the Crusades (e.g. Southern 1970: 17, 308; Küng 1978: 168). The image of the wandering Jew, the migrant, the outsider, implied 'a kind of *vampire*, committing ritual murder on Christian children and consuming their blood', 'a *hidden hand* secretly manipulating the course of history', and 'a *parasite* preying on the host society' (Cohen 1988: 16). Later, as pre-Christian Roman anti-Judaism gave way to Constantinian anti-Judaism, so religious anti-Judaism gave way to a secular *antisemitism*. Due to the growth of secularisation and nationalism, associated *inter alia* with the French Revolution, religious anti-Judaism gave way to an antisemitism articulated in terms of 'race'. In Poliakov's words, 'if contemporaries formed an imaginary image of a Jewish race, they did so because a theologically condemned caste already existed' (1975: 458–9; see also Brown 2000: 78). In the age of capitalism and Enlightenment, the wandering Jew person-ified the free movement of capital and of ideas (Cohen 1988: 16–17), so that eventually the Jew would be portrayed as 'a cut-throat capitalist bleeding the workers to death *and* as a free-thinking socialist poisoning the hearts and minds of Young England' (1988: 17), or, indeed, of any other 'nation'.

Of course, this was not a simple progression, for two reasons (Bauman 1989). First, the movement from religious anti-Judaism to secular anti-semitism was not an automatic switch. From its inception, Christianity was, in a sense, defined vis-à-vis Judaism (1989: 37–8), but a Jewish person could always convert to Christianity. In medieval Europe, this was quite acceptable – the Jewish people were, after all, a distinctive group, but, within the system of feudal relations, they constituted but one distinctive group among many (1989: 57), and conversion would confirm the superiority of the faith of Christendom (1989: 58–9). The *modern* view of a human being as *tabula rasa*, with a perfectible human nature, threatened to erase the boundary between the Jewish people and the rest of society. Therefore, according to Bauman:

> If it was to be salvaged from the assault of modern equality, *the distinctiveness of the Jews had to be re-articulated and laid on new foundations, stronger than human powers of culture and self-determination.* In Hannah Arendt's terse phrase, Judaism has to be replaced with Jewishness.
>
> (1989: 59; original emphasis)

In other words, secular antisemitism articulated in 'racial' terms did not emerge from religious anti-Judaism, nor was it an automatic consequence of modernity and secularisation. Rather, it was constituted by an acceptance of some features of modernity and secularisation, and resistance against some of their consequences.

Second, the antisemitism that culminated in the Holocaust was not constituted by a primitive anger against a (theologically or otherwise) condemned population. Not only was the *Endlösung* dependent on a system of formally rational bureaucracy and technology, which could not have been sustained by anger alone (notoriously, had *Kristallnacht* been repeated every day, it would have taken nearly 200 years to murder the six million Jews who were killed in the death camps [1989: 89–90]), but the antisemites' *perception* of antisemitism was of a very different order. It was not that the

Jews had a crime to expiate, nor was it simply that their perceived 'racial' inferiority made them unworthy of possessing any rights, including the right to life. Rather:

> ... it was the perpetual and ubiquitous homelessness of the Jews that more than anything else set them apart. ... Hitler believed that having no territorial state, the Jews could not participate in the universal power-struggle in its ordinary form of a war aimed at land conquest, and thus had to reach instead for indecent, surreptitious and under-hand methods which made them a particularly formidable and sinister enemy; an enemy, moreover, unlikely ever to be satiated or pacified, and hence bound to be destroyed in order to be rendered harmless.
>
> (1989: 35)

The existence of the Jewish people qua diaspora was at odds with the nationalist ethos, both in terms of the 'natural' association of 'people' (*Volk*) with 'homeland' (*Land*), and in terms of the expansionist calling of the nation state.

EUROPEAN EXPANSION AND COLONISATION

This expansionism began before nation state hegemony, by the end of the fifteenth century. Economic and political power in Europe had consolidated in the emergent nation states of the north and west of the continent (Kiernan 1972: 12–13; Wallerstein 1974). Trade, travel and exploration, as interdependent elements in attempts by the feudal ruling classes to resolve major economic crisis (Fox-Genovese and Genovese 1983: 10), widened European contact with populations elsewhere. Thus, the context within which representations of the Other were generated and reproduced changed. Up to this point, the non-Muslim Other (the crucial exception being the Jews, as we have already seen) was outside the European arena. Moreover, discourse about the Muslim Other was for a long time generated in the context of European subordination to a greater economic and military force.

However, once emergent European city and nation states began to expand their material and political boundaries to incorporate other parts of the world within a system of international trade (Braudel 1984: 89–174), subsequently linked with colonial settlement, the popula-tions they confronted were within the arena of Europe in an economic and political sense, though not spatially. When colonisation became an objective, a class of Europeans initiated direct relationships with indigenous populations, a contact increasingly structured by competition for land, the introduction of private property rights, the demand for a labour force, and the perceived obligation of conversion to Christianity. Collectively, these were embodied in the discourse of 'civilisation'.

Europeans who travelled in pursuit of trade, military advantage, religious mission or curiosity carried expectations derived from extant verbal and written accounts of the Other (e.g. Dickason 1984: 18, 80). They came therefore with intentions and objectives that influenced their perceptions of those populations with whom they came into contact, perceptions that were sustained and discursively reworked. Thus, Columbus reported finding 'savage' but not 'monstrous' people (Friedman 1981: 198). Representations based on the empiricism of direct experience permitted a transformation in the content of representations of the Other, but the existence of the Other as a mirror of what the European was not remained largely unquestioned. Travellers' accounts were published, for profit, education and entertainment, with the result that representations of the Other circulated throughout Europe (e.g. Dickason 1984: 67). Significantly, travellers' sense of the normal served to identify the abnormal characteristics of people with whom contact was established and of their mode of life. Hence, with regard to Africa, Curtin has observed that 'the reporting often stressed precisely those aspects of African life that were most repellent to the West and tended to submerge the indications of a common humanity' (Curtin 1965: 23). A negative representation of the Other therefore defined and legitimated the 'positive' qualities of author and reader (cf. Febvre and Martin 1976: 281; Hakluyt 1972: 33).

However, non-European peoples were not represented in a homogenous manner. Travellers who went east, into Russia and Central Asia, tended to describe the people they met using the words 'barbarous', 'tyrant' or 'infidel' (Hakluyt 1972: 63, 80, 86, 123, 245). Rarely was reference made to their physical appearance or cultural practice. The discourse of tyrant and infidel reproduced earlier discourses of the Muslim world, and signified religion as the means by which to establish a Self–Other dialectic. On the other hand, travellers to the Americas, Africa and India remarked consistently on the skin colour of the indigenous populations, on other physical characteristics such as hair type, and on their partial or complete nakedness (Jordan 1968: 4; Cole 1972: 64–5; Hakluyt 1972: 105–8, 267; Sanders 1978: 211–25).

These populations were often represented as savages and/or cannibals

(Dickason 1984). John Hawkins described Dominica as 'an island of cannibals' (Hakluyt 1972: 107) and Thomas Cavendish wrote of a population on the South American mainland: 'In this river there are great store of savages which we saw, and had conference with them: they were men eaters, and fed altogether upon raw flesh and other filthy food' (1972: 279). James Lancaster described the inhabitants of the Cape of Good Hope as 'black savages very brutish' (1972: 361), a view endorsed by seventeenth-century travellers who described them as 'beasts in the skins of men' and as being halfway between man and ape (Novak 1972: 188). Seeking the Northwest Passage, Martin Frobisher made contact with people living in the northern polar region. He described them as fierce and cruel, and their appearance and cultural practices as follows:

> They are men of a large corporature, and good proportion: their colour is not much unlike the sunburnt country man who laboureth daily in the sun for his living. . . . I think them rather anthropophagi, or devourers of man's flesh than otherwise: for that there is no flesh or fish which they find dead (smell if never so filthily) but they will eat it, as they find it without any other dressing.
>
> (Hakluyt 1972: 192–4)

The use of the term *anthropophagi* is an instance of the way in which Plinian categorisation shaped travellers' representations several centuries later and is consistent with the argument that the attribution of cannibalism consistently (and misleadingly) occurs in Western representations of the Other (Arens 1979).

Such references were not the only representations that accompanied the signification of skin colour and nakedness. Columbus distinguished between *canibales* and *indios*; the latter he represented as exhibiting kindness and deference and no evidence of bestiality (Sanders 1978: 93–4, 123–4). Francis Drake described the population of the island of Batjan in the Moluccas in the following manner:

> The people of this island are comely in body and stature, and of a civil behaviour, just in dealing, and courteous to strangers. The men go naked, saving their heads and privities, every man having something or other hanging at their ears. The women are covered from the middle down to the foot, wearing a great number of bracelets upon their arms.
>
> (Hakluyt 1972: 186)

Two English travellers to Virginia described the Indians that they met as 'most gentle, loving and faithful, void of all guile and treason, and such as live after the manner of the golden age' (1972: 274). Indeed, some people described as savages were also described as 'harmless', such as the indigenous population of Newfoundland by Humphrey Gilbert (1972: 236).

After initial contact, more complex representations were constructed, including positive elements. For example, a respect developed for aspects of the life of Native North Americans, including their perceived strength and agility, and their hunting and fishing skills (Nash 1972: 68). The Caribs were represented as depraved by virtue of their supposed cannibalism, but were also attributed with courage and strength (Robe 1972: 45). For some observers, certain Indian populations were represented as living in a condition of original harmony and egalitarianism (Baudet 1976: 26–8, 35–6). Thus the existence of non-Europeans was interpreted as a measure of the loss within Europe of an earlier 'golden age' or 'paradise' (cf. Popkin 1974: 129; Baudet 1976: 10–11). This discourse served to identify the observers as living in an unnatural, depraved condition, desirous of rediscovering their ideal prelapsarian conditions. This supports the argument that the conception of the 'noble savage' existed long before Rousseau (Symcox 1972: 227–8; Baudet 1976: 11; Friedman 1981: 163–77; Dickason 1984: 59, 81).

Nevertheless, the majority of descriptions in Hakluyt's collection of accounts of non-European peoples are pejorative. In addition to the examples already cited, South American Indians were described as 'a warlike kind of people' and 'very ugly and terrible to behold' (Hakluyt 1972: 139), Indian Brahmins as 'a kind of crafty people, worse than the Jews' (1972: 259), the Javanese as 'heathen' (1972: 293), and the population of an island off the African coast as 'treacherous' (1972: 362). Hence, if there was no single representation, neither was there an equality of negative and positive meanings. European representations were hierarchically ordered around the view that Europeans were superior by virtue of their 'civilisation' and achievements (including world travel and trade): the condition of the Other was represented as proof of that interpretation.

These representations were instrumental. For example, Columbus initiated the idea that those Indians who were named Caribs were, by custom, eaters of human flesh and, by a process of linguistic transformation, this name gave rise to the label 'cannibal'. Spanish explorers and colonisers in the Caribbean and Mexico increasingly applied the term to peoples with whom they established contact, although in the written records of the period there is no first-hand witness account of human flesh being eaten. The increasing use of the term correlates with indigenous resistance to the Spanish presence, attempted military subjugation of indigenous peoples, and their induction into unfree labour (Sanders 1978: 101; Arens 1979: 44–77).

Thus, these representations refracted a purpose, as discovery was followed by settlement, and settlement by the introduction of systems of unfree labour (Miles 1987a) to exploit the natural resources for the benefit of the European ruling classes. Contact and interaction did not occur in a neutral context, but in a context of conflicting interests and unequal military resources, usually effected by force. The European classes involved in this process (re)constructed representations of these indigenous populations, both to legitimate their actions and in response to their experience of those populations. Consequently, there was a complex interaction between class interests and empirical observation. The representations of the Other that resulted from this were neither absolutely homogeneous, nor static (see, for example, George 1958; Walvin 1986: 77), because colonisation had neither a singular character nor a universal course, and because it had political and ideological repercussions in Europe.

Given the temporal length, spatial extent and complexity of colonisation, it is impossible to offer here a comprehensive analysis of representations of the colonised Other. There are reasons to focus briefly on British representations of African populations (for representations of other colonised populations, see, for example, Kiernan 1972; Bearce 1982). First, Africa was involved in many different phases of British colonialism over a period of four hundred years and therefore representations of the African populations constitute a central pillar of British colonial history. Second, representations of the African as Other become increasingly interwoven with justifications for, as well as opposition to, the enslavement of Africans in the Americas. This has led to over-deterministic assertions that economic interests required a theory of inherent inferiority in order to justify African slavery (e.g. Fryer 1984: 134), a functionalist assertion that raises important theoretical questions.

When evaluated in the light of historical evidence, such claims are difficult to sustain, not least because they fail to explain the development of earlier representations of Africans. Functionalist accounts are incomplete by virtue of their simplistic, non-dialectical nature. Nevertheless, despite this specific focus upon representations of Africans, it should be noted that representations of other colonial Others exhibit both continuity and discontinuity with the former. One example of continuity is the attribution of excessive and unrestrained sexuality to different colonised populations (e.g. Kiernan 1972: 59, 255–60).

As we have seen, European discourse noted African skin colour and nakedness in order to signify difference. It noted that Africans were not Christians, and as a result they were represented as 'heathens' (see Jordan 1968: 20–1). Thus, this European discourse reflected back what the African was not in order to affirm difference, employing both phenotypical and cultural criteria (Curtin 1965: 30). Additional characteristics were attributed to the African during the seventeenth and eighteenth centuries and after, in the course of which the African was known to Europeans, and particularly the British, as a slave, both in the colonies and within Britain (Fryer 1984: 155; Walvin 1986: 80–2).

One of these characteristics was a potent sexuality. African women were considered to be especially solicitous of sexual intercourse, while African men were thought to possess an unusally large penis and to be particularly virile and lusty (Jordan 1968: 151, 158–9; Fryer 1984: 140, 159). The African was attributed with a bestial character and there was much speculation about the origin and consequences of the supposed physical similarities between Africans and apes, both of which were 'discovered' by Europeans at the same time in a common geographical location. Some Europeans suggested that sexual intercourse occurred between Africans and apes (Jordan 1968: 28–32, 238; Fryer 1984: 138). Furthermore, the African was considered lazy, superstitious, ferocious, and a coward, as well as polite, noble, and respectful of the elderly (Curtin 1965: 222–4; Barker 1978: 104). Additionally, the early charge of cannibalism was elaborated throughout the colonial period (Barker 1978: 129).

This emphasis on physical and animalistic characteristics was used to advance a conception of the African as living in a condition of savagery, a definition which placed the African far below the European on the European scale of human progress (Curtin 1965: 63–5; Walvin 1986: 77). In other words, the African was less civilised, a barbarian, by virtue of supposedly looking more like a beast and behaving in ways that approximated to the behaviour of beasts (Jordan 1968: 24–5, 97). Although for a majority of European opinion, this condition of barbarity and savagery was negatively evaluated, it was regarded by a significant minority, particularly during the eighteenth century, as expressive of moral superiority because the African was thought closer to nature (Curtin 1965: 48–51; Fryer 1984: 145). Here we find the reproduction of the discourse of the noble savage.

For most of the seventeenth and eighteenth centuries, the alleged difference was explained in environmentalist terms (Barker 1978: 79). The physical appearance of the African, and specifically the colour of the African's skin, increased in significance as a sign of differentiation (Jordan 1968: 216–17, 512). By the late eighteenth century the claim that blackness was the result of God's curse was no longer considered satisfactory, and the argument that climate was the key determinant increased in significance (Jordan 1968: 525). Specifically it was proposed that the heat of the sun in tropical regions either burnt the skin, or caused it to change colour as protection against the heat. Additionally, some argued that once this transformation had occurred, blackness became an inherited characteristic (Curtin 1965: 40–1; Jordan 1968: 11; Barker 1978: 85). Climate was also believed to determine cultural characteristics. For example, the attributed quality of laziness was also explained by reference to the heat of the sun.

However, climate was not considered to be the sole environmental determinant. Samuel Stanhope Smith argued in 1787 that the human species had originated in Asia in a 'civilised' form and that subsequent migrations were followed by 'degeneration' into savagery and gradual alterations in physical appearance. The causes of these transformations were identified as climate, the state of society and habits of living. Smith placed considerable emphasis upon the latter two factors and this environmentalist argument continued to predominate in American and European discourse in the late eighteenth century (Jordan 1968: 487, 513–15; also Popkin 1974: 139; Barker 1978: 52, 79).

Environmentalist arguments implied that the characteristics attributed to the African were, in principle, subject to modification. If the African was a savage, this was a human condition that could be improved (Barker 1978: 99; also Curtin 1965: 66). Hence Stanhope Smith, for example, claimed that Africans in America were becoming more capable of instruction and that their physical appearance was undergoing modification (Jordan 1968: 515–16). Environmentalism therefore sustained strategies for 'civilising' the African: heathenness and savagery could be changed through missionary work and plantation production (e.g. Curtin 1965: 123–39, 259–86). The idea of the 'civilising mission' was particularly significant during the nineteenth century (Kiernan 1972: 24).

This discourse had implications for the economic role that many Africans were forced to perform in the Americas. African slavery in the Americas was justified, first, by the claim that Africans (unlike Europeans) were specifically suited to work under tropical conditions (Curtin 1961: 104, 1965: 116; Barker 1978: 61). The logic of environmentalism implied that this suitability could be acquired, although this seemed to be less readily accepted by Europeans concerning themselves, implying inconsistency in environmentalism as an explanation for the hypothesised differences between Europeans and Africans. This ambiguity was partially removed in the nineteenth century with the emergence of the discourse of 'race'. Second, it was justified by the argument that it enabled Africans to escape from savagery. Entry into slave relations of production permitted Africans to step along the road of 'progress' towards 'civilisation', placing them initially in an economic position similar to the European poor (Kiernan 1972: 242; Barker 1978: 68, 151–2, 160, 198, also chapter 4).

THE SIGNIFICANCE OF SCIENCE

The idea of 'race' took on a new meaning in Europe with the Enlightenment and the development of science from the late eighteenth century (Banton 1987: 28–64; see also Eze 1997). From this time, 'race' increasingly came to refer to a biological type of human being, and science purported to demonstrate the number and characteristics of each 'race', and a hierarchical relationship between them. Thus it was claimed that every human being either belonged to a 'race' or was a product of several 'races', and therefore exhibited the characteristics of that 'race' or those 'races', and that the biological characteristics of each 'race' determined a range of psychological and social capacities by which they could be ranked.

Stated in its most extreme form, 'race' was believed to determine economic and cultural characteristics and development (cf. Barzun 1938: 19–21; Banton 1977: 47). This was a discourse of 'race' that may be described as biological determinism (cf. Gould 1984: 20; Rose et al. 1984: 3–15). Thereby, the Other was represented as biologically distinct, a 'race' apart, with fixed capacities. There is now a considerable literature on the ideological career of the idea of 'race' (e.g. Gossett 1965; Banton 1977, 1987; Stepan 1982; Augstein 1996), some aspects of which are particularly relevant to this study.

First, the scientific assertion of the existence of different biologically constituted 'races' led to a clash with religious ideas about the nature and development of the human species. Biblical interpretation suggested that the human species was divinely created, and that all human beings, past and present, were descended from Adam and Eve. This implied some ultimate homogeneity of the human species. One way of harmonising these assertions was to claim that God had responded to human sin by damnation: those damned, and their descendants, were marked by distinctive features (such as black skin). Another, with an equally long pedigree, placed less emphasis on divine intervention. This argument maintained that environmental factors (such as the influence of the sun) had modified the original and single biological form represented by Adam and Eve, creating a number of different types that were subsequently reproduced by hereditary means. Using this latter argument, many 'race' scientists of the eighteenth and nineteenth centuries claimed that their explanation for 'race' differentiation was consistent with Christian theology.

In the late eighteenth century, scientific analysis revived an objection which had been articulated in the sixteenth century by Hakluyt (see Sanders 1978: 223–4): that phenotypical features did not change when members of 'races' moved to different geographical locations and were subjected to different environmental conditions. The example of Africans enslaved in the Americas was often cited to support this view, as was that of Europeans in the tropical colonies. The conclusion was that environmental factors, including climate, were incapable of altering the physical features of 'race'. The implication was that distinct 'races' of human beings had always existed, and that 'racial' hierarchy was therefore natural, inevitable and unalterable. This assault on environmentalism led to a fundamental conflict with Christian theology (Stanton 1960: 69, 169; Haller 1971: 69–79; Stepan 1982: 36–46). The conclusions to which it gave rise were accorded even greater legitimacy as science occupied an increasingly ascendant position over theology. By the mid-nineteenth century this theory of polygenism was dominant, and many of its key assumptions survived into the post-Darwinian era (Stocking 1968: 39, 45–6, 55).

Second, the scientific discourse of 'race' did not replace earlier conceptions of the Other. Ideas of savagery, barbarism and civilisation predetermined the space that the idea of 'race' occupied, but were themselves reconstituted by it. Thus, extant imagery was refracted through the representational prism of 'race', and environmentalism declined in importance (Miles 1982: 111–12). For example, 'civilisation' was initially considered attainable by all human beings, including the most 'savage', given sufficient time and assistance, but this was challenged in the late nineteenth century by the scientific idea that the human species was divided into permanent and discrete biological groups. As a result, savagery became a fixed condition of the 'Negro' or African 'race', a product of a small brain, and civilisation became an attribute of large-brained 'white' people (Stocking 1968: 35–7, 121–2).

Third, in generating and reproducing the idea of 'race', many scientific writers drew upon and criticised each other's work, seeking new methods of measurement and solutions to emergent anomalies. The science of phrenology originated in the work of Gall and Spurzheim in Germany and was developed by George Combe in Scotland (Gossett 1965: 71–2), a friend of Samuel Morton, an American, who published *Crania Americana* in 1839 and *Crania Aegyptiaca* in 1844 (Gould 1984: 50–69). The cephalic index (a measurement of skulls that divided the length of the skull by the breadth) was invented by Anders Retzius in Sweden (Gossett 1965: 76). F. Tiedeman, a German anatomist, measured brains in order to establish differences between 'races', his results stimulating a critical reply from Josiah Nott in the United States (Gossett 1965: 77). With George Gliddon, Nott had a major impact on 'race' theory with *Types of Mankind*, first published in 1854, which appeared in at least nine editions before the end of the century (Gossett 1965: 65; Banton 1977: 50–2). Thus the increasingly international character of the scientific enterprise facilitated the formulation of the discourse of 'race'. Consequently, the scientific idea of 'race' had a widespread circulation, and its proponents represented *various* Others (Africans, North American Indians, Indians) as 'racially' different and inferior to 'Caucasians'.

Fourth, although the *ideas* of biological type and hierarchy remained constant, the *forms* of classification and the *content* of attribution changed over time. For most of the late eighteenth and early nineteenth centuries, 'race' classifications were based on skin colour, hair type and nose shape, but there was increasing emphasis on the dimensions of the skull (Benedict 1983: 22). This became prominent during the early nineteenth century (Curtin 1965: 366), and considerable effort was expended in assessing, for example, cranial capacity, facial angle and cranial index. Indeed, there was much debate about the relative validity of these different measures. The science of 'race' therefore underwent a complex evolution. In part, this complexity was due to its essential error: as each attempt at classification broke down under the weight of logical inconsistency and empirical evidence, a new classification was formulated. It was also due to increasing sophistication of measurement (Stocking 1968: 57).

For example, in late eighteenth-century Germany, Peter Camper claimed to distinguish between 'races' by facial angle, the angle that a line from the chin to the top of the forehead forms with a horizontal line at the base of the chin. He drew the most extreme contrast between 'Greeks' and 'Negroes' (Gossett 1965: 69–70). Somewhat different arguments, but leading to the same conclusion, were advanced by phrenology, which divided the brain into a number of sections, each of which was the basis of a different faculty. It was argued that each 'race' was distinguished by a distinct variation in size and interrelation of these different sections, and not by the weight of the brain or capacity of the skull (Stepan 1982: 21–8). Combe claimed, for example,

> The HINDOOS are remarkable for want of force of character. . . . Power of mental manifestation bears a proportion to the size of the central organs, and the Hindoo head is small, and the European large, in precise conformity with the different mental characters. . . . The Hindoo brain indicates a manifest deficiency in the organs of Combativeness and Destructiveness; while, in the European, these parts are amply developed. The Hindoo is cunning, timid and proud; and in him Secretiveness, Cautiousness and Self-Esteem are large in proportion to the organs last mentioned.
>
> (Combe 1830: 605–6)

On this basis, 'phrenology justified empire-building' (Fryer 1984: 171). Samuel Morton measured differences between 'races' by filling skulls with mustard seed or lead shot, from which he derived a measure of cranial capacity. He claimed to demonstrate significant differences in cranial capacity between five different 'races' (Caucasian, Mongolian, Malay, American and Ethiopian), although in his final conclusions these 'races' were further subdivided into 'families' (see Gould 1984: 54–5). Morton's craniometry was a major influence on Nott and Gliddon (see Stanton 1960; Gould 1984: 30–72), who assumed that there was a correlation between cranial capacity and innate intelligence. Louis Gratiolet offered evidence that the coronal suture of the skull closes, thereby arresting the growth of the brain, at different times for different 'races'. He concluded that this closure occurred earlier among 'Negroes' than 'Whites' (Gossett 1965: 75; Gould 1984: 98). The list goes on.

Fifth, those who formulated the idea considered themselves to be members of a 'race', but they also identified a hierarchy of 'races' within Europe. Efforts were made in the late nineteenth century, for example, to identify the different 'races' of which the British population was composed, using hair and eye colour and skull measurements (Beddoe

1885). Concerning Europe as a whole, various classifications were devised, the most common being a distinction between Teutonic (or Nordic), Mediterranean and Alpine 'races' (Ripley 1900: 103–30). In the USA, this classification was combined with an argument that human intelligence was fixed and hereditary in order to produce a hierarchy of acceptable and unacceptable immigrants (Kamin 1977: 30–51; Gould 1984: 146–233).

Within Europe, representations of the Other as an inferior 'race' focused *inter alia* on the Irish (Curtis 1968, 1971) and Jews (Mosse 1978). This was sustained partly by claiming biological superiority for the Nordic 'race'. In Germany, Günther (1970) interpreted European history in a book titled *The Racial Elements of European History* (first published in 1927) using the scientific idea of 'race' to refer to human groups with distinct and measurable physical and mental characteristics. He identified the Nordic 'race' as especially creative, with a need for conquest, a special aptitude for military science and a low crime rate, and he feared social decay in Europe as a result of 'the running dry of the blood of the . . . Nordic race' (1970: 198). Portentously, he stated that 'the question put to us is whether we have courage enough to make ready for future generations a world cleansing itself racially and eugenically' (1970: 267). Günther was only one of a large number of scholars (and activists) who used a scientific discourse of 'race' to assert a superiority of the Nordic 'race' and inferiority of Jews (Mosse 1978: 77–93, 113–27).

Sixth, the scientific conception of 'race' has been shown to be mistaken, although a number of scientists continue to assert its key ideas in various forms. The exposure of the error had a long genesis that began with the work of Charles Darwin and finished with the emergence of population genetics. The first step was the formulation of a theory of evolution that questioned the validity of the idea of fixed and permanent biological species. However, when the human species was located in evolutionary theory in Europe in the latter half of the nineteenth century, the idea of 'race' was retained, the argument being that each 'race' could be ranked on an evolutionary scale. Thus, what came to be known as Social Darwinism (Jones 1980; Clark 1984, 1988) asserted that there was a struggle for survival among different human 'races', in the course of which those with lesser intelligence or capacity for 'civilisation' would disappear. 'Disappearance' was evidence of a 'natural' inability to evolve. Thus, evolutionary theory was developed initially in a way that endorsed the idea of discrete biological 'races', and the classifiers of the human species continued to produce their typologies (Haller 1971: 121–52; Banton 1977: 89–100; Stepan 1982: 47–110).

A further decisive development was the identification of the statistical limitations of phenotypical measurement by those who continued to defend the utility of such measurement. The work of Boas in the early twentieth century is particularly important because he also demonstrated the influence of the social environment on physiological features by use of the cephalic index (e.g. Boas 1940: 60–75). Boas believed in the existence of biological 'races', but rejected the argument that they were fixed because of evidence that phenotypical features such as head form responded to environmental influences (Stocking 1968: 170–80). He also argued that, although the world's population could be divided into 'races' using phenotypical criteria, each such category contained within it a range of variation that overlapped with the variation of any other category: 'With regard to many characteristics of this kind, we find that the difference between the averages of different races is insignificant as compared to the range of variability that occurs within each race' (Boas 1940: 42). So, although two populations may have a different average height, it does not follow that any two individuals selected from these populations will demonstrate the same difference. In other words, group differences do not correspond to individual differences (cf. Stocking 1968: 192–3).

The full implications of Darwin's evolutionary theory could only be explored with the emergence of a science of genetics that identified the biological basis of evolutionary processes. Genetics shifted attention partly away from phenotypical differences such as skin colour and analysed biological features that were not evident to the naked eye and that, in a complex interaction with the environment, determined biological changes in the human species. It was generally concluded after the Second World War that the scientific conception of 'race', grounded in the idea of fixed typologies and based upon phenotypical features, did not have any scientific utility. Moreover, the evidence showed no causal relationship between physical or genetic characteristics and cultural characteristics. Genetics demonstrated that 'race', as defined by scientists from the late eighteenth century, had no scientifically verifiable referent (Boyd 1950; Montagu 1964, 1972).

SCIENCE AND 'RACE' TODAY

This paradigm shift is frequently taken to be a consequence of the widespread revulsion felt at the Nazis' 'final solution' (*Endlösung*). However, the credibility of the science of 'race' was in decline *before* 1933, when Hitler came to power. Richards (1997: 68–71), writing about the science of 'race' in psychology, compared the number of papers which espoused a 'race psychology' perspective and were published in psychology journals, with those which espoused an 'anti-race psychology' perspective, and concluded that the latter perspective was ascendant as early as 1931. There is a consistent pattern of science being chronologically out of step with its use, at least as far as the legitimation of the exclusion and exploitation of the Other is concerned. The idea of 'race' was rarely used during the slave trade era (Barker 1978: 42, 52, 164), and the scientific legitimation of the term did not *predominate* until the nineteenth century (Jordan 1968: 532), possibly as late as 1840 (Curtin 1965: 29). Thus, it seems ironic that the *Endlösung* occurred at the time when science itself was increasingly critical of the validity of 'race' typologies.

However, the term has not been eradicated from either scientific or everyday language. Some physical anthropologists have continued to assert a 'race' classification using phenotypical features in spite of genetic and other contrary evidence (e.g. Hooton 1947) and the famous UNESCO statements on the nature of 'race' gave some varying, but heavily qualified, approval to this approach (see Montagu 1972: 9, 142, 150). On the other hand, many geneticists have argued that populations can be better distinguished from each other by identifying different frequencies of variable genes, also acknowledging that the distinction between populations is determined arbitrarily (Boyd 1950: 202–7; Bodmer 1972: 90; Cavalli-Sforza 2001: 25–31). Some argue that these populations, distinguished not by phenotypical features but by genetic frequencies, should be labelled 'races', while others reject this argument. For example, Luca Cavalli-Sforza points out that the genetic variation between Australian Aborigines and Africans is greater than that between Australian Aborigines and Asians (2001: 62–5), and, in any case, there is more genetic variation within groups which have been constructed as 'races' than between them (Bodmer and Cavalli-Sforza 1976: 588–603). The paradigm shift in genetic science is described by Paul Gilroy as follows:

Biologists like Richard Lewontin and Steven Rose have reminded as that we stand on the threshold of a transformed understanding of the visible differences coded inside human bodies. The old notions of 'race' are likely to look very different, less natural, and more unstable than they now do when confronted with a pattern of predispositions to health, illness and longevity that does not obey the predictive rules of Linnean racial typology. Perhaps a new, as it were 'postracial', genetic science will appear before long. It is already being prefigured in several forms, not all of which will respect a vestigial racial theory as the frontier of some enhanced eugenic ambitions.

(2000: 218)

In light of the different conceptions of the 'race' idea, and of the claims by some scientists that it has no scientific value at all, it is difficult to identify any utility in continuing to use the term in scientific or social-scientific analysis (cf. Montagu 1972: 63; Jones 1981; see Miles 1982: 18–19).

To illustrate the argument in more detail, we focus on the allegation of 'racial' differences in IQ. Some psychologists and other writers have postulated a correlation between 'race' and IQ, arguing that there is a consistent difference between 'black' and 'white' people, which is at least partly a consequence of innate 'racial' differences. In response, Richards comments:

In essence the situation has been that for the *majority* of psychologists, geneticists and anthropologists the question has remained 'scientifically' closed – it is meaningless and unresearchable. The controversy is not so much alive as undead. On the other hand the minority pro-differences camp, consisting primarily of a small group of, occasionally quite eminent, psychometricians (though not all psychometricians I must stress) has managed to muster enough allies to keep the controversy culturally alive. . . . A highly controversial reading of the 'socio-biology' approach during the later 1970s and 1980s reinforced this, leading many to fear a return to Social Darwinism, of which Scientific Racism was a central dogma. . . . I am referring here to the short-lived wave of right-wing readings of E.O. Wilson's new 'Socio-biology' which found within it a 'scientific' rationale for economic deregulation and insistence on the 'instinctive' basis of traditional sex-roles, heterosexuality, selfishness, aggression and competitiveness.

(1997: 262, 288n; original emphasis)

The integration of racism with sexism and homophobia is discussed in Chapter 6, while the significance of right-wing economics is discussed further below. In his conclusion, Richard argues strongly against those who accuse opponents of the pro-differences position on 'race' and IQ of being ideologically driven and ignoring 'the facts':

One is bound to conclude that those psychologists who continue to advocate the pro-differences position are knowingly doing so in bad faith. Their higher loyalty to what they see as the white race's cause in an ongoing racial war overrides any duty of integrity in relation to egalitarian and non-white scientific colleagues and intellectuals – whom they despise. . . . There was a time when race differences seemed a legitimate and meaningful area of scientific enquiry. That time has long passed. What persists is a farce in which scientific etiquette requires that we pretend we are all playing by one set of rules when one party is only interested in honing its skills in cheating.

(1997: 281)

Some disagree with the Richards's claim that the pro-differences camp is of marginal significance, and it does not automatically follow that those who would give it a greater significance are actually in agreement with it. Nevertheless, there seems to be a weighting towards the political right wing. D'Souza articulates this argument as follows:

In 1988 two social scientists, Mark Snyderman and Stanley Rothman, polled over six hundred psychologists and educators anonymously to find out what they believed about IQ tests. They discovered that most experts are convinced that such tests do measure intelligence and not simply the ability to succeed at taking tests. Moreover, 45 percent said that IQ differences between blacks and whites were partly hereditary; only 15 percent insisted that such differences were entirely due to environmental factors; others refused to answer or said the data were insufficient to arrive at a reasoned conclusion. 'There has been a real shift in the scholarly community,' Christopher Jencks says. 'The hereditarian position enjoys much wider support than it did twenty years ago, and the extreme environmental position is now considered dubious.

(1995: 442)

D'Souza does not provide a reference to Jencks here, but the statement is consistent with his position. However, it is misleading, because Jencks has argued that the gap is eradicable (see Jencks and Phillips 1998).

Nevertheless, there have been some concerted attempts to 'reveal' a hereditary difference, notoriously *The Bell Curve* by Herrnstein and Murray. This book contains nearly 900 pages, including 58 pages of bibliography, 93 illustrations (bar charts, histograms, etc.) and 44 tables. Simply put, their argument is threefold: there are 'racial' differences in intelligence that are 'natural', 'hereditary' or 'genetic'; those who argue differently are ideologically or pragmatically driven and unconcerned with 'the facts' or 'the truth'; and affirmative action programmes in the United States are misconceived (their 'scientific' evidence 'proves' this) and should be abolished (but they will probably remain in place for ideological reasons, and this will lead to disaster).

We consider these claims in turn. First, they claim that there are 'racial' differences in intelligence that are 'natural', 'hereditary' or 'genetic'. The assumptions built in to this claim are: (i) that IQ is an accurate measure of intelligence; (ii) that there are discrete races, enabling racial differences to be measured; and (iii) that these differences are not primarily caused by environmental factors, such as poverty, education, or culture. On the face of it, they do not claim that intelligence is entirely genetic, but they estimate (in what are ultimately meaningless terms) that the hereditability of IQ is between 40 and 80 per cent, probably over 60 per cent (Herrnstein and Murray 1994: 23, 105). The balance is explained as the result of environmental factors, though they also assert that these factors are influenced by 'the cognitive stratification of society' (1994: 108), which, it would seem, is ultimately structured by innate differences in intelligence. They do not demonstrate that IQ tests are an accurate measure of intelligence, but they trace, briefly, the development of intelligence testing from Francis Galton in 1869 (1994: 1ff.), apparently in order to establish its respectability, and complain that opponents of intelligence testing were ideologically driven and used insulting language about its proponents (1994: 7–13).

They try consistently to demonstrate that IQ differences are not due to environmental factors: if, for example, the low score of African-Americans was due to the history of discrimination, including slavery, then one would expect Africans, in Africa, to have a higher average IQ; however, Africans had a lower IQ than African-Americans (1994: 288–9, 565). They neglect to state that the African tests were conducted in English, a non-native language for many of the subjects (Kamin 1999: 398–9). However, they address a similar criticism, concluding: 'The correlations between the verbal and arithmetic subtests were substantially *higher* [original emphasis] for Latinos born abroad', who would have less knowledge of English, 'than for whites, blacks, or Latinos born in the United States, the opposite of what would be expected if English fluency were a problem for the foreign-borns' (Herrnstein and Murray 1994: 668). So, presumably, we must conclude on the basis of 'the scientific facts' that knowledge of English makes it more difficult to take intelligence tests in English, and ignorance of English makes it easier.

Second, the claim that their opponents are ideological axe-grinders is common among proponents of these theories, but is refuted by Richards, as we have shown above. Claims about a typology of 'race' have been repeatedly contradicted by scientific evidence, and, in a number of notorious instances, the scientific proponents of 'race' classification have been shown (e.g. in Gould 1984; Richards 1997; Montagu 1999) to have consciously or unconsciously falsified their evidence in order to claim 'scientific' support for their arguments. However, even if it were true that the world's population is permanently divided into some form of biological hierarchy, the political case against unequal treatment, which denies a common humanity, remains. All people should have the right to economic and political circumstances that permit the realisation of their faculties and abilities. This has been denied on the slave ships and plantations, in the concentration and death camps, under the Reserve and migrant labour system, and in all circumstances where the law is used to segregate and disadvantage particular populations. This right deserves to be defended, while at the same time considering the extent to which it can be realised in a capitalist society.

Third, the opposition to affirmative action programmes is a common mantra of the American right, but it has nothing to do with science, even if Herrnstein and Murray's findings are scientific and valid (which they are not). It is a non sequitur. The argument is that spending money on improving the situation of people and groups with a lower IQ is a waste of money, since their intelligence is largely inherited. This applies particularly to attempts to improve their skills, most importantly through state education. However:

> It simply does not follow that the state should withdraw resources from those who are regarded as having a poorer genetic constitution. No one would reasonably argue, for example, that spending on health should be diverted away from those with genetic disabilities to those who are perfectly healthy.
>
> (Cartwright 2000: 334)

Clearly, scientific discourses of 'race' are not what they were in the nineteenth century, but they are not dead either. The connection with eugenics may be, at most, tenuous, but the assertion of 'racial' differences in intelligence is made by a number of scientists including Herrnstein and Murray (1994), J. Philippe Rushton (1997) and Richard Lynn (1991).

The similarities between sociobiology and the currently fashionable evolutionary psychology might lead one to suppose that the latter, like the former, is influenced by scientific conceptions of 'race'. However, this appears not to be so. Rushton's work is the exception rather than the rule, and evolutionary psychologists who continue to argue for the scientific status of a concept of 'race' are marginalised by their peers. Cartwright, in a textbook on evolutionary psychology/biology, is at pains to demonstrate 'that Darwinism provides no ammunition for the eugenicist and little comfort for the racist' (2000: 337), though he also argues that the possibility of racism having some kind of evolutionary function must be considered. He writes:

> . . . racism exists and is in need of an explanation as well as a cure. We must consider the slightly frightening prospect that racism has some adaptive function. To offer an explanation is of course not to condone the behaviour. If we explain racism sociologically, for example, which is commonly done, this neither supports racism nor excuses it. Nor, crucially, does it undermine the sociological approach. If there is a biological basis to racism, it is something that we must face squarely.
>
> (2000: 336)

Whatever its faults, this is not what we will identify as scientific racism, but the danger is present for evolutionary psychology and biology, and indeed for sociology, that explanations for racism can be turned into justifications. This may be part of the historical explanation for the emergence and popularity of scientific racism: the academic must not abrogate responsibility for the uses to which his or her research may be put, but cannot predict these uses either.

CONCLUSION

In the light of this historical panorama, a number of conclusions can be drawn. First, the process of representing the Other entails a dialectic of representational inclusion and exclusion. By attributing a population with certain characteristics in order to categorise and differentiate it as an Other, those doing so establish criteria by which they themselves are represented. In the act of defining Africans as 'black' and 'savages', and thereby excluding them from their world, Europeans in the eighteenth and nineteenth centuries were representing themselves as 'white' and 'civilised'.

Moreover, using the discourse of 'race' to exclude and inferiorise, that same discourse, but with inverted meanings, served to include and superiorise: if the population of Africa was represented as a 'race', then the population of Europe is simultaneously represented as a 'race', albeit a supposedly superior one. Hence, the act of representational exclusion is simultaneously an act of inclusion, whether or not Self is explicitly identified in the discourse.

Second, for the European, the Other has not been created exclusively in the colonial context. Representations of the Other have taken as their subject not only the populations of Africa, the Asian subcontinent and the Americas, but also the populations of different parts of Europe, as well as inwardly migrant populations, notably from North Africa and the Middle East. Moreover, the Other has been created not only externally to the nation state but also within, notably in the Jewish case. Consequently, debate about the nature and origin of representations of the Other cannot be *confined* to the analysis of European colonialism.

Third, representations of the Other are holistically neither static nor unitary. They have undergone transformation over time, in response to changing circumstances, including the economic and political position of those producing and reproducing the representations. The character-istics attributed to the Other, the evaluation of those characteristics, and the explanations offered for difference, have therefore been altered, though rarely holistically. The African's skin colour has remained a constant feature of European representations, but savagery and bestiality have not. Indeed, the evaluative content of European representations has not been consistently negative, and we have seen examples where the attributed qualities have been positive. Moreover, those people who constitute the object of representation, who are created as the Other, also change over time. For example, for a long time in European history, the primary Other was found in the Muslim world rather than in central and southern Africa.

Hence, when analysing representations of the Other, it is necessary to analyse the context, including the class position of those producing and reproducing these representations, their dynamic and heterogeneous nature, and their more constant features. One cannot assume that contemporary representations are simply inherited from the past. Rather, contemporary representations are always the product of historical legacy and active transformation in the context of prevailing circumstances, including the pattern of class relations (cf. Cohen 1988).

Fourth, for the European, and other populations, somatic features (particularly skin colour) have been used to represent the Other long before European colonisation. However, exteriorisation by reference to blackness has not consistently correlated with the attribution of additional, negatively evaluated characteristics, and hence the representation of the African within the Greco-Roman world differs in a number of important respects from that created and reproduced in north-west Europe from the seventeenth century. Moreover, representations of the Other have not been based on somatic characteristics alone. Cultural characteristics have also been used, such as European representations of the Muslim world, which extensively utilised images of barbarism and sexuality in the context of a Christian/heathen dichotomy.

Fifth, the development of the discourse of 'race', and its subsequent incorporation into the discourse of science, did not entail a complete break with earlier representations of the Other. Within Europe, scientific discourse and its application to the human species took place in a context of an existing pattern of representation and inferiorisation that it incorporated and theorised by new criteria of secularised validity. Because the emergence of science did not displace earlier hierarchies of inferiority, including those which used somatic differences to identify the Other, analyses of representations of the Other that focus exclusively on the career of the discourse of 'race' arbitrarily detach that history from its roots.

This is not to minimise the gradual epistemological shift from religion to science as the criterion by which to measure and evaluate the nature of the social and material world. This transformation was highly significant in so far as it permitted and rationalised a method of inquiry that sought to investigate a level of reality that lay below that revealed by immediate and unmediated observation, and to advance explanations which were not confined to references to 'divine will'. Nevertheless, the development of science did not guarantee accuracy and veracity, partly because the agenda for scientific investigation was shaped by additional interests and by international economic and political relations.

As a result, in many different contexts, people have continued to identify the Other by reference to phenotypical features (especially skin colour) that therefore serve as indicators of an alleged significant difference. Moreover, they have continued to use the idea of 'race' to label that difference. As a result, certain sorts of social relations are defined as 'race relations', social relations between people of different 'races'. Indeed, states legislate to regulate 'race relations', with the result that the reality of 'race' is apparently legitimated in law (Guillaumin 1980, 1995; Banton 1991, 2001). Thus the idea of 'race' has continued to be used in common-sense discourse to identify the Other in many societies, although largely without the sanction of science since the 1950s, if not the 1930s.

II

CONCEPTUALISING RACISM

2

THE UNITY OF RACISM: A CRITIQUE OF CONCEPTUAL INFLATION

INTRODUCTION

Against the background of the historical review of representations of the Other in Chapter 1, we move to consider the problem of defining racism. Some analysts will describe all those representations of the Other as racism, while others will want to distinguish different categories of discourse, labelling only some as instances of racism. Thus, if there was general agreement between these groups of writers that the content of Chapter 1 constituted an accurate, if not complete, history of discourses of the Other, their disagreement would result largely from their different concepts of racism. The previous chapter therefore provides an initial historical contextualisation for the conceptual problem to be considered in the next three chapters.

In using racism as a concept to describe and explain aspects of the structure and processes of concrete social formations, it is necessary first to know to what the word refers, what particularity it identifies. That this is considered to be problematic may appear surprising, given the widespread understanding of, for example, Nazi discourse about the Jews, the justifications for apartheid in South Africa, official legitimations of

British colonial settlement and rule, or slavery in the United States. Nevertheless, the concept of racism is contested. In essence, the debate concerns the scope of the concept, and in two senses.

First, for those who define the concept as referring to a particular instance of *ideology*, there is disagreement about the form and content of that ideology. We explore this disagreement, starting from Barker's (1981) concept of the 'new racism', continuing with the development of this concept in the work of other writers. Second, some writers have claimed that the concept should be used to refer not only to ideology but also to intentional practices and/or unintended processes or consequences – such consequences are central to the concept of 'institutional racism'. In sum, there have been different cases of conceptual inflation whereby the concept has been redefined to refer to a wider range of phenomena. The purpose of this chapter is to review critically these cases of conceptual inflation, while Chapter 3 reviews the opposite problem of conceptual deflation, and Chapter 4 offers a resolution of some of the problems identified. We begin with a brief overview of the emergence of the concept of racism in order to outline the baseline for the analysis of conceptual inflation and deflation.

THE CONCEPT OF RACISM

Although the word 'racism' is now widely used in common-sense, political and academic discourse, readers may be surprised to learn that it is of very recent origin (cf. Leech 1986). There is no reference to the word in the *Oxford English Dictionary* of 1910 (although there are entries for 'race' and 'racial'). The *OED Supplement* of 1982 defines racism as 'the theory that distinctive human characteristics and abilities are determined by race' and records its first appearance in the English language in the 1930s. Anglophone critics of scientific theories of 'race' prior to the 1930s did not use a concept of racism to identify their ideological object. For example, in a wide-ranging critique published in the late 1920s, Friedrich Hertz (1928: 1–19) referred to 'race hatred'. In the late 1920s and 1930s, the term *'racisme'* was used in French critiques of German nationalism, the earliest example apparently being an *Action Française* writer who, in 1927, argued for an equivalence of the concepts of 'racism', 'subjective nationalism', 'pan-Germanism', 'xenophobia', 'bellicosity' and 'imperialism' (cited in Taguieff 2001: 93). This may be regarded as a somewhat racist use of the word 'racism', and such a judgement would be reinforced by the right-wing nationalist standpoint of *Action Française*, and Charles

Maurras's (a founder and leading figure of *Action Française*) use of the concept of racism in the 1890s as a *positive* self-designator: to be 'racist' was to be 'truly French' (Taguieff 2001: 85–6). In German, the term racism was used as a title for a book written by Magnus Hirschfeld in 1933–4, subsequently published in English translation in 1938. In *Racism*, Hirschfeld set out to refute arguments of the nineteenth century that claimed the mantle of science to sustain a notion of the existence of discrete 'races', hierarchically ordered. However, he did not offer any formal definition of racism, nor did he clarify how racism is to be distinguished from xenophobia, another concept employed in his argument (1938: 227).

The original definition and use of the word arose from the coincidence of two processes. The first, outlined in Chapter 1, was the growing body of scientific evidence that undermined the idea of 'races' as natural, discrete and fixed subdivisions of the human species, each with its distinct and variable cultural characteristics and capacity for 'civilisation'. The second was the reaction to the rise of Fascism in Germany and the use of the 'race' idea, legitimated partly by reference to science (albeit an increasingly anachronistic science) by Hitler and the German Nazis in their identification of Jews as an alien and inferior 'race' (Maser 1970). As the campaign against Jewish people in Germany unfolded (see Krausnick *et al.* 1968; Peukert 1987), there developed elsewhere in Europe and North America an increasing awareness of the way in which the discourse of 'race' was being used to legitimate the exclusion and genocide of Jewish people and other sections of the German population. It became an imperative for some academics and scientists, as well as political activists, to formulate a coherent rejection of the way in which the 'race' idea was utilised in Nazi Germany.

These two developments reinforced each other. There was an intensification of the debate about the scientific status of the discourse of 'race', evident in the publication during the 1930s and 1940s of a number of books which were explicitly critical of either a certain usage of the idea or, in certain instances, the idea itself (e.g. Huxley and Haddon 1935; Barzun 1938, 1965; Montagu 1974 [first published in 1942]; Benedict 1983 [first published in 1942]). These writers used the newly created *concept* of racism (and racialism) in different ways, and differed in the extent of their acceptance or rejection of 'racial' classification.

The prominence and significance of the concept of racism was then elevated following the end of the Second World War. Knowledge of the consequences of Hitler's 'final solution' to the 'Jewish question'

(Dawidowicz 1977; Fleming 1986) led to new initiatives after 1945 to prevent the discourse of 'race' from being used for similar political purposes in the future. The most significant was undertaken by UNESCO, and claimed the status of science, and of international collaboration and unanimity, to legitimate its objectives. During the 1950s and 1960s, UNESCO assembled, on four separate occasions, a group of scientists of international reputation who were asked to summarise the scientific evidence concerning the nature of 'race'. The objective was to demonstrate that the barbarism of the *Endlösung* rested on 'a scientifically untenable premise' (Montagu 1972: x). Of the four UNESCO statements on 'race', only the fourth explicitly addressed the issue of a definition of racism. The first three statements were intended primarily to demolish 'the myth that race determines mental aptitude, temperament, or social habits' (Montagu 1972: x). The fourth statement broadened the framework of discussion in order to address directly the definition of a concept of racism.

This statement defined racism as a falsification of the scientific knowledge about human biology: 'Racism falsely claims that there is a scientific basis for arranging groups hierarchically in terms of psychological and cultural characteristics that are immutable and innate' (Montagu 1972: 158). This definition includes those arguments that mistakenly identify a hierarchy of human groups, each of which is somehow naturally and inevitably distinct from all others.

The essence of this definition was incorporated directly into the social sciences in the 1960s and 1970s by writers such as Van den Berghe (1978: 11) and Banton (1970). The latter defined the concept of racism in the late 1960s as 'the doctrine that a man's behaviour is determined by stable inherited characters deriving from separate racial stocks having distinctive attributes and usually considered to stand to one another in relations of superiority and inferiority' (Banton 1970: 18). He was referring exclusively to nineteenth-century scientific arguments about 'race'. As a result, given that those ideas had been largely discredited by science, Banton concluded that racism was dead (1970: 28; see also Puzzo 1964: 586). Banton subsequently defined this nineteenth-century scientific doctrine as 'racial typology' rather than racism (1977: 27–8, 47, 1980: 28) and so, at least to his satisfaction at that point in time, abolished racism as a concept in sociological analysis (1987: ix). We will return to these arguments later. Their importance to this point is to establish the context for the development in Britain during the 1980s of the debate about the meaning of the concept of racism.

THE NEW RACISM

Barker's (1981) concept of the 'new racism' referred to an allegedly 'new' political discourse within the British state in the 1970s, one that asserted that it was natural for people to prefer to live among 'their own kind', and therefore to discriminate against those not considered part of that community. Such arguments either made no mention of the idea of a hierarchy of 'races' or sometimes specifically rejected the idea. Barker argued that the new racism emerged in Britain as part of a broader revision of Conservative Party ideology in the wake of its electoral defeat in 1974. One dimension of this revision focused on immigration. Immigration was regarded as having brought to Britain a population that destroyed the cultural homogeneity of the nation and that, as it grew in size, threatened to 'swamp' the culture of 'our own people'. Barker identified the 'core of the new racism' as:

> ... a theory of human nature. Human nature is such that it is natural to form a bounded community, a nation, aware of its differences from other nations. They are not better or worse. But feelings of antagonism will be aroused if outsiders are admitted ... Each community is a common expression of human nature; all of us form exclusive communities on the basis of shared sentiments, shutting out outsiders.
>
> (1981: 21–2)

Identifying this theory of human nature as a form of racism, Barker did recognise the necessity to define the general concept of racism. In doing so, he claimed that:

> ... the prevalence of a definition of racism in terms of superiority/ inferiority has helped conceal how common is a form of racism that does not need to make such assertions – indeed, can make a positive virtue out of not making them. It is indeed a myth about the past that racism has generally been of the superiority/inferiority kind.
>
> (1981: 4)

Theories and arguments are identified as racism if they see 'as biological, or pseudo-biological, groupings which are the result of social and historical process' (1981: 4).

This concept of new racism was taken up by other writers in the Marxist tradition, notably a group who wrote *The Empire Strikes Back* in the name of the Centre for Contemporary Cultural Studies (CCCS 1982: 27, 29, 48;

see also Gilroy 1987). Like Barker, they focused attention on an ideology that was seen to be an integral part of a wider ideological realignment within the Conservative Party in the context of an organic crisis of British capitalism in the 1970s. This ideology largely dispensed with notions of biological superiority and inferiority, and formulated a notion of the Other as naturally different in cultural terms, with a natural 'home' outside Britain. There is much that is similar here with Barker's analysis. What is less clear than in Barker's analysis is their definition of the concept of racism.

As with Goldberg's (1993) later work, the CCCS offers a description of the nature of racism, but, unlike Goldberg, they do not offer the hope of a 'grounded' definition. Indeed, they do not identify any criteria by which racism can be distinguished from any other ideology. They argued that racism is not a fixed, static ideology but is contradictory and constantly undergoing transformation (CCCS 1982: 9–11). They claimed that racism has deep historical roots, so that ideas and arguments derived from imperialist history are continually being reworked and given new meanings as a result of contemporary endogenous political–economic forces, and combined with new ideas and images (1982: 11–12, 48, 66, 68, 70, 74). We fully concur with these arguments. However, the CCCS collective made no attempt is made to identify the characteristics that would permit an ideology to be identified as racism. Many, if not all, ideologies are flexible and fluid and many, if not all, have a historical chronology, so these criteria do not permit us to identify what is distinctive about *racism* as an ideology.

Indeed, if racism is always in a process of transformation, it is particularly important to identify the criteria by which this ever-changing ideology can be identified. Presumably there must be some transhistorical features which identify the different racisms as instances of a specific form of ideology, distinct from other ideologies such as nationalism and sexism, for example, but we are never advised what they might be. Additionally, the CCCS text assumes, but fails to demonstrate, that the arguments of a group within the Conservative Party are hegemonic, reduces the parameters of contemporary British racism to the arguments of this small group and, most importantly of all, operates with an (undefined) conception of the new racism which is derived from a single empirical instance.

The work of this CCCS collective was influenced by the important work of its previous Director, Stuart Hall (1978, 1980). Hall recognised that racism is a 'rational abstraction' that identifies a particular phenomenon, but warned against 'extrapolating a common and universal structure to racism, which remains essentially the same, outside of its specific historical location' (1980: 337). However, if there are 'historically-specific racisms' (1980: 336), they must have common attributes that identify them as different forms of racism. For example, capitalist social formations are similarly historically specific, but they share common attributes, and hence the 'rational abstraction', capitalism, which refers to those social formations characterised by *inter alia* generalised commodity production and the commodification of labour power. Hall does not specify what the many different racisms have in common qua racism.

Nevertheless, implicit in Hall's argument is a use of a concept of racism that refers to ideology. He identified racism as 'one of the dominant means of ideological representation through which the white fractions of the class come to "live" their relations to other fractions, and through them to capital itself' (1980: 341). He recommended an investigation of the 'different ways in which racist ideologies have been constructed and made operative under different historical conditions', asserting: 'In each case, in specific social formations, racism as an ideological configuration has been reconstituted by the dominant class relations, and thoroughly reworked' (1980: 341–2). In his analysis of British indigenous racism, Hall examined the way in which the 'black' presence is identified as 'the enemy within', a signifier of crisis in British society. He explained: 'This ideology, which is formed in response to a crisis, must of course, to become a real and historical political force, connect with the lived experiences of the "silent majorities"' (1978: 30). Hall therefore uses the concept of racism in a narrower sense than that of the analytical tradition founded in events in the United States in the 1960s, as we shall see. Moreover, his suggestion that the analytical task is to identify the historically specific racisms (and their real material conditions of existence) constituted the theoretical groundwork for the specification of the 'new racism' by Barker and its use by the CCCS collective.

In comparison, Barker's analysis has the virtue of explicitly defining the concept of racism, even if it is a definition that we find problematic (Miles 1987b). In order to define the arguments of a particular faction within the Conservative Party as an instance of racism, Barker has inflated the definition to refer to all arguments that mistakenly identify a socially defined and constituted group as being a biological or pseudo-biological entity, that is to say, a 'natural' collectivity. Thus, nineteenth- and twentieth-century arguments that assert that, for example, the French people have a natural set of common characteristics that justify their constituting a nation state is an instance of racism. So is the claim that women are the weaker sex. In other words, Barker's definition of racism eliminates the distinction between racism and, respectively, nationalism and sexism.

Barker is also mistaken in his historical claim that racist ideologies have not generally asserted a hierarchy of superiority and inferiority. The historical material in Chapter 1 demonstrates clearly that a large proportion of European and North American representations of the Other have asserted such a hierarchy, certainly since the sixteenth century and probably earlier, although these have not always been expressed in terms of inherent biological differentiation. Nevertheless, identification with the Christian religion was crucial to the establishment of a hierarchy of the saved and the damned within Europe, and to the legitimation of war with the Muslim world. Significantly, Barker cites no examples to sustain his case. For these, and other reasons (see Miles 1987b), the concept of the new racism is problematic because the definition of racism is problematic.

BEYOND THE NEW RACISM?

Barker's work nevertheless opened up the discussion in Britain about both the concept of racism and the historically specific racism that many writers considered had become hegemonic in Britain by the 1980s. In this debate, other labels were employed to denote a form of racism that does not necessarily assert biological superiority and inferiority. These included 'cultural racism' and 'differentialist racism'.

Solomos (1993) does not explicitly accept Barker's analysis, nor does he utilise these other concepts, but he (rightly) recognises that Barker identified a significant political and media discourse of the late 1970s and early 1980s. He cites Barker's contribution as the identification of a tendency 'to deny the importance of racism in British society and . . . to deny that hostility to the presence of black communities in Britain is a form of racism', and of the argument that people naturally prefer to live 'with their own kind and not become a multiracial society' (1993: 193). Solomos situates this tendency and argument within a range of discourses, including new-right nationalism, opposition to anti-racism, and an emphasis on 'defending the interests of the white British majority against the claims of minority communities' (1993: 196). Solomos' analysis is perceptive and persuasive but also fails to confront the issue of the scope of the concept of racism. In order to avoid the excessive inflation of the concept of racism, it must be *demonstrated* (and not merely asserted) that such ideologies embody racism.

Gilroy's most recent work (2000: 32–4) continues to acknowledge Barker's contribution to the debate about the new racism. Gilroy observes that phenomena similar to those identified by Solomos were visible elsewhere: including the United States, 'where five great raciocultural agglomerations (Asians, blacks, Hispanics, whites, and Native Americans) appeared and took on many of the fateful characteristics associated with eighteenth-century racial groups'; and continental Europe, 'where conflicts between migrant workers and their resentful hosts were re-articulated as the grander cultural and religious opposition between Christian universalism and resurgent Islamic fundamentalism' (2000: 33). He also argues that the articulation of cultural difference is not always distinguishable from the articulation of biological difference, nor is it necessarily more benign from victims' perspectives (when connected with violence or exclusionary practices, for example). So, he concludes, 'the era of that New Racism is emphatically over' (2000: 34). Racism still exists in a pseudo-scientific form, with a biological referent, though he emphasises the differences between the 'new' genetic racism and the 'old' scientific 'raciology'. Indeed, superseding the 'new racism' analysis, for Gilroy, means recognising the 'new' genetic racism as 'a distinctive phenomenon that needs to be apprehended and countered as such' (2000: 34).

Certainly, this 'new' genetic racism uses a distinctive vocabulary. However, as Gilroy recognises, this discourse is neither hegemonic nor even dominant in the biological and genetic sciences. Furthermore, it is unclear what is *ideologically* distinctive about the 'new' genetic racism. It is a racism that represents the world's population as divided biologically, and negative (though not necessarily hierarchical) evaluations are made about some groups constructed by this division. Moreover, these latter groups are often faced with exclusionary practices and violence, and are concentrated in certain sectors of (or outside) the labour market.

Barker, Gilroy and others unnecessarily attempt to distinguish different 'forms', or 'types', of racism *chronologically*. Miles (1992: 115–16, 1993: 86) observes that Taguieff (1987, 1990, 2001) translates Barker's chronological distinction into a more satisfactory analytical distinction, between *racisme inégalitaire* (discriminatory or inegalitarian racism) and *racisme différentialiste* (differentialist racism). In the former, there is hatred of the Other, and a conception of a hierarchy or inequality of 'races'. In the latter, there is no such conception – Otherness is appreciated, to the extent that it is considered better for different 'races' to remain separate, develop separately, and, thus, maintain their distinctiveness. The consequence of this, in contemporary French and European politics, is anti-immigrant sentiment, manifest in exclusionary practices, violence and demands for 'repatriation'.

Taguieff shows a genius for developing classifications and typologies of racism that is unmatched by any of his contemporaries, as is the subtlety, complexity and sophistication of his work. Some (e.g. Wieviorka 1995) imply that his work undermines the concept of the unity of racism, which is necessary as a foundation of inquiry and defence against conceptual inflation. As Taguieff's sub-divisions of racism multiply, this is a matter of concern. However, the distinction between *racisme inégalitaire* and *racisme différentialiste* is consistent with the definition of racism that this book advocates and our attempt to limit conceptual inflation. The former articulates an explicit concept of 'race' and a negative evaluation of one or more 'races'. The latter articulates a concept of 'race' that is at least as strong (i.e. the foundation of difference), and the Other is evaluated as incapable of being compatible with Self – it is 'them' who must be isolated from 'us', not vice versa.

INSTITUTIONAL RACISM

A second kind of conceptual inflation is also rooted in the 1967 UNESCO statement on 'race'. The statement offered a further definition of racism as 'antisocial beliefs and acts which are based on the fallacy that discriminatory intergroup relations are justifiable on biological grounds' (Montagu 1972: 158). While the statement failed to justify or explore the implications of this inflation of the scope of the concept to include practices as well as discourse, other writers have since pursued the logic of this inflation in two, interrelated, directions. The first has been to define as racism all processes that, intentionally or otherwise, result in the continued exclusion of a subordinate group. The second has been to define as racism all activities and practices that are intended to protect the advantages of a dominant group and/or to maintain or widen the unequal position of a subordinate group. In both instances, the dominant and subordinate groups are usually designated by reference to skin colour, as 'whites' and 'blacks' respectively. Consequently, racism is, by definition, effected (intentionally or otherwise) by 'white' people to the disadvantage of 'black' people. We will later refer to this latter claim as a significant deflation of the concept of racism.

These definitions of racism were shaped by the political struggle of African-Americans against their position of inequality in the United States. The experience of material deprivation and exclusionary practice in the southern states and northern cities of the United States gave rise to political resistance which increased in scope and intensity during the twentieth century. In the context of resistance in the 1960s, Carmichael and Hamilton published *Black Power* (1968), a book that presented what became a very influential political analysis and strategy. They defined racism as 'the predication of decisions and policies on considerations of race for the purpose of *subordinating* a racial group and maintaining control over that group' (1968: 3). They distinguished between overt, individual racism and covert, institutional racism (which they also described as internal colonialism). The former was defined as explicit actions by individuals and the latter as those actions and inactions which maintain 'black' people in a disadvantaged situation and which rely on 'the active and pervasive operation of anti-black attitudes and practices' (1968: 5). Thus, the concept of racism was expanded in meaning to include not only beliefs but, more importantly, all actions, individual and institutional, which had the consequence of sustaining or increasing the subordination of 'black' people.

A number of American academics took up this idea of institutional racism and attempted to give it greater coherence and analytical power in an academic context where the dominant concept was prejudice and the dominant paradigm was social psychological, locating the origin of the problem in the cognitive errors of individuals (Henriques 1984: 65–81). Not all of these attempts achieved these objectives. Knowles and Prewitt (1969), for example, failed to offer a formal definition of institutional racism but seemed to use it to mean practices within institutions which ensure that 'black citizens . . . are consistently penalised for reasons of color' but which may be neither intentional nor motivated by 'conscious bigotry' (1969: 4–7). Blauner was more careful to define his concepts explicitly. He argued that the definition of the racism should be extended to refer not only to individual prejudiced attitudes but also to processes that sustain 'white' domination:

> The processes that maintain domination – control of whites over non-whites – are built into the major social institutions. . . . Thus there is little need for prejudice as a motivating force. Because this is true,

the distinction between racism as an objective phenomenon, located in the actual existence of domination and hierarchy, and racism's subjective concomitants of prejudice and other motivations and feelings is a basic one.

(1972: 9–10)

Thus, Blauner expanded the concept of racism to refer to two different phenomena that are very similar to Carmichael and Hamilton's distinction between individual racism and institutional racism. Significantly, Blauner did not identify criteria for identifying either 'prejudice' or those processes that 'maintain . . . control of whites over non-whites'.

The second direction we identify is represented by Wellman, who also extended explicitly the definition of racism to denote more than 'prejudiced beliefs'. While Wellman used the concept to refer to personal prejudice, he argued that 'the essential feature of racism is . . . the defense of a system from which advantage is derived on the basis of race' (1977: 221–2) and hence he claimed that 'racism is a structural relationship based on the subordination of one racial group by another' (1977: 35). As well as accepting the concept of a 'racial group', Wellman defines racism on the basis of its effects, not its ideological content:

A position is racist when it defends, protects, or enhances social organisation based on racial disadvantage. Racism is determined by the consequences of a sentiment, not its surface qualities. . . . White racism is what white people do to protect the special benefits they gain by virtue of their skin colour.

(1977: 76)

Hence, both Blauner and Wellman inflate the definition of racism to include not only discourses (whether formal or disaggregated), but also (and more importantly) all actions and processes (whatever their origin or motivation) which result in one group being placed or retained in a subordinate position by another (cf. Williams 1985: 329–30). The concept of racism is used therefore to refer to a range of phenomena (beliefs, actions, processes) but with a specific emphasis on their consequences for the domination of one group by another. These groups are defined, respectively, as 'black' and 'white', and consequently racism is conceived as something that 'white' people think about and do to 'black' people.

These American theories have been as influential as they are controversial. The concept of institutional racism was noted by a number of

British analysts in the late 1960s and early 1970s (Leech 1986: 85) and, since then, has been used to analyse the British situation (e.g. Sivanandan 1982; Miles and Phizacklea 1984; Parekh 2000). The use of the concept is explained in part by the historical context. Although theories of biological inferiority were rarely articulated publicly by the 1960s, descendants of those people who had been colonised and the subject of nineteenth-century theories of 'race' had migrated from the British colonies and ex-colonies to the 'mother country'. There they were concentrated in some of the worst housing and employed in largely manual jobs, despite certain forms of 'racial' discrimination being declared illegal during the 1960s. Accordingly, attention began to turn away from explicit expressions of racism (qua ideology) and from intentional and individual discriminatory actions. As in the United States, the problem was identified as one of determining the cause of 'black disadvantage', and the meaning of racism was inflated to expedite this task.

Yet the concept of institutional racism was introduced and used with little analytical rigour (Mason 1982; Williams 1985; Phillips 1987). For example, the term occupied a central position in Sivanandan's influential writing of the 1970s and 1980s (e.g. 1982: 61, 84, 109, 113, 138) and yet he offered no formal definition. Although he implied a distinction between racism, institutional racism and racialism, these concepts were not defined and defended systematically. In an early paper, Sivanandan distinguished between racism and racialism, using the former to refer to 'an explicit and systematic ideology of racial superiority' and the latter to refer to the unequal treatment of different 'races' (1973: 383). In a later set of essays, he defined racialism as simply attitudes and behaviour, and racism as the systematisation of these attitudes and behaviour into 'an explicit ideology of racial superiority and their institutionalisation in the state apparatus' (1982: 170n). Subsequently, he used the concept of racialism to denote racial prejudice and racial discrimination (1983: 2). Later still, he defined racialism as individual prejudiced attitudes, and racism as 'structures and institutions with power to discriminate' (1985: 27).

Within Sivanandan's analysis, the meanings of these terms shift without explanation: at one point, racialism is used to denote discriminatory treatment, and at another, individual prejudice, while racism first denotes a particular and explicit ideology, later those institutions with the power to discriminate. In this latter example, racism seems to have been equated with institutional racism, denoting any institution with the power to discriminate rather than a systematic ideology of 'race'. Viewed collectively, these writings demonstrate a transition to a conception (not always explicitly defined) of racism that uses the term to refer primarily, though not exclusively, to institutional discriminatory practices. The concept of racism therefore focuses upon practices to the exclusion of ideology: 'It is the acting out of racial prejudice and not racial prejudice itself that matters. ... Racism is about power not about prejudice' (Sivanandan 1983: 3). Logically, x is what matters, therefore x is racism.

During the 1990s, the concept of institutional racism moved to centre stage in Britain, in large part as a result of the political and public attention paid to violence against British citizens of Caribbean and Asian origin. The Macpherson report defined institutional racism as follows:

> The collective failure of an organisation to provide an appropriate and professional service to people because of their colour, culture or ethnic origin. It can be seen or detected in processes; attitudes and behaviour which amount to discrimination through unwitting prejudice, ignorance, thoughtlessness and racist stereotyping which disadvantage minority ethnic people.
>
> (Macpherson 1999: §6.34)

Here, the concept of institutional racism is inflated even further than in the aforementioned American works. It includes inaction as well as action, ignorance as well as beliefs, of a dominant group when it has the effect of widening the unequal positions between a dominant and subordinate group. In the same paragraph, it is explicitly stated that institutional racism:

> ... persists because of the *failure* of the organisation openly and adequately to recognise and address its existence and causes by policy, example and leadership. *Without* recognition and action to eliminate such racism it can prevail as part of the ethos or culture of the organisation. It is a corrosive disease.
>
> (1999: §6.34; added emphasis)

The report is consistent in defining racism from the victim's perspective. This approach reaches a zenith with the recommendation that a 'racist incident' be defined as 'any incident which is perceived to be racist by the victim or any other person' (1999: §47.12).

We have already referred to Banton's (2001: 184) claim that 'the concept of a *racial group* is the price to be paid for a law against indirect discrimination' – similarly, such an inflated concept of racism and institutional racism is perceived as necessary in the struggle against racism and violence inspired by racism. This is particularly true of the definition of a racist incident, which was framed so as to compel the British police to take seriously incidents of violence which may have been motivated by racism. Analytically, however, defining racism from the victim's perspective is antithetical to a definition of racism as ideology, and facilitates a greater (potentially infinite) conceptual inflation. One could conceivably claim that *any* action (or inaction) on the part of another individual (or group) constitutes racism, irrespective of whether or not the claim is justified by or reflective of an ideological motivation for the action (or inaction).

Collectively, these arguments about institutional racism offer a very different concept of racism from that of racism as ideology. First, the concept has a generalised rather than a specific referent: it identifies as racism all those beliefs, actions and processes that lead to, or sustain, discrimination against and the subordination of 'black' people. Second, it denies that intentionality or motivation are measures of the presence or absence of racism. While an explicit motive or intention to subordinate may be evident, it is not considered a necessary condition for the identification of racism. Third, by definition, racism is a prerogative of 'white' people. Fourth, although there are important exceptions (e.g. Sivanandan 1983, 1985), it asserts or assumes a theory of stratification in which the terms 'white' and 'black' have analytical status. The social formation under analysis is identified as constituted by the presence of two (homogeneous) groups, 'whites' and 'blacks', which have a hierarchical relationship with each other. In that hierarchy, 'blacks' are a subordinated totality and totally subordinated while 'whites' are a dominant totality and totally dominant. By implication, the struggle between these two groups constitutes the primary, if not the sole, dynamic within the social formation. Thus, the significance of racism is simultaneously enlarged and de-contextualised.

CONCLUSION

Viewed in broad perspective, this analytical inflation of the concept of racism surveyed in this chapter occurred for two (interrelated) reasons. First, the long history of the interdependence of capitalist development and the subordination of colonised populations began a new chapter with the migration of colonised people from the peripheries of capitalism (overseas colonies in the case of Europe, or the southern plantations in the case of the United States) to the metropolitan centres. Within the peripheries of capitalism in the eighteenth and nineteenth centuries, the exploitation of colonised labour power in unfree relations of production placed the colonised in a subordinate position to the emergent proletariat of the core, legitimated by representations of the Other which identified the colonised as belonging to biologically inferior 'races'.

During the second half of the twentieth century, and following the migration from periphery to centre, it became apparent that the commodification of 'black' labour power was widely (although not exclusively) accompanied by subordination 'below' the position occupied by a majority of indigenous labour power (evident in the concentration of migrant labourers in the poorest quality housing and in semi- and unskilled manual labour, for example). Many analysts concluded that the essential structure of 'black' subordination had not changed, even if the ideological justification had. The point of emphasis became the continuity of structural subordination rather than ideological transformation. Consequently, the meaning of racism was inflated to take account of this.

Second, from a radical, and certainly from a Marxist, perspective, this transformation sustained an argument that linked racism and capitalism functionally and causally. Thus, the political critique of capitalism could be broadened and capitalism could be damned for yet another reason. Morally, this critique was sustained by the horror and outrage concerning the Holocaust, which ensured that the word racism took on a new sense of disapproval after 1945. There were therefore good political and moral reasons to continue to employ the concept because it carried with it a strong negative evaluation. To label someone or something as an instance of racism was to place the person or event outside the boundaries of civilisation. We consider in Chapter 4 whether or not this inflation of the concept of racism was the only analytical response possible. Before we do so, we first consider a deflation of the meaning of the concept of racism that paralleled the inflation of the concept discussed in this chapter.

3

THE DIVERSITY OF RACISM: A CRITIQUE OF CONCEPTUAL DEFLATION

INTRODUCTION

The conceptual inflation discussed in the preceding chapter has been accompanied by a parallel and sometimes interrelated conceptual deflation. That is to say, when one examines the discussion about the meaning and scope of the concept of racism as it has developed since the late 1960s, and taking as one's point of reference the historical origin of the concept, we find that its meaning has been limited in a number of ways. We identify a number of such instances in this chapter, all of which result in a significant curtailment of the explanatory power of the concept of racism. Our objective is to sustain a concept of racism that emphasises the diversity of the phenomenon and that conceives of it as an ideological phenomenon that works through a Self/Other dialectic.

'WHITE' RACISM

Dictionary definitions of racism frequently allude to a belief in a hierarchy of 'races', or the superiority of one 'race' over other 'races'. In the academic literature, however, one of the most common and influential deflations of the concept of racism has been its (re)definition as an exclusively 'white' phenomenon. As we have seen in the previous chapter, a number of analysts in the United States concluded during the 1960s and 1970s that only 'white' people express racist sentiments and act in a racist manner (e.g. Wellman 1977). This argument has been endorsed and developed by Katz, who argued not only that 'racism is a White problem in that its development and perpetuation rest with White people' (1978: 10) but that racism is a psychological disorder 'deeply embedded in White people from a very early age on both a conscious and an unconscious level', This has, as a result, 'deluded Whites into a false state of superiority that has left them in a pathological and schizophrenic state' (1978: 14–15). Thus, the concept of racism is defined to refer to all actions, inactions, sentiments and silences that sustain 'black' subordination, and also to a form of schizophrenia that all 'white' people 'have', in the sense that it structures the totality of their experience and being-in-the-world.

It follows that 'white' people lack the capacity to understand, analyse and explain racism, and that 'white' involvement in exposing and resisting racism is only further evidence of a racist and colonising mentality because it implies that the victims are unable to act as autonomous beings on their own account. These arguments are articulated more in the political than the academic arena, although an echo is apparent in the problematic category of 'white sociology' (CCCS 1982: 133–4). Some might conclude that the writing of this book is, by definition, a failure because 'white' sociologists are incapable of understanding the 'black' experience, though it is unlikely that they would make the concomitant assumption that only 'white' people are able to understand what motivates racism.

We reject these arguments, in part because of the racialised essentialism on which they are based. Let us explore this in a grounded manner. It is true that the experience of people of Caribbean and Asian origin in Britain, for example, is different from that of the 'indigenous' population in so far as sections of the latter, as well as the British state, articulate racism and practise discrimination against the former. It is also true that acceptance of racist and colonial imagery can lead to closure of the space within which resistance to racism is formulated and practised by members of the 'indigenous' population. The mistake is to assume that, as a result, all Caribbean and Asian experience is different from that of the indigenous population and that all members of the indigenous population consistently engage in such acts of closure. It is a mistake because such assumptions inaccurately generalise about a socially constructed category on the basis of the experience of a sample in particular contexts, and because they deny a relative objectivity in order to advance an absolute subjectivity. Expressed empirically, it is evidently a mistake because there is a long tradition of 'white' people being involved in anti-racist activities of many kinds.

In other words, there is no single truth about racism that only 'black' people can know. To assert the contrary is to condemn 'white' people to a universal condition that implies possession of a permanent essence that inevitably sets them apart. As Said (1995: 322) has remarked, 'the notion that there are geographical spaces with indigenous, radically "different" inhabitants who can be defined on the basis of some religion, culture, or racial essence proper to that geographical space is . . . a debatable idea'. Armed with the notion that truth is relative and negotiated, and hence with the assumption that one may advance claims that may subsequently be refuted, there is no reason to believe that the amount of melanin in one's skin naturally or inevitably prevents one from contributing to an understanding of the nature and origin of racism. Indeed, one can only succeed in that task if, in a society in which skin colour is signified, others with a different skin colour participate in the realisation of that objective.

The concept of institutional racism, qua a reductionist concept implying that only 'whites' are racist and only 'blacks' the victims of racism, can be criticised on a number of grounds (cf. Miles 1982: 72–9). Importantly, this deflation of the concept has as a consequence a concomitant inflation of the concept, as we have seen and will see again. The criticisms are fourfold. First, the concept is inseparable from a theory of stratification that is simplistic and erroneous because it states or assumes that the sole or primary division within a society is between 'white' and 'black' people. This suppresses or denies the existence of class divisions, and the (unequal) distribution of 'white' and 'black' people to different class positions. Consequently, the simplistic definition of ('white') racism as 'prejudice + power' (such as in Katz 1978: 10) ignores class and other divisions within the 'white' population, and hence the differential access to power among that population. Racist beliefs and sympathy for Fascist politics among sections of the 'white' working class in Britain (e.g. Phizacklea and Miles 1980: 175) are therefore more accurately understood as a response to powerlessness rather than the consequence of the possession of power.

Moreover, 'black' people in the United States do not constitute a homo-geneous population, occupying a common economic position subordinate to all 'white' people. There is now a very considerable literature in the United States about the uneven distribution of not only African-Americans across the sites of different classes but also of Mexican-Americans, Asian-Americans and other ethnicised populations (e.g. Massey 1986; Small 1994; Kitano and Daniels 2001). Moreover, if racism is defined as the prerogative of 'white' people and as the consequence of any action which sustains the subordination of 'black' people, it is not clear how one can conceptualise and explain, for example, the continued situation of economic disadvantage of sections of the 'black' population in American cities where 'black' people occupy positions of power in the political administration (cf. Gurnah 1984: 12).

Similarly, it is not clear how one can conceptualise the continued economic disadvantage of (often female) 'black' employees of the small, but growing, 'black' bourgeoisie and petite bourgeoisie in Britain (see, for example, Hoel 1982; Anthias 1983; Mitter 1986). It could be claimed that, because those in positions of power are 'black', it follows by definition that their (conscious or unconscious) actions cannot be racist, but this contradicts the conceptualisation of racism as all those *acts* that have as their consequence the creation or maintenance of disadvantage. This problem is evident in, for example, Sivanandan's (1985: 14) use of quotation marks when referring to the 'black' petite bourgeoisie, suggesting that when 'black' people occupy positions of economic, political and administrative power they become less 'black'.

Second, this concept of racism is ultimately teleological. If, as Katz (1978: 10) argues, racism is a disease that all 'white' people 'have', and if racism is 'perpetuated by Whites through their conscious and/or unconscious support of a culture and institutions that are founded on racist policies and practices', then all 'white' actions (and inactions) are racist. The definition is all-inclusive, with the result that, for example, if a 'white' person suggests that some particular act is not racist, this can only be interpreted as evidence of a 'delusion' because, by definition, all 'whites' are sick and all acts that sustain the status quo are racist. In other words, the concept has no discriminatory power. And yet the analytical objective of identifying a phenomenon as racism is to distinguish it (by reference to specified criteria) from others that do not exhibit those qualities and can therefore be defined as 'not racism'. But in an inherently and holistically racist society, there can be no actions carried out by 'whites' which have the quality of 'not racism'. The concept therefore assumes what should be demonstrated, explained and contextualised (though certainly not minimised) in every particular instance. This particular deflation of the concept of racism leads dialectically to a concomitant universalisation of racism.

Third, the definition of racism as a structural domination of 'black' by 'white' limits the scope of analysis to a limited range of historical instances. It excludes many conjunctures in which, by another definition, a racist ideology has been expressed in order to legitimate exclusionary practices, but where the object of racism was not 'black' people (Miles 1993: 128–69). For example, in the nineteenth century, the Irish in Britain were widely defined as a distinct 'race', and although the stereotype of the Irish was not consistently negative, it was nevertheless a stereotype which attributed specific characteristics to the Irish 'race' in a deterministic manner (Curtis 1968, 1971; Walvin 1986: 93). As recently as the 1920s, an official report to the General Assembly of the Church of Scotland identified the Irish 'race' as a threat to the existence of the Scottish 'race' and its positive cultural attributes, stereotyped the Irish as criminals, claimed they were intending political domination, and called for controls over Irish immigration to Scotland (see Miles and Muirhead 1986). The idea of the Irish as an inferior 'race' was accompanied by widespread violence against them, by active trade union opposition to their employment, and discrimination by employers (Miles 1982: 135–45). In turn, this had significant effects on the expression of racism in Scotland after 1945 (Miles and Dunlop 1986, 1987).

In the United States in the early twentieth century, a campaign for controls on the entry of certain European populations was organised on the basis of the attribution of 'racial' inferiority. It was argued, citing evidence supplied by psychologists, that the population of Europe was made up of different 'races', with differing innate intelligence, and that an increasing proportion of immigrants to the United States, originating from Southern and Eastern Europe, were of inferior 'race'. In comparison with people of British, German and Scandinavian 'stock', Italian, Polish, Russian and Jewish immigrants were said to have naturally inferior intelligence. Advocates of immigration control claimed that the increasing presence of this Southern European 'race' in the United States was lowering the average level of intelligence and predicted dire consequences. The Johnson–Lodge Immigration Act was passed in 1924 with the intention of preventing 'race deterioration' as a result of immigration from Europe (Kamin 1977: 30–51; Gould 1984: 224–32).

Furthermore, as we saw in Chapter 1, the idea of 'race' has been used to identify and exclude Jewish people. Throughout nineteenth-century Europe, older representations of the Jews as ritual murderers, wanderers, and conspirators bent on world domination were revitalised and given new force through the idea of 'race', legitimated by science. This ideological confluence sustained an idea of the distinctiveness of, and conflict between, Aryan and Jewish 'races'. In Nazi Germany, in a wider context of economic and political crisis, the idea of the Jewish people as a degenerate, unproductive and criminal 'race', as simultaneously a 'race' of exploiters and revolutionaries (Mosse 1978: 178, 219), was a key factor in the evolution of a state policy of genocide. The significance of the science of 'race', supported by the Nazi state, was evident in the continuation of anthropological measurements of Jewish people in the concentration camps, alongside human vivisection, the subjects of which were also usually Jewish (Biddiss 1975: 17; Mosse 1978: 227–8).

If one retains a definition of racism as all actions, intended or otherwise, by 'white' people that have the consequence of sustaining their dominance over 'black' people, the three examples just discussed cannot be accepted for consideration. Reflecting on more recent events, such a definition also excludes consideration of, for example, recent genocides in Rwanda and Bosnia, the conflict in the Middle East, and the upsurge of hostility to Russian Jews following the collapse of communist regimes in Central and Eastern Europe. Using such a definition, these must all be defined as instances of some other phenomenon, despite the articulation of the idea of 'race' and its legitimation of discrimination and/or murder. Clearly, a concept of racism that is formulated by reference to a single historical example (the United States) and then applied uncritically to another (Britain) has a degree of specificity that seriously limits its analytical scope.

The fourth problem is that the distinctions between belief and action, and between intentionality and unintentionality, are obscured. In the case of the concept of institutional racism, this is presented as a virtue insofar as it is argued that the intentionality or otherwise of actions is secondary to their consequences. The interrelations between belief and action, and between intended and unintended consequences, are complex. Beliefs may not be accompanied by logically appropriate actions, and some actions are inconsistent with beliefs. Actions can produce consequences consistent with motivations and intentions, but they often have unanticipated outcomes. These 'inconsistencies' are omnipresent in social life, and give rise to major methodological problems for the determination of 'causality'. They are largely marginalised by this homogeneous concept of racism.

There are a number of reasons to object to this marginalisation. Whether disadvantage is the consequence of intentionality and a belief in the existence and inferiority of certain 'races', or of the unintentional outcome of decisions or taken-for-granted processes by people who do not hold such beliefs, invites distinct interventionist strategies. In other words, if the determinants are different, so should be the responses to prevent them from occurring in the future. Moreover, where there is no consistent or logical connection between ideas and actions, an analysis of the prevalence of racist beliefs may be an unreliable guide to the extent of discriminatory behaviour, and vice versa. Defining racism by reference to consequences absolves the analyst (and activist) from the task of identifying the diverse processes that create and reproduce disadvantage. Yet there are many forms and determinants of disadvantage. The claim that the concept 'racism' identifies only those actions that have 'black' disadvantage as their consequence excludes a large number of actions and processes. Particularly, and circularly, it assumes that these actions are in some way exclusive in that they occur only where 'black' people are present and therefore because of the meaning attached to their 'blackness'. The advocates of this argument explicitly assert the exclusive nature of racism when they argue that it refers to what 'white' people do to 'black' people. Where the concept of racism is used to identify certain negative beliefs about people defined as 'black' and/or actions that intentionally exclude, there is a clear measure of the exclusivity of disadvantage.

If the presence of certain beliefs and of intentionality are defined as irrelevant to the identification of racism, the problem of exclusivity is correspondingly intensified. For example, it is often argued that 'word of mouth' recruitment to jobs is an instance of institutional racism because, in a workplace where no 'black' people are employed, such a process will therefore exclude them, irrespective of the intention and beliefs of the employer. But such a procedure excludes individuals from any group that is not represented in the place of work. Thus, if women, Irish or Jewish people are not present, then they too are excluded by this method of recruitment, and hence the practice of 'word of mouth' recruitment does not only exclude 'black people'. There are analytical implications. Is the exclusion of women, Jewish and Irish people to be defined as institutional racism? If not, how are these instances to be conceptually differentiated? And if they are, by what logic does one identify institutional racism as a specific phenomenon when other people are also excluded by the identical practice?

To identify racism as an exclusive phenomenon, affecting only certain groups of people, it is essential to demonstrate that the consequences are exclusive or cannot be explained in any other way. In other words, if neither specific beliefs nor intentionality are necessary criteria by which to identify racism, the potential to make a spurious correlation is considerably increased. Hence, systematic comparative analysis is essential: it is necessary to demonstrate that 'black' people collectively are treated in a certain manner or experience a particular disadvantage, and that the same treatment and disadvantage are not experienced by any other group. Demonstrating that something does not happen to another group is, methodologically, much more difficult than demonstrating that something does happen to one particular group. As a result, assertions that particular practices constitute an exclusive instance of institutional racism are often difficult to substantiate.

SCIENCE, IDEOLOGY AND DOCTRINE

We pursue our discussion of the ways in which the definition of the concept of racism has been constrained or deflated by reference to the writing of two British sociologists who engaged in a debate about the concept in the late 1960s and during the 1970s. Both Michael Banton and John Rex went on to make important contributions to our understanding of the history of racism, of its relationship to discrimination and of the multiple consequences of the expression of racism, although their work is grounded within very different paradigms (e.g. Rex 1970, 1986; Banton 1977, 1987).

We noted in Chapter 2 that, at the end of the 1960s, Banton had concluded that racism was no longer a viable concept in a world where the doctrine of 'racial typology' no longer had any legitimacy or support. Banton's rejection of the concept of racism – based on a deflation of its scope – is indicative of four problems that arose from the fact that this original concept of racism was shaped by the particular historical context, and political strategies, of the 1930s and 1940s. First, the concept of racism was forged largely in a conscious attempt to withdraw the sanction of science from a particular meaning of the idea of 'race'. This required a rejection of this product of nineteenth-century science, with the result that what had previously been considered to be a scientific fact had been transformed into an ideological category. However, in the process of effecting this transformation, racism was defined narrowly to refer exclusively to this specific ideological object. As a result, when the concept was applied to other social contexts or when the social context changed, it failed to identify an object. In the absence of an explicit, nineteenth-century discourse of 'race', with its correlate assertions, the analyst could only conclude that racism had evaporated.

This issue had been recognised by those who drafted the fourth UNESCO statement on 'race' in 1967. The statement noted that the widespread exposure of the falsity of assertions that the human species is composed of a hierarchy of biologically distinct groups had transformed the content of racism:

> Whenever it [racism] fails in its attempts to prove that the source of group differences lies in the biological field, it falls back upon justifications in terms of divine purpose, cultural differences, disparity of educational standards or some other doctrine which would serve to mask its continued racist beliefs.
>
> (Montagu 1972: 159)

Therefore, the deflation of the scope of the concept of racism, to refer solely to a nineteenth-century conception, led to its exclusion from some discourses and analyses, a consequence of which was a corresponding inflation of the concept in order to maintain its place in the lexicon. However, there is an alternative to Banton's rejection of the concept of racism. Returning to the notion of historically specific racisms, we can refer to this very specific ideological product of nineteenth-century science as 'scientific racism' (thus partially reflating the scope of the necessarily wider concept of racism). Comas (1961) was an early advocate of this conceptualisation. Miles (1982: 21), along with others (e.g. Rich 1986: 13), has followed and elaborated this conceptual strategy. This of course presumes a generic definition of racism, of which this scientific form is but one instance, a matter that is a central concern of this book.

Second, the original definition of racism tended to remain inextricably entangled with, and consequently to legitimate, the idea of 'race'. Because the definition of racism was confined to refer to the nineteenth-century discourse of 'race', in a context where either the idea of 'race' was given scientific legitimacy, or was not explicitly rejected on the grounds of having no real referent, the concept of racism, while rejecting as unscientific the formulation that 'race' determines culture, left the idea of 'race' unquestioned and unchallenged. Thus, racism was exposed as a false doctrine, but it was conceded (sometimes by default, sometimes explicitly) that the human species was nevertheless divided into 'races'. In other words, the concept of 'race' remained, sanctioning some form of biological classification as meaningful and descriptively useful. This ambiguity became the focus for an extended critique of what Miles has described as the 'race relations' paradigm (e.g. 1982, 1993).

Third, because racism became a label attached to a set of beliefs about 'race' used to justify exclusionary actions and, ultimately, genocide, the historical context ensured that the concept of racism carried with it a prominent moral and political content. To label a set of assertions as racism, and the person who articulated them as a racist, consequently associated those ideas and persons with Hitler and Fascism. Hence, within a liberal and humanitarian tradition, the ideas and arguments that the concept of racism came to denote were morally reprehensible and politically unacceptable to those writers who coined and employed the term. Thus, it was a concept that claimed scientific justification for its rejection of the claims of nineteenth-century scientific investigation while simultaneously expressing a clear value judgement about what were acceptable beliefs.

Fourth, this early definition of racism, by focusing on the product of nineteenth-century scientific theorising, tended to presume that racism was always, and therefore only, a structured and relatively coherent set of assertions, usually sustained by reference to formally organised empirical evidence. This is demonstrated in Banton's early definition of racism as a *doctrine*. Such a definition excludes less formally structured assertions, stereotypical ascriptions and symbolic representations which draw meaning from unstated assertions or assumptions of causal determination, and which do not meet the criterion of constituting an explicitly 'logical' structure.

One of the members of the 1967 UNESCO group was John Rex. In the course of a critique of Banton's analysis of the concept of racism, Rex later advanced an argument similar to that contained in the UNESCO statement. Suggesting that biological arguments that identify and justify group differentiation have functional substitutes derived from different discourses, Rex argued that:

> . . . the common element in all these theories is that they see the connection between membership of a particular group and of the genetically related sub-groups (i.e. families and lineages) of which that

group is compounded and the possession of evaluated qualities as
completely deterministic.

(1970: 159)

In other words, the concept of racism refers to any argument, irrespective
of form and content, that suggests that the human species is composed
of naturally occurring discrete groups in order to legitimate social
inequality. This conception of racism refers to the function rather than
the content of discourses: the definition does not focus on a particular
ideological content but on the intention and/or consequence of any
deterministic assertion about group differences. While this widens the
definition to include any deterministic attribution of qualities to a group
identified as biologically or culturally distinct in order to justify inequality
– and therefore includes arguments or statements such as 'women should
not be put in positions of responsibility because their emotional character
prevents them from making rational decisions', which might otherwise be
designated as sexist, and 'I don't go to Italian restaurants because Italians
are rude' – it also deflates the definition because it has become, at least in
part, a functionalist definition of racism that must therefore exclude purely
descriptive statements when they are not intended to, or when they do not
explicitly, justify inequality (cf. Miles 1982: 72–9).

Rex's critique of Banton's position did nevertheless highlight the
limitations of a concept of racism that confined its scope to the necessary
appearance of doctrine. Defining racism, as we do, as ideology rather
than a doctrine includes within its scope relatively unstructured, incoherent
and unsupported assertions, stereotypical ascriptions and symbolic representations; in short, beliefs that are consciously held but not logically
structured. This is the stuff of everyday life, characterised as it is by
discourses that usually consistently fail to meet the standards of formal,
logical debate. It is the stuff that Gramsci sought to understand through
his concept of common sense. However, it does not include *unconscious*
attitudes and assumptions, nor, for that matter, exclusionary practices and
violence. Contrast this with Wieviorka's (1995) influential analysis.
Wieviorka distinguishes between three strands of racism that together
comprise what he defines as the unity of racism, and that can be summarised
as: prejudices, assumptions, attitudes and opinions; exclusionary practices,
or behaviours of discrimination, segregation and violence; and racism as an
ideology, doctrine, or political programme. In comparison, our definition
may look too narrow. Yet, it is possible to synthesise the two positions in

the following way: racism is primarily an ideology, but it is articulated and manifest in a plurality of forms (Brown 2000: 86).

THE DIALECTIC OF SELF AND OTHER

Emerging from our critique of the inflationary and deflationary elements in the debate about the concept of racism over the past fifty years or so is a definition of racism as an ideology that is characterised by its content. More specifically, to this point, it is a content that asserts or assumes the existence of separate and discrete 'races', and attributes a negative evaluation of one or some of these putative 'races'. But this formulation may incorporate a further significant and unreasonable limitation on the scope of the concept. In other words, it may constitute another instance of conceptual deflation. As we pointed out in the Introduction, this negative evaluation is usually of a 'race' or 'races' to which the person articulating the racist ideology does not regard himself or herself as belonging. In other words, the emerging definition of racism is, to this point, premised on the identification of a negatively evaluated Other. However, there are examples of ideologies where the primary emphasis is focused on a positive conceptualisation of Self as a 'race'.

For example, the racism of the Third Reich was premised on a categorisation of the Self as an Aryan 'race' (we will introduce the concept of racialisation in Chapter 4 to identify this process theoretically), a 'race' that was attributed with an excessively positive evaluation. For Hitler, 'race' determined culture and historical development, and he identified the Aryan 'race' as chosen to rule the world and as the guarantor of civilisation (Dawidowicz 1977: 44–8). Consequently, and subsequently, the idea that the Aryan 'race' was engaged in a struggle for survival with the Jewish 'race' was embodied in the Nuremberg Laws of 1935. They were intended to maintain the purity of German 'blood' in order to ensure the continued existence of the German people, and they made marriage and sexual relations between Jews and Germans illegal (Dawidowicz 1977: 98–101). Jews were declared in law to be non-Germans:

> This legal definition, separating German Jews from Germans, laid the foundation for the liquidation of these 'parasites' who were poisoning the German blood and the German nation. Arguments invoking genocide were frequently phrased in terms of biological pollution and racial hygiene.
>
> (Seidel 1986: 21)

Thus, it was the conceptualisation of the Self as a superior 'race' (Aryans) that solicited the conceptualisation of the Other as the inferior 'race' (Jew) and that resulted in genocide. Elsewhere, the racism of the Ku Klux Klan has been legitimated in terms of 'defending' the 'superiority' of 'the white race'. Indeed, 'white' supremacism – in the United States, Nazi Germany, South Africa, Europe and elsewhere – is frequently seen as more threatening and insidious than racisms that prioritise the inferiorisation of the Other, racisms that can be described as heterophobic (anti-Other). In other words, although the historical evidence may suggest that racism is usually premised on the negative stereotyping of the Other, this is not always the case.

The key conclusion to be drawn from this discussion is that it is necessary to analyse the Self/Other dialectic as a coherent, yet historically specific, unity that is found at the core of all racisms. Identifying the dialectic by reference to its two extremes, there is an explanatory utility in considering a twofold classification of racism as ideology: one based on heteroracialisation (i.e. an attribution of the 'racially' defined Other with negative characteristics); the other on autoracialisation (i.e. an attribution of the 'racially' defined Self – 'Us' – with positive characteristics). This classification was developed by Taguieff (1987: 163ff., 2001: 120ff. in Hassan Melehy's translation). Autoracialisation (*autoracisation*, translated by Melehy as 'self-racialisation') is part of a 'series' that leads to the imagining and consolidation of difference, 'purification' of the 'race', and extermination of the Other. Heteroracialisation (*hétéroracisation* or 'other-racialisation'), on the other hand, leads to inequality, domination and exploitation (1987: 163, 2001: 120). The latter, according to Taguieff (1987: 163-4, 2001: 121), is the 'normal' foundation of racism, while the former represents the extreme form of racism, 'the unconditional fear of the Other' which can only be assuaged by 'the *total destruction* of the Other' (1987: 166, 2001: 123). The former may represent a constructed 'race' or 'races' in a negative manner; the latter necessarily represents all 'races' other than one's own in a negative manner and as an absolute threat. Thus, it too is a form of racism, although it is also the case that Self and Other are racialised dialectically, without a necessary programme of extermination.

Taguieff's conceptualisation and suggested distinction between autoracialisation and heteroracialisation has been the focus of critical debate (e.g. Wieviorka 1995). We cite the distinction here, less to endorse it in some absolute sense, but rather because it serves to remind us of a potential limitation of deriving a definition of racism as ideology too quickly and too literally from the immediate historical context in which the concept was first formulated. Political considerations may well encourage us to focus first upon the way in which racism identifies an Other as a 'race' and attributes negatively evaluated characteristics to that population. But, as we have observed above, the imagination of the Other is simultaneously an imagination of the Self, each reflecting and refracting a kaleidoscope of contrasting attributes. We might therefore conclude that the moment of racism as ideology is one in which Self and Other simultaneously embrace and repel by reference to a set of imagined attributes that carry a duality of evaluations, negative and positive. Conceptually, this is its unity. But, historically, the ideological content, the specific groups represented as Self and Other, and the consequences are always diverse.

CONCLUSION

The analytical problems explored in this chapter express a tension evident the evolution of the concept of racism. While the origin of the concept is closely related to the central role of racism in the rise of Fascism in Western Europe during the 1930s, much of its post-1945 evolution has been shaped by the need to understand colonialism, either to comprehend its legacy in a post-colonial context or to explain the response of the state and its citizens in Western European countries to migrations from ex-colonies. Many of the central features of the colonial model were carried over into the analysis in the United States of the rise of the civil rights movement and the struggle of African-Americans against their subordination. This was achieved by means of a focus upon the legacy of slavery and its origin in the colonising project and by means of the theory of internal colonialism. Consequently, we have been offered definitions and theories of racism that are so specific to the history of overseas colonisation that they have limited value in explaining any other context. Moreover, many of these theories simultaneously transpose the duality of coloniser and colonised into the duality of 'white'and 'black', further limiting the explanatory power of the resulting theory and concepts. We conclude that we need to seek for a concept of racism that has the ability to grasp and comprehend the diversity of the phenomenon to which it refers.

4

ON SIGNIFICATION

INTRODUCTION

This chapter has two interrelated objectives. The first, in light of the problems identified in the previous two chapters, is to reconsider the definition of the concept of racism. This will involve a clarification of the relationship between the concept of racism and a number of related concepts, principally 'race', ethnicity, racialisation, ethnicisation and institutional racism. Second, it is instructive to reflect on these related concepts themselves – although we emphasise the problematic nature of the concept of 'race', it is not the only problematic concept in this field of study.

These objectives will be realised by reflecting theoretically on the nature of the social process by which meanings are attributed to real or imagined human characteristics. Thus, a concept of racism will be derived analytically rather than inductively from consideration of a single empirical instance. This theoretical work will produce no more than a *concept* of racism, and it makes a concession to (the entirely respectable philosophical doctrine of) essentialism by identifying what many different instances of racism have in common qua racism. On the specificity of each instance, the variety of representational content and context, and 'grounded' discussions of the nature and definition of racism, these are matters for historically and ethnographically specific analysis, examples of which are discussed in Chapters 5 and 6.

'RACE'

The theoretical work begins with the idea of 'race', from which the concept of racism was initially derived. The word 'race' continues to be used in at least three different anglophone discourses. Within the scientific field, it appears in the discourse of the biological sciences, specifically genetics, and of the social sciences. Additionally, it is widely used in everyday (including political) discourse, and constitutes a key element of common sense (the accumulated, taken-for-granted, and often contradictory set of assumptions and beliefs employed by people to impose an ideological structure upon the social world, within which they can then act). These uses are differentiated, yet interrelated.

Within genetics, debate continues about the validity of using an 'old' concept to refer to a 'new' phenomenon, that is to the patterns of genetic variation which are not visually observable and do not correlate with evident phenotypical variation. Although the scientifically legitimate object of analysis has changed from phenotypical difference to genetic variation, there is no unanimous view that this should be reflected in a change in scientific terminology. Hence, the idea of 'race' is sometimes retained within the biological sciences to refer to populations differentiated by genetic frequency (Miles 1982: 18–19; also Montagu 1964: 23; Jones 1981). Certainly, there is no scientific justification for using the term to refer to a discrete hierarchy of 'races' distinguished by phenotypical features such as skin colour. In the latter sense, as far as the biological and genetic sciences are concerned, 'races' do not exist (see Montagu 1972; Rose et al. 1984: 119–27).

However, in the everyday world, the facts of biological difference are secondary to the meanings that are attributed to them and, indeed, to imagined biological difference. Where the discourse of 'race' is employed, there are two levels of selection involved. The first is the selection of biological or somatic characteristics in general as a means of human classification. The second is the selection from the available range of somatic characteristics, those that are designated as signifying a supposed difference between human beings. Human beings exhibit a very wide range of phenotypical difference: height, weight, length of arms and legs, ear shape, width of feet, breadth of palm, hair colour, extent of body hair, facial structure, eye colour and so on can all be used to differentiate and categorise. Thus, when the idea of 'race' is employed, it is the result of a process of signification whereby certain somatic characteristics are attributed with meaning and are used to organise populations into distinct groups that are defined as 'races'.

People differentiated on the basis of the signification of phenotypical features are usually also represented as possessing certain cultural characteristics (such as diet, religious belief, mode of dress, language, etc.). As a consequence, the population is represented as distinctive by virtue of a specific profile of (sometimes real and sometimes imagined) biological and cultural attributes. The deterministic manner of this representation means that all who possess the signified phenotypical characteristics are assumed to possess the concomitant cultural characteristics. Further, it follows that the human species is conceived as consisting of a number of distinct collectivities, and that every individual is attributed with membership of one of those collectivities.

In Europe, North America, and Australasia, the idea of 'race' is now usually (though not exclusively) used to differentiate collectivities distinguished by skin colour, so that 'races' are either 'black' or 'white' but never 'big-eared' and 'small-eared'. The fact that only certain physical characteristics are signified to define 'races' in specific circumstances indicates that we are investigating not a given, natural division of the world's population, but the application of historically and culturally specific meanings to the totality of human physiological variation. This is made equally evident by historical evidence that records that certain populations have been categorised as different 'races' at different historical times and in different places. Thus, the use of the word 'race' to label groups so distinguished by some combination of phenotypical and cultural attributes is one moment in the ongoing social construction of reality: 'races' are socially imagined rather than biological realities.

These processes of signification and representation have a history. Chapter 1 demonstrates that, within Europe, somatic characteristics have been signified for several centuries as a means of representation of human beings, and that skin colour has been commonly selected from the range of somatic features as the primary sign by which the Other can be created. The use of the discourse of 'race' to refer to the populations differentiated by somatic characteristics is, however, more recent. While this form of representation has been discredited scientifically, the fact that the idea of 'race' continues to be employed in common sense testifies to its continuing practical rather than scientific utility. Husband has commented: "'Race' as a means of categorising people theorises the "social facts" of colour difference in a rigid and absolute way which carries all the implicit naturalness and authority of "race" thinking' (1982: 16). The signification of phenotypical features is therefore pragmatic and instrumental, not an end in itself. Its practical utility is not simply representational. Because it seeks to claim the authority of a natural (and therefore unalterable) difference, it is the prelude to exclusionary practices, the consequence of which are patterns and structures of inequality between the populations so differentiated.

Since the early part of this century, some North American and European social scientists have defined the study of this and consequent processes as the study of 'race relations' (e.g. Rex 1970, 1986; Banton 1977, 1987; George 1984). As Miles (1982: 22–43, 1984a, 1987a: 7–11, 1993: 27–52) has argued, these writers have employed uncritically the common-sense notion of 'race', reified it and then attributed it with the status of a scientific concept. Similarly, Guillaumin has argued:

> Whatever the theoretical foundations underlying the various inter-pretations of 'racial' relations, the very use of such a distinction tends to imply the acceptance of some essential difference between types of social relation, some, somewhere, being specifically racial. Merely to adopt the expression implies the belief that races are 'real' or correctly apprehensible, or at the best that the idea of race is uncritically accepted; moreover it implies that races play a role in the social process not merely as an ideological form, but as an immediate factor acting as both determining cause and concrete means.
>
> (1980: 39)

Thus, perversely, social scientists have prolonged the life of an idea that should be consigned to the dustbin of analytically useless terms: 'There are no "races" and therefore no "race relations"' (Miles 1993: 42). Unfortunately, social scientists have frequently assumed that it is possible to overcome the problems inherent in using the term 'race' analytically by simply using scare quotes – that is, substituting 'race' for race. This has the virtue of emphasising that 'race' is not a real attribute of human biology, but socially constructed and discursively perceived. However, 'race' is too often used as a code-word for race – even with quotation marks, the term is used to denote common-sense categories of human being, usually identified by skin colour.

The discourse of 'race' has been a European discourse projected onto various Others, and, subsequently, onto the European Self. However, it has not remained exclusively a discourse of subordination. During the twentieth century, those who have been its object have often accepted their designation as a biologically distinct and discrete population, as a 'race', but have inverted the negative evaluation of their character and capacities. Consequently, the discourse of 'race' has been transformed into a discourse of resistance. Certain somatic characteristics (usually skin colour) have been signified as the foundation for a common experience and fate as an excluded population, irrespective of class position and cultural origin. This has served as a basis for a political appeal to 'race' (commonly in the form of an appeal to 'blackness') in order to bring about a political mobilisation against material and political disadvantage as well as colonial rule. One of the best-known instances is the rise of the Black Power movement in the United States in the 1960s (see Seale 1970). The political content, objective and strategy of such mobilisations vary considerably, but they all have in common at least an implicit acceptance of the legit-imacy and accuracy of the European discourse by means of which they have been constituted as different. Indeed, the inversion of the negative evaluation serves to reinforce at a deeper level the process of signification by which the Other was originally constituted (cf. Fanon 1967: 188–9; Chachage 1988) and therefore, in the course of resistance, the discourse of 'race' is further legitimated.

It is not denied that there are somatic and genetic differences between human beings. Neither is it denied that phenotypical (and sometimes genetic) characteristics are signified in the 'real world' as indicative of meaningful differences between human beings, and that at a certain historical period the idea of 'race' was employed to name the collectivities so distinguished. What is at issue is the scientific status of the terms used to analyse this representational process, this historical construction and reproduction of common sense in the European world, and its economic and political concomitants and consequences. If 'races' are not naturally occurring populations, the reasons and conditions for the social process whereby the discourse of 'race' is employed to label, constitute and exclude social collectivities requires explanation rather than be assumed to be a natural and universal process. In other words, the construction and reproduction of the idea of 'race', is something that requires investigation. This task is circumvented by the transformation of the idea itself ('race') into an analytical concept. Thereby, what needs to be represented as a social process and explained is reconstructed as a social fact that can be used to explain other social facts.

The analytical task is not to explain 'race relations'; rather, it is the generation of concepts with which one can grasp and portray the historical processes by which notions of 'race' become accepted and/or used in a plurality of discourses. In particular, because 'race' and 'race relations' are ideological notions which are used both to construct and negotiate social relations, the concepts that are employed to analyse that social process should reflect that fact consistently, something which is not achieved by simply placing the word 'race' inside quotation marks. Only then will we have a scientific language that allows the deconstruction of the idea of 'race', rather than a language that reifies and thereby legitimates it.

ETHNICITY

> . . . the sociologist must be very careful in searching for the influence of races on any social phenomenon. For to solve such problems the different races and their distinctions from each other must be known. This caution is the more essential because this anthropological uncertainty might well be due to the fact that the word 'race' no longer corresponds to anything definite. Indeed, on the one hand, the original races have only a paleontological interest, and on the other the narrower groups so designated today seem to be peoples or societies of peoples, brothers by civilisation rather than by blood. Thus conceived, race becomes almost identical with nationality.
>
> (Durkheim 2002: 33)

In this passage from *Suicide* (first published in 1894), Durkheim inadvertently identifies one reason why many social scientists prefer to use the term 'ethnicity' to 'race': the latter has no objective biological referent, whereas the former relates to social and cultural norms and symbols. Durkheim could have referred to ethnicity rather than nationality. Given that nationality is so often associated with nation states, citizenship and passport ownership, 'ethnicity' may capture the sense of Durkheim's argument rather better. The term 'ethnicity' is often prefered to the term 'race' for these reasons, and because its use is 'an admission by politicians, policy-makers, and so on, that the facts of cultural difference constitute a valid parameter for their deliberations' (Miles 1982: 71). However, the term is not always used so carefully, nor is it always distinguishable from the concept of 'race' (1982: 44–71).

Anthropological research has employed extensively the concept of ethnicity and the related concept of ethnic group. In the late 1960s, Fredrik Barth suggested a common anthropological understanding of the term 'ethnic group'. He proposed that the term designated a population that:

1. is largely biologically self-perpetuating
2. shares fundamental cultural values, realised in overt unity in cultural forms
3. makes up a field of communication and interaction
4. has a membership which identifies itself, and is identified by others, as constituting a category distinguishable from other categories of the same order.

(Barth 1969: 10)

Barth believed that these four characteristics were 'close enough to many empirical ethnographic situations' (1969: 10), thereby justifying this particular concept of ethnic group. We find this to be a very problematic claim. First, Barth's first criterion is so close to the meaning of the idea of 'race' as to be indistinguishable from it. Second, the migration of human genes has negated such biological self-perpetuation (see Cavalli-Sforza *et al.* 1994; Cavalli-Sforza 2001). Third, the number of groups that fulfil these criteria is very small, and yet the concept of ethnicity (like 'race'), has a universal connotation (such that it is presumed that every human being belongs to an ethnic group). That being said, Barth was not unaware of difficulties with this concept of ethnic group, noting that ethnic groups do not develop in isolation from one another and that the boundaries between groups are usually at least blurred.

Barth's formal definition of ethnic group demonstrates in a nutshell the problems with the concept of ethnicity qua an inherent attribute of human beings and/or groups of human beings. It is often used as a politically correct code word for 'race' – that is, it signifies a group that is identified as an ethnic group according to common-sense phenotypical indicators. On this criterion, African-Americans in the USA or Asians in Britain might constitute an ethnic group (though not necessarily 'white' people, because 'ethnic' often connotes 'Other' or 'minority'). Sometimes, the ethnic group is smaller and more local. For example, 'ethnic cleansing' was added to the lexicon in the early 1990s to denote mass murder and forced migration within the conflicts in Bosnia and Herzegovina, and other parts of the Balkans. There, the ethnic groups were identified as Serbian, Croatian, Bosnian Muslim, Romani ('Gypsy') and Albanian. In this context, phenotypical indicators of ethnicity were less important than cultural, linguistic or religious ones, but the use of mass rape as an instrument of war suggests that 'other' ethnic groups were perceived as biologically distinct and self-perpetuating, and that this distinctiveness and self-perpetuation could be negated by forced insemination. The difference between such a concept of ethnic distinctiveness and a concept of 'racial' distinctiveness is entirely elusive.

This is not new. In 1935, Huxley and Haddon argued that there was no scientific evidence to sustain the idea of distinct and discrete 'races', and that 'racial biology' was pseudo-science. Much of their argument consisted of a scientific refutation of classifications based on somatic characteristics and an evaluation of the contribution of genetics to an understanding of human variation, from which they concluded that the word 'race' should be dropped from scientific vocabulary, to be replaced by 'ethnic group' (Huxley and Haddon 1935: 108, 164, 268).

Their justification for this recommendation was, at least in part, political. They argued that the term 'race', like many other pseudo-scientific terms, could be used to 'rationalise emotion' (1935: 262), and that science had a responsibility to identify the truth value of ideas employed in political life (1935: 287). They made reference to the then contemporary situation in Germany, specifically denying that Nordic or Jewish 'races' existed, and identifying Nazi theories of 'race' as a 'creed of passionate racialism' (1935: 277). They continued: 'Racialism is a myth, and a dangerous myth at that. It is a cloak for selfish economic aims which in their uncloaked nakedness would look ugly enough' (1935: 287). This myth of racialism was explained as an attempt to justify nationalism.

However, Huxley and Haddon's text demonstrates a contradiction over the significance of biological classification. They argued that 'any biological arrangement of the types of European man is still largely a subjective process' (1935: 166), but proceeded to construct one using 'those characters which are the most convenient and readily observed' (1935: 169), specifically skin colour, and hair and nose type. They concluded:

We can thus distinguish three major groupings of mankind:

(1) Black woolly hair, dark brown or black skin, and a broad nose.
(2) Wavy or curly hair of any colour from black to flaxen, dark brown to white skin, and a typically medium or narrow nose with usually a high bridge.
(3) Straight lank dark hair, yellowish skin, nose with a tendency to be broad and low-bridged.

(1935: 169–70)

Thus, they reproduced a taxonomy that differed only from nineteenth-century classifications in that it did not label these groups as 'Negroid', 'Caucasian' and 'Mongoloid' and described them as 'ethnic groups' rather than 'races'. The ontological difference, however, was and remains non-existent.

Our reference to Barth also highlights an absence of any correlation between the dimensions of ethnicity identified. Biological similarity, values, linguistic/physical proximity and group identification do not necessarily (nor, in most cases, do they empirically) correlate in the formation of an 'ethnic group'. And we have noted Barth's recognition of the boundary problem inherent in this concept of ethnicity. This is a problem shared with those who seek to employ a concept of 'race': the mistake is to assume the existence of a finite number of discrete ethnic groups. Even though cultural factors are embedded in the concept of ethnicity, there is still a boundary problem. Where does one culture begin and another end? How many cultures are there? For these reasons, the concept of ethnicity, qua an inherent human attribute, while having the virtue of connoting socio-cultural norms rather than putatively biological characteristics, is as problematic as the concept of 'race'. Furthermore, where negative judgements are made about one or more cultures, and where the ethnic groups are regarded as 'biologically self-perpetuating', the ethnic ideology seems to be indistinguishable from racism.

However, we do not advocate consigning the concept of ethnicity to the same analytical dustbin as a concept of 'race'. It is when the concept of ethnicity is used to denote an inherent attribute of human beings that it loses any referent and becomes meaningless. However, it can be used in a relational and contextually specific manner:

> . . . ethnicity is essentially an aspect of a relationship, not a property of a group. . . . Ethnicity is an aspect of social relationship between agents who consider themselves as culturally distinctive from members of other groups with whom they have a minimum of regular interaction.
>
> (Eriksen 1993: 12)

Because ethnicity is not considered a human attribute, or an attribute of a group, it is not necessary to regard all human beings as 'possessing' an ethnicity nor to produce a taxonomy of ethnic groups, each with a set of identifying characteristics. In the light of this, Eriksen sets out a number of conditions which must be fulfilled to warrant categorisation as an ethnic group, such as contact between different sub-groups within the ethnic group, 'a social identity (based on a contrast *vis-à-vis* others) characterised by metaphoric or fictive kinship', and political or organisational aspects (1993: 12). Thus, the concept of ethnicity can be applied to a number of groups, in a relational context where members of these groups identify themselves as culturally distinctive, such as 'urban ethnic minorities', 'indigenous peoples', 'proto-nations' or 'ethnonationalist movements', or 'ethnic groups in . . . states with culturally heterogeneous populations' (1993: 13–14). Eriksen admits that the application of the concept is problematic in all these cases, but it provides an analytical programme for investigating the development of ethnic consciousness, that is, ways in which agents interactively produce concepts of themselves as culturally distinctive and metaphorically kin.

In other words, as with the concept of 'race', the analytical task is not to explain what ethnicity 'is', or how it functions, or how it determines the life chances of individuals or groups; rather, it is the generation of concepts with which one can grasp and portray the historical processes by which notions of 'ethnicity' become accepted and/or used in a plurality of discourses.

ETHNICISATION

If ethnic groups are no more objective or real than 'races', we need to then ask how they are constituted. We refer to this as a process of ethnicisation, a process that is both economic and cultural in character. The concept of ethnicisation has been usefully developed by Wallerstein (1995: 122). He argues that the continuous migration of people (both forced and voluntary) has been accompanied by 'an ethnicisation of the world's work force, such that in any given locale, the population is seen as divided into various ethnic groupings (whether the marker of such ethnicity is perceived skin colour, language, religion, or some other cultural construct)' (1995: 122). Significantly, Wallerstein insists that skin colour is a cultural construct that may be used as a signifier of ethnicity.

Wallerstein continues with the definition of his concept of ethnicisation, elaborating its mechanism and consequences, then emphasises its changing nature:

> There tends to be at all times a high correlation of households between their ethnic stratum (as defined locally) and their occupational or class

location. Of course, the details constantly change – the definition of ethnic boundaries, which ethnic group correlates with which ethnic stratum – but the stratification principle is an enduring feature of the capitalist world-economy, serving both to reduce overall costs of labour and to contain thrusts to delegitimise the state structures.

(1995: 122)

For Wallerstein, ethnicisation is connected with class struggle and with fluctuations in the world economy. As the doyen of world systems theory, his language and concepts are technical, but it is instructive to see how these connections are understood:

This process of ethnicisation has a clear downside in terms of any balance sheet. It creates the structural foundation of continuous struggle both between upper and lower ethnic strata, and among ethnic strata at the lower level. These struggles tend to become more acute each time there is a cyclical downturn in the world-economy, which is half the historical time. The struggles have frequently deteriorated into violent forms, from minor riots to wholesale genocides.

(1995: 122)

Not only is the process of ethnicisation connected with class and the world economy, but there is also a link with racism that underlines our contention that constructions of 'race' and 'ethnicity' are inseparable, as are class identities and other identities. He ends with a description of the present (at the time of writing) that may also be read as an indication of future ethnic conflict in the capitalist world economy:

The crucial element is that the ethnicisation of the world's work force has required an ideology of racism, in which large segments of the world's population have been defined as under classes, as inferior beings, and therefore as deserving ultimately of whatever fate comes their way out of the immediate political and social struggles. These 'civil wars' have not grown fewer with time but, if anything, have become more oppressive and deadly in the twentieth century. This is a very large minus in the balance sheet of our current world-system.

(1995: 122)

The functionalist reading of the role of racism is worthy of further reflection but the more immediately interesting question that this passage invokes is the nature of the relationship between what he describes as ethnicisation and what we will define as racialisation.

Other writers have developed a concept of ethnicisation, although with different emphases. For example, Essed (1991: 189, 210ff.) conceives of ethnicisation (or 'ethnisation') in the labour market as a repressive form of tolerance. She compares the United States and the Netherlands, arguing that the ideal of multiculturalism, in the Dutch case, implies the dominant group 'tolerating' minority ethnic groups, while the dominated groups 'must believe in the "goodwill" of the dominant group' (1991: 210). Thus, there is an ethnicised structuring of the labour market, with the aim of providing an economy, social services and appropriate policies for each ethnic group, *through the agency of members of that group* that encourages an objectification of the dominated groups, the 'ethnic minorities', by the dominant 'white' group, and a conception of 'whiteness' as 'the norm' (1991: 189, 194–6, 210ff.). *Inter alia* for these reasons, this system of 'pillarisation' in the Netherlands has declined since the early 1990s (e.g. Rath *et al*. 1997). Elsewhere, Essed points to changing forms of racialisation, in the context of a constant *presence* of racialisation, and draws a parallel between racialisation and ethnicisation. Indeed, she seems to use these two concepts interchangeably, in the context of a broader argument:

> . . . the particular content of systems of racial meanings can change historically, but the presence of a system of racial meanings is a permanent feature of European culture that has been constantly activated throughout the United States in the past few centuries and in the Netherlands in more recent times. Social relations are racialised (or ethnicised) when they represent racially or ethnically identified differences in position and power. Because 'race' is an organising principle of many social relations, the fundamental social relations of society are racialised relations. However, it is only when these racial or ethnic dimensions of social relations are called upon or activated through practice that racial and ethnic relations are created, reinforced, or reproduced. In other words, even when specific relations are racialised and when these relations underlie and structure social relations, racism does not necessarily have to occur in a specific time or place.
>
> (1991: 52)

The concept of ethnicisation as a process that structures and stratifies the labour market is close to an alternative (or, rather, more focused) conception of racism which has been offered by one of the authors of this book. Miles (1987a: 188) conceives racism as 'a potential ideological element of signification by which to *select* and to *legitimate* the selection of a particular population, whose labour power will be exploited in a particular set of unfree production relations'. The processes of racialisation and ethnicisation, and the ideology of racism, all have a material impact on the economic infrastructure of the capitalist world economy.

However, ethnicisation is not an exclusively economic process. As we have already argued, the major strength of the concept of ethnicity is that it denotes the cultural characteristics of a group (whereas its major weakness is a reluctance to escape the biological and somatic presuppositions inherent in the notion of 'race'), so the process of ethnicisation is also a process of cultural differentiation and consequent group formation and reproduction. This process is usually carried out by the ethnicised majority, hence, it is usually a process of hetero-ethnicisation. Hargreaves defines ethnicisation in the following terms:

> In the present context, membership of a minority ethnic group is defined by the objective fact of common origins in a territory outside the state in which the group now resides, and within which (an)other group(s) occupies/occupy a dominant position. Those foreign origins may be direct (in the case of immigrants) or indirect (in the case of their descendants). Whether this territorial or biological legacy is of real social significance depends to a large extent on how it is perceived by different social actors. A minority ethnicised group is one whose members are considered by members of the majority population to be in a significant sense separate from the national community; racialised minority groups (categorised by somatic features such as skin colour) are a sub-type of ethnicised minorities.
>
> (1995: 36)

In the light of this formulation, we define ethnicisation as a dialectical process by which meaning is attributed to socio-cultural signifiers of human beings, as a result of which individuals may be assigned to a general category of persons which reproduces itself biologically, culturally and economically. Where biological and/or somatic features (real or imagined) are signified, we speak of racialisation as a specific modality of ethnicisation.

RACIALISATION

The concept of racialisation is more widely used and understood. One of its earliest uses was by Fanon in a discussion of the difficulties facing decolonised intellectuals in Africa when constructing a cultural future

(1967: 170–1). Banton (1977: 18) utilised the concept more formally to refer to the use of the idea of 'race' to structure people's perceptions of the world's population. His usage was limited, and by implication, its scope was confined to scientific theories of racial typology as used to categorise populations. In the 1980s, Reeves distinguished between 'practical' and 'ideological' racialisation, using the former to refer to the formation of 'racial groups' and the latter to refer to the use of the idea of 'race' in discourse (1983: 173–6; see also Troyna and Williams 1985). This is an extension of Banton's use of the concept, not only by virtue of drawing this distinction but also because his concept of ideological racialisation refers to any circumstance where the idea of 'race' is employed in discourse. Hence, Reeves analysed the way in which the discourse of 'race' had entered British political discourse and, in turn, had been reified in legislation since 1945. Omi and Winant use the concept to 'signify the extension of racial meaning to a previously racially unclassified relationship, social practice or group. Racialisation is an ideological process, an historically specific one' (1986: 64). This definition corresponds closely to Reeves's concept of practical racialisation.

In these usages, there is minimal agreement that the concept be used to refer to a representational process whereby social significance is attached to certain biological (usually phenotypical) human features, on the basis of which the people possessing those characteristics are designated as a distinct collectivity. Banton and Reeves both specify that such a process only occurs where the collectivity is explicitly defined as a 'race'. Thus, for these two writers, the process of racialisation begins with the emergence of the idea of 'race', and continues for the duration of the employment of the idea of 'race' to categorise the world's population (cf. Guillaumin 1980: 49).

Miles (1982: 120, 150) uses the concept of racialisation as a synonym for the concept of 'racial categorisation', defined as 'a process of delineation of group boundaries and of allocation of persons within those boundaries by primary reference to (supposedly) inherent and/or biological (usually phenotypical) characteristics' (1982: 157). For reasons of analytical clarity, we use only the concept of racialisation, but defined as above in order not to limit its application to historical contexts where the idea of 'race' is present. This is because, as is shown in Chapter 1, phenotypical characteristics such as skin colour were signified in European social formations and discourses to constitute discrete collectivities before the emergence of the idea of 'race'. For example, within the Greco-Roman world, the African's skin colour was signified as a means of collective representation, and a similar process occurred during the period of European exploration from the fifteenth century. In other words, the idea of 'race' has a pre-history, during which the representation of the Other was effected through the signification of certain physical features subsequently identified as the criteria by which a person's 'race' was determined. Similarly, in much contemporary discourse in Europe and North America, categories such as 'white' and 'black' are used to label individuals, and hence to constitute groups, but often in the absence of any explicit discourse of 'race'.

We therefore employ the concept of racialisation (for other uses, see, for example, Young 1992: 257–8; Solomos 1993: 72–3, 136–9; Mac an Ghaill 1999: 19–22, 68–70; and especially Barot 2001) to denote those instances where social relations between people have been structured by the signification of human biological characteristics in such a way as to define and construct differentiated social collectivities. The characteristics signified vary historically and, although they have usually been visible somatic features, other non-visible (imagined and real) biological features have also been signified. The concept therefore refers to a process of categorisation, a representational process of defining an Other, usually, but not exclusively, somatically. The defined collectivity is considered (implicitly if not explicitly) to constitute a naturally occurring, discrete breeding population and therefore subsumes a pattern of gender differentiation. The concept of racialisation, by highlighting the process of categorisation as one of attributing meaning to somatic characteristics, presumes a social psychological theory that explains the nature and dynamics of the process (e.g. Billig 1976: 322–69).

Racialisation is a dialectical process of signification. Ascribing real or imagined biological characteristics with meaning to define the Other necessarily entails defining Self by the same criteria. When Greco-Roman and later Northern European explorers and merchants defined Africans as 'black', they were implicitly defining themselves at the opposite end of a dichotomy or continuum, that of skin colour. The African's 'blackness' therefore reflected the European's 'whiteness': these opposites were bound together, each giving meaning to the other in a totality of signification. Similarly, when Africans were later identified by Europeans as constituting an inferior 'race', Europeans were simultaneously, if only implicitly, defining themselves by reference to the discourse of 'race', albeit with a different evaluative connotation. Thus, Self and Other were similarly encapsulated in a common world of (European) meanings. By virtue of sharing in that common world of meaning, the Other may adopt the content of the racialised discourse to identify itself as Self. Thus, populations that were racialised and excluded by the European discourse of race have appropriated and legitimated that discourse as a means by which to identify Self and Other. In so doing, the evaluative content has usually been changed from negative to positive: what for Europeans was once a sign of inferiority has been transformed into a source of pride.

Since the eighteenth century, as we saw in Chapter 1, the world's population has been sorted in European thought into 'races', and relations between 'races' perceived as shaped, if not determined, by supposedly inherent characteristics. Moreover, even if the idea of a hierarchy of 'races' is no longer articulated in the formal political arena, it is still widely assumed that 'races' exist as distinct, biologically defined, collectivities. Thus, the idea of 'race' continues to be widely employed as a universal descriptive category to designate collectivities to which Self and Other belong. The concept of racialisation therefore alludes to the historical emergence of the idea of 'race' and to its subsequent reproduction and application.

Furthermore, the racialisation of human beings entails the racialisation of processes in which they participate and resultant structures and institutions. Thus, where human beings are identified as collectivities by reference to physical features, the interrelations between those collectivities are effected *inter alia* by means of extant political institutions and processes. This is dramatically evident where 'races' are defined in law as discrete collectivities and where the law actively structures relations between those collectivities, but it also occurs where somatic signification is effected and negotiated through less formal mechanisms. Consequently, issues such as who occupies positions of leadership, or the topics placed on the political agenda, may be shaped by meanings attributed to phenotypical variation: thus, demands may be made that 'black' people be represented within decision-making structures or that 'white kith-and-kin' should be given a privileged status in immigration law. In such circumstances, the political process is racialised in the sense that it assumes a particular representational content by representing 'race' as the determinant and object of political relations.

In sum, we use the concept of racialisation to denote a dialectical process by which meaning is attributed to particular biological features of human beings, as a result of which individuals may be assigned to a general category of persons that reproduces itself biologically. This process has a long history in precapitalist and capitalist societies. The particular content of the process of racialisation, and its consequences (including its articulation with political and economic relations), cannot be determined abstractly or derived formally from the primary features of the mode of production but are matters for historical investigation.

RACISM

We have, in Chapter 2, provided an account of the origin of racism as a word and concept. Its origin and the subsequent wide-ranging debate about the meaning of the concept have given rise to a complexity of meaning and usage that calls out for clarification. Against the background of the preceding discussion of ethnicisation and racialisation, we offer a clarification in two stages. First, we argue that the concept should be used to refer to an ideological phenomenon. Then, and second, we identify the specific representational characteristics that must exist to warrant description as racism.

The case for limiting the use of the concept to refer to ideology is based on the assumption that the analytical value of a concept is determined by its utility in describing and explaining social processes. As we have demonstrated, the inflation of the concept has resulted in it being used to connote a wide range of practices and processes. Not only does such a concept lack discriminatory power, but it also makes the identification of determinacy more difficult. Moreover, there is no necessary logical correlation between cognition and action. The conceptual ability to make these distinctions serves the interests of analytical accuracy and of formulating potentially successful interventionist strategies intended to negate both racist ideologies and the disadvantage that accrues from exclusion. We refer to the latter phenomenon as 'exclusionary practice', though it is important to note that inclusion and exclusion refer to different moments in a single act or process: to include is simultaneously to exclude, and vice versa. In reality, racism often exists in a mutually reinforcing unity with exclusionary practice but we wish to insist on the validity of the analytical distinction.

If the concept of racism is more precisely defined as an ideological, representational phenomenon, distinguished analytically from exclusionary practice, what are its primary defining characteristics? We propose that it be identified by its ideological content rather than function. The distinguishing content of racism as an ideology is, first, its signification of some biological and/or somatic characteristic(s) as the criterion by which populations are identified. In this way, these populations are represented as having a natural, unchanging origin and status, and therefore as being inherently different. In other words, this process of racialisation conceives of a plurality of 'races'. Second, one or more of the groups so identified must be attributed with additional (negatively evaluated) characteristics and/or must be represented as inducing negative consequences for (an)other group(s). Those characteristics or consequences may be either biological or cultural.

Because ideologies are produced and reproduced in a context of inequality, and therefore of relations of domination and subordination, these ideological representations are never equally weighted. The ideological struggle is uneven (but also continuous). Within the hierarchy of domination at any historical moment, there will usually be at least one racialised group that is represented as possessing a range of (negatively evaluated) biological and/or cultural characteristics. It follows that such a naturally defined collectivity constitutes a problematic presence: it is represented ideologically as a threat (cf. Miles 1982: 78–9).

The ideology of racism has a number of additional characteristics. First, because it presumes a process of racialisation, it has a dialectical character insofar as the representation of Other simultaneously refracts a representation of Self. If the Other is a naturally constituted collectivity, then so is Self. Racism is therefore a representational form which, by designating discrete human collectivities, necessarily functions as an ideology of inclusion and exclusion: for example, the signification of skin colour both includes and excludes in the categorisation process. Furthermore, it is the *negative* characteristics of Other which mirror the *positive* characteristics of Self (see Roediger 1994). Racism therefore presupposes a process of racialisation but is differentiated from that process by its explicitly negative evaluative component.

Second, racism may take the form of a relatively coherent theory, exhibiting a logical structure and adducing evidence in its support, but it also appears in the form of a less coherent assembly of stereotypes, images, attributions, and explanations that are constructed and employed to negotiate everyday life. Too many of the contributions to the debate about the nature of racism as an ideology have a fascination with the writing of fellow intellectual practitioners but maintain a silence about the way in which representations of the Other have been created and reproduced in everyday life. Racist assertions can be coined as easily in the factory or office as in a university library, and such assertions can be manifest in unconscious prejudices as well as exclusionary practices. One of the major limitations of the original concept of racism was therefore that its object was largely textual, and this was reflected in the definition of racism as a doctrine.

Hence, and third, racism refracts in thought certain observed regularities, and constructs a causal interpretation that can be presented as consistent with those regularities and that constitutes a solution to perceived problems. An emphasis on racism solely as a 'false doctrine' fails to appreciate that one of the conditions of existence of ideologies (which by definition constitute in their totality a false explanation, but which may nevertheless also incorporate elements of truth) is that they can successfully 'make sense' of the world, at least for those who articulate and use them (cf. Cohen 1992: 80). Put another way, the ideology of racism can constitute a description and explanation of the way in which the world is experienced to work. As explanation, specific racisms may indeed exhibit considerable creativity in the way that they combine direct observation with racialised categories. Therefore, at least part of the ideological content of racism will vary with the class position of its exponents because *Erlebnis* (lived experience of the world) and its consequent problems vary with class position.

This can be demonstrated with two examples. First, during the nineteenth century, the competitive pre-eminence of British capital ensured that the British bourgeois and merchant capitalist classes occupied for a long period of time a position of unrivalled economic and political domination within the capitalist world economy. The productive and technological superiority of British capitalism, supported by a superior navy and military, was especially evident when its representatives and advocates were engaged in further expansion of the British Empire in Africa and India in the nineteenth century. There was, in other words, a real material difference between the conditions of the British bourgeoisie and merchant capitalists and the populations of Africa and India where commodity production was either hardly evident or had been partially, if not wholly, destroyed by the former modes of production that sustained them. That difference, which was experienced as real, required explanation. An argument that the British bourgeoisie was part (if not the pre-eminent members) of an inherently superior 'white race', with a biological capacity for invention, democracy and the spread of 'civilisation', not only justified colonial strategies (Thornton 1965) but, perhaps more importantly,

made sense of the British bourgeois *Erlebnis*. The falsity of the
was in inverse proportion to its effectivity as an explanation
for real material differences. Moreover, it was an account of the world
that recognised and offered an explanation for the (long-established)
signification of certain physical differences between coloniser and colonised.
Indeed, the idea of 'race' served to link the observed material differences
and signified phenotypical differences in a total, causal explanation (Miles
1982: 113–19).

Second, in many areas of working-class residence in Britain, the decline
of capitalist production and the decay of the urban infrastructure (consequences of the uneven development of capitalism) coincided temporally
with the arrival and settlement of migrants from the Caribbean and
Asian subcontinent during the 1950s and 1960s. While the determinants
(rather than the consequences) of the changing composition and mobility
of capital were not immediately, visibly evident, the presence of populations
signified historically as inferior 'races' was, and remains so. Consequently,
economic decline and migrant settlement were experienced as causally
related by sections of the indigenous working class. Thus, a real problem
of exclusion from access to material resources and services, and the search
and struggle for a resolution to that problem, has been racialised. The
idea of 'race' is used to define the Caribbean and/or Asian migrants as
an illegitimate, competing Other whose presence has either caused or
intensified the struggle for housing, social services and employment, from
which it is concluded, apparently logically, that the problems could be
resolved by excluding the Other. For this reason, this specific instance of
working-class racism does not have to be explained by proposing a capitalist
conspiracy or by identifying small groups of people who gather to celebrate
Hitler's birthday and can only see Jewish and 'black' people as biologically
degenerate. Rather, it seeks a significant part of the explanation in the active
attempt to interpret and explain the working-class *Erlebnis* (e.g. Phizacklea
and Miles 1979; Miles and Phizacklea 1981).

This evidence gives empirical substance to Hall's theoretically derived
assertion that the expression of racism within the working class is a form
of representation by which sections of the working class live out their
experience of the capitalist mode of production (1980: 341). It confirms
more generally that racism:

> . . . is not a set of mistaken perceptions. . . . [It arises] because of the
> concrete problems of different classes and groups in the society.

Racism represents the attempt ideologically to construct those conditions, contradictions and problems in such a way that they can be dealt with and deflected at the same moment.

(Hall 1978: 35)

Therefore, racism can successfully (although mistakenly) make sense of the world and provide a strategy for political action. It follows that, to the extent that racism is grounded in economic and political relations, strategies for eliminating racism should not concentrate on trying *exclusively* to persuade those who articulate racism that they are 'wrong', but on changing those particular economic and political relations.

The fourth distinguishing content of racism as an ideology is that the concept does not identify a specific historical content. Rather, it identifies the general characteristics that a discourse must possess to qualify as an instance of racism. In other words, racism is not a single, static ideology, one that is identified by the persistence of a specific set of assertions, images and stereotypes. Empirically, there 'have been many significantly different racisms – each historically specific and articulated in a different way with the societies in which they appear' (Hall 1978: 26; also 1980: 342). Again, the importance of this can be illustrated by recent as well as historical research.

Returning to the nature of working-class racism, Phizacklea and Miles emphasised the specificity of the racism identified among some of the working class in London in the 1970s by noting the relative insignificance of stereotypes derived from Britain's history as a colonial power (1979: 97–8, 119–20, 1980: 173–4). It was not that the imagery of, for example, 'black savagery' was absent. It was sometimes articulated as context, but it was of little value in explaining the economic and political realities of a shortage of housing and a variety of social facilities and services in London in the 1970s (although it may have had a greater utility in explaining the representation of African-Caribbean male youth as especially prone to criminal assault). The specific racism identified in that context was one in which skin colour served to identify the Other, and the Other was considered to have a privileged and illegitimate access to resources (e.g. Phizacklea and Miles 1979: 111).

The fluidity of racism can also be demonstrated historically. Jordan's (1968) immensely detailed account of the changes as well as the continuities in American representations of the African illustrates this. Drawing on this and other work, we showed in Chapter 1 that European and North

presentations of Africans in the eighteenth century considered
uropeans, to be human beings but nevertheless a distinct
being, distinguished by skin colour but also *inter alia* by a potent
sexuality, bestiality and laziness, all of which were negatively evaluated.
Consequently, the African was ranked below the European on a hierarchy
of acceptability. During the nineteenth century, the idea of 'race' assumed
increasing prominence, and accordingly there was an important change
in the representation of the African as Other. Many of the negatively
evaluated characteristics continued to be attributed to the African but
the overall nature of the African when compared with the European was
re-evaluated.

Thus, skin colour, potent sexuality, bestiality, etc. were no longer
considered environmentally determined or evidence of degeneration, but
among the inherent characteristics of the African 'race'. This was a racism
which represented the African as essentially different from the European
and therefore confined the African as Other to perpetual inferiority, unlike
that of the eighteenth century, which presented the African as a form of
deviation from a (European) norm, assuming that the attributed inferiority
was a temporal condition.

In response to specific events during the nineteenth century, there were
significant shifts in the content of British representations of the colonised
Other. The Indian Mutiny of 1857 had a profound impact on British
conceptions in both India and Britain. The predominant representation of
the population of India had been of a docile, industrious Hindu, but in the
immediate aftermath of the mutiny the Indian was increasingly represented
as deceptive, fanatical and cruel. The image of the scheming, bloodthirsty
Oriental was not new, but was more widely articulated (and elaborated by
the addition of the image of the Indian as 'nigger') in an attempt to
comprehend the events of 1857 and to justify the imposition of direct
British rule over India. Although in the longer term the (contradictory)
myth of the effete Hindu persisted, the ideological reaction to the events
of the mid-nineteenth century in India demonstrated the fluidity of racism,
the responsiveness of its authors to real events and the ability creatively to
reshape the ideology.

Similarly, events in the Caribbean in the mid-nineteenth century
provided an occasion for a change in British representations of the African,
although this took the form of a simple reinforcement of existing
representations. The Jamaican revolt of 1865 was widely interpreted as
evidence of the innate savagery and inferiority of the African 'race', and the

need for strong government to prevent a retreat into barbarism: the association of the African with savagery and barbarism in the European mind has a long history, as we have seen, but the events of 1865 strengthened the view in the British public mind that these were biologically determined characteristics (Bolt 1971: 102–8, 178–205, 209–10).

Thus, racisms differ on a number of dimensions, all of which are historically variable: the group that is identified as its negative object; the features signified as natural; the characteristics attributed to both Self and Other and the respective evaluations of these characteristics. Yet they are not historically random. While it is important to identify and explain the dynamic content and fluidity of racism, there are also certain historical continuities. Again, as we saw in Chapter 1, certain European representations of the African have remained prominent for long periods of time. Different racisms are therefore not necessarily independent of each other, nor are they continually created anew in any absolute sense. Rather, any one instance of racism will be the product of both a reworking of at least some of the substance of earlier instances, and a creation of novel elements.

In sum, we use the concept of racism to denote a particular form of (evaluative) representation that is a specific instance of a wider (descriptive) process of racialisation. As a representational phenomenon, it is analytically distinguishable from exclusionary practices. Such a distinction is essential to the task of explanation because it does not foreclose the identification of the reasons why racialised populations occupy disadvantaged positions in current or historical social formations. Having demonstrated that a racialised population has been intentionally or unintentionally excluded from, for example, the labour market, it does not necessarily follow that this is a consequence of racism. Exclusionary practices may be partially or wholly motivated by or expressive of racism, but this must always be demonstrated rather than assumed to be the case.

INSTITUTIONAL RACISM

Finally, we argue for the retention of the concept of institutional racism in a more precise form than those that we criticised in Chapter 2. In a sense, every racism is institutional because racism is not an individual but a social creation. Hence, strictly speaking, individuals are not racist. Rather, it is an ideology that is racist. Here, however, we propose that the concept of institutional racism refer to two sets of circumstances: first, circumstances where exclusionary practices arise from, and therefore embody, a racist discourse but which may no longer be explicitly justified by such a discourse; and second, circumstances where an explicitly racist discourse is modified in such a way that the explicitly racist content is eliminated, but other words carry the original meaning.

What both circumstances have in common is that the racist discourse becomes silent, but is nevertheless embodied (or institutionalised) in the continuation of exclusionary practices or in the use of the new discourse. The continuing practice or the new discourse is expressive of an earlier, racist discourse. Hence, the concept of institutional racism does not refer to exclusionary practices *per se* but to the fact that a once present discourse is now absent and that it justified or set in motion exclusionary practices that therefore institutionalise that discourse. An ideology of racism is thereby embodied in a set of practices. This warrants classification as institutional racism only where the process of determinacy can be identified. Thus, in order to determine the presence or otherwise of institutional racism, one assesses not the consequences of actions but the history of discourse and its manner and moment of institutionalisation in order to demonstrate that prior to the silence (or transformation), a racist discourse was articulated.

Both of these forms of institutional racism can be illustrated by a British example, the first by reference to immigration law (e.g. Macdonald 1983). None of the post-1945 British Immigration Acts employed an explicitly racist discourse: they did not make explicit reference to 'black' people and they contained no statement of intent to exclude people defined as a distinct 'race' – unlike, for example, the Special Restriction (Coloured Alien Seamen) Order of 1925 (see Gordon and Reilly 1986; Rich 1986: 122–30). Nevertheless, when the political context in which the legislation was passed is examined, we find that a racist ideology was present and that the legislation was introduced in order to realise racist objectives.

During the late 1940s and early 1950s, the British government used various administrative devices to restrict the entry of 'coloured' (to use the language of the historical period) Commonwealth citizens, and even considered legislation to prevent their entry and settlement in Britain, which was then their right. During the late 1950s, and especially after the attacks on British citizens of Caribbean origin in 1958, there were increasing demands from politicians to restrict the rights of entry of these Commonwealth citizens because, it was alleged, they were more likely to engage in criminal acts and to carry contagious diseases. There was public pressure to restrict 'coloured' immigration from the electorate because it assumed dire consequences for housing and state benefits; increasingly supported by MPs, this was sufficient to allow the Conservative Government to legislate in 1962 in the way that had been desired a decade earlier (e.g. Joshi and Carter 1984; Miles 1984b; Miles and Phizacklea 1984; Carter et al. 1987; Harris 1987).

Subsequent legislation was intended to ensure that the objectives of the 1962 Act were more effectively achieved. Thus, the 1968 Commonwealth Immigrants Act withdrew the right of 'coloured' UK passport holders to enter Britain, while the 1971 Immigration Act extended the right of entry and settlement to several million 'white' people. A key feature of the political context for this legislation was the prominence of Enoch Powell, who, in a series of speeches, racialised the people of Asian and Caribbean origin in Britain and alleged a range of negative consequences for 'our own people' arising from their presence in Britain (Smithies and Fiddick 1969; Schoen 1977; Miles 1988). Additionally, the state's own legitimation of its legislation that came to predominate in the 1960s, but that was emergent in the late 1950s, is a prime instance of a racialised discourse that contributed to the institutionalisation of racism.

The legitimation claimed that strict immigration control was essential to ensure good 'race relations'. This maxim alleged that, as a result of immigration, a number of different 'races' were living in Britain and, to ensure that they could co-exist without conflict, the number of 'coloured people' living in Britain had to be limited. This was because, in the words of a Government White Paper, *Immigration from the Commonwealth*, published in 1965, 'the presence . . . of nearly one million immigrants from the Commonwealth with different social and cultural backgrounds raises a number of problems and creates various social tensions in those areas where they have concentrated'. The immigrant presence was therefore the cause of problems that had to be solved, 'if we are to avoid the evil of racial strife and if harmonious relations between the different races who now form our community are to develop'. Hence, the discourse that paralleled and legitimated immigration legislation was explicit in confirming the strategy of withdrawing from certain 'races' the right of entry to Britain because they created social problems.

This maxim illustrates the second form of institutional racism, a form whereby a racist discourse is simultaneously superceded by and reconstituted in an apparently non-racist discourse. During the 1950s, British MPs agitating for immigration legislation were explicit in demanding that the legislation apply exclusively to 'coloured people'.

In this respect, they were only demanding what the first two post-war governments were considering largely in secret (Joshi and Carter 1984; Carter *et al.* 1987). However, in light of the (accurate) accusation of racism, such explicit references became less common in the formal statements of politicians who increasingly referred only to the need for 'firm immigration control'. More recently, the need to prevent a 'flood' of 'bogus asylum seekers' entering Britain has been alleged. Given that the original agitation had explicitly identified 'coloured immigrants' as constituting a problematic presence, and given that immigration continued to be represented as creating a 'race relations' problem, the apparently more neutral language of 'immigration' and 'immigrant' therefore carried a set of additional, implicit meanings. As a result, they were widely understood to refer specifically to 'coloured' immigrants. One interesting instance of this coding is the way in which, during the late 1960s, opinion poll questions eliciting views on 'repatriation' referred sometimes to 'immigrants' and sometimes to 'coloured immigrants' (Miles 1988). This coding was also central to the discourse of the New Right in the 1980s (see, for example, Palmer 1986).

The concept of institutional racism therefore refers to circumstances where racism is embodied in exclusionary practices or in a formally non-racialised discourse. But, in both cases, it is necessary to demonstrate the determinate influence of racism. As we have already argued, exclusionary practices that result in disadvantage for racialised groups cannot be assumed to be determined wholly or in part by racism.

CONCLUSION

In confronting the problem of the meaning of the concept of racism in the context of conceptual inflation and deflation, we have sought a solution by situating it in a set of interrelated concepts. Thus, rather than assent to an ever-broadening concept of racism, we have argued that it should be more narrowly defined as an ideology if it is to be of serious analytical value. Consequently, our interest is in the production and reproduction of meanings. However, we have also recognised the empirical significance of many historical transformations that have occurred and that have stimulated conceptual inflation and deflation. Most significantly, although explicit expressions of a belief in the existence of a hierarchy of biologically distinct 'races' are much less widely articulated, especially in the formal public arena, a discourse of 'race' continues, along with a signification of somatic features and an attribution of (negatively and positively) evaluated characteristics to groups so defined. We have argued that such a discourse should be defined as racism. But we have also argued that the expression of racism is an integral component of a wider, historical process of racialisation that is interlinked with exclusionary practices and with the expression of other forms of exclusionary ideology. In a social context structured by historical change and, in a post-colonial and post-Fascist era, by a desire to obscure intentionality, our conceptual framework warrants a greater degree of complexity and sophistication than is allowed by those who employ the concept of racism in a loose or undefined manner.

III

CONTEXTUALISING RACISM

5

RACISM AND CLASS RELATIONS

INTRODUCTION

We have discussed racialisation and racism as representational phenomena in the previous chapter. We now move to discuss their determination and effects in the wider context of economic and political relations. In this chapter, we confront the interrelation between racialisation and racism and the historical development of capitalism as a mode of production within a developing world economic system. We undertake this task against the background of a history of economistic analysis (with a strong tendency to present racism as 'functional' to capitalist development in general) that has largely given way to a cultural analysis that neglects the economic basis of capitalism and social relations of inequality.

We regard racialisation and racism as historically specific and necessarily contradictory phenomena. Racism has appeared in a number of different forms, but it has a varying interaction with economic and political relations in capitalist and non-capitalist social formations. Racialisation and racism are not exclusive 'products' of capitalism but have origins in European societies prior to the development of the capitalist mode of production and have a history of expression within social formations dominated by non-capitalist modes of production in interaction with the capitalist mode.

In other words, racism is an ideology with conditions of existence that are, at least in part, independent of the interests of the ruling class and the bourgeoisie within capitalist societies.

To define racism as functional to capitalism is to presuppose the nature and outcome of its interaction with economic and political relations, and with other ideologies. Such a definition mistakenly assumes that a homogeneous ruling class inevitably and necessarily derives economic and/or political advantages from its expression. The use of racism to limit the size of the labour market is not necessarily in the interests of those employers experiencing a labour shortage, nor of those who require skilled labour, while racism and exclusionary practices that result in civil disturbance will not necessarily be welcomed by capitalists whose business activity has been disrupted as a result, or by the state that may need to increase expenditure to maintain social order.

Hence, we analyse racism as a necessarily contradictory phenomenon. The expression of racism, and the subsequent structuring of political and economic relations, has a variety of temporally specific consequences for all those implicated in the process, and whether or not they are advantageous will depend upon class position and conjuncture. Racism is therefore a contradictory phenomenon because what is 'functional' for one set of interests may be 'dysfunctional' for another, and because the conditions that sustain its advantageous expression are rarely permanent, and changed circumstances may clash with the continued expression of racism. The effectivity of racism is therefore historically specific and hence knowable only as a result of historical analysis rather than abstract theorising. The objective of this chapter is to illustrate and elaborate these claims.

SLAVERY

We begin with slavery, a subject which has provoked a great deal of mythologising in Western nation states. To express this in a tongue-in-cheek manner, readers in Britain will know that the Whigs abolished slavery in the British Empire in the early nineteenth century, and that this spelled the global death of slavery. American readers will know that slavery was actually abolished in America, and therefore world-wide, in 1862 by Abraham Lincoln. Of course, the reality is somewhat different, and slavery continues to exist in the present day (see, for example, Index on Censorship 2000). Like capitalism, it is a mode of production that produces its own inequalities, which have overlapped and do overlap with inequalities that are produced, sustained and legitimated through the ideology of racism. Indeed, there exists a strong consciousness, particularly in the United States, that racism – particularly as manifest in exclusionary practices – is a consequence of slavery. Racism in its modern manifestation is seen as the reaction of 'white' Americans to the loss of slaves who they considered their property, a desire to ensure that 'black' people would 'know their place' and that 'white' supremacy would be maintained, albeit to a lesser degree. Omi and Winant express this notion of historical continuity as follows:

> In the Americas, the conquest represented the violent introduction of a new form of rule whose relationship with those it subjugated was almost entirely coercive. In the U.S., the origins of racial division, and of racial signification and identity formation, lie in a system of rule which was extremely dictatorial. The mass murders and expulsions of indigenous people, and the enslavement of Africans, surely evoked and inspired little consent in their founding moments. . . . *By no means has the U.S. established racial democracy at the end of the century, and by no means is coercion a thing of the past.* But the sheer complexity of the racial questions U.S. society confronts today, the welter of competing racial projects and contradictory racial experiences which Americans undergo, suggests that hegemony is a useful and appropriate term with which to characterise *contemporary* racial rule.
>
> (1994: 67; added emphasis)

This is one of several reasons why analyses of racism in the USA do not transfer easily to Europe (and vice versa) where in the modern period slavery has been largely externalised to colonies and was rarely used as a relation of production within Europe. Hence, in European discourses, racism is more often perceived as the consequence of colonialism than slavery. However, in this context, the controversial nature of some of Dinesh D'Souza's arguments can be more readily appreciated by a European reader. He argues that slavery was not a racist institution, because:

> Slavery was practiced for thousands of years in virtually all societies: in China, India, Europe, the Arab world, sub-Saharan Africa, and the Americas. In the United States, slave-owning was not confined to whites: American Indians and free blacks owned thousands of slaves. Thus slavery is neither distinctively Western nor racist. What is uniquely Western is the abolition of slavery. The American founders articulated

principles of equality and consent which formed the basis for emanci-
pation and the civil rights movement.

(1995: 22)

Although D'Souza's work has been controversial, and his right-wing
agenda is not disguised – indeed, this argument seems to culminate with
a rejectionist standpoint on the reparations issue (1995: 113) – he does
have a point. Slavery as a mode of production does not *necessarily* have
anything to do with racism. It existed before racism, some Africans were
sold into slavery by other Africans, and some slave owners in the United
States were defined as 'black'. However, it is noticeable that many historical
examples of slavery have prioritised the enslavement of 'foreigners', while
the enslavement of members of one's own group, nation or tribe has often
been taboo. Furthermore, in the colonial period, slavery was legitimated
by the ideology of racism, and its most significant manifestations were the
transportation of human beings from Africa to the Americas, where they
were defined as the 'black' slaves of 'white' slave owners. In other words,
although slavery was not exclusively practised by 'white' people against
'black' people, this became the norm in the Americas.

As a mode of production, slavery is a form of unfree labour, and, as such,
is central to the understanding of racism. Elsewhere, as we have seen, Miles
defines racism in the following terms:

> I conceive racism (which has additional, secondary conditions of
> existence and reproduction) as a potential ideological element of signif-
> ication by which to *select*, and to *legitimate* the selection of, a particular
> population, whose labour power will be exploited in a particular set of
> unfree production relations.
>
> (1987a: 188)

Racism as ideology and racism as an unfree relation of production are
complementary and inseparable. Furthermore, slavery has co-existed with
capitalism (Miles 1987a), so the articulation of racism has had features
common to the contexts of both modes of production. Importantly, in
each case, its articulation as an ideology has legitimated the mode of production and racialised as well as ethnicised the labour market. Consequently,
people classified as a racialised ethnic group have been concentrated in
certain sectors of, or outside, the labour market. In the contexts of slavery,
capitalism and, as we shall see, colonialism, this has been part of the wider
macro-social structure.

COLONIALISM AND UNFREE LABOUR

This mode-of-production oriented analysis is now a less-common approach to the study of colonialism and racism. Indeed, one of the most important contributions of the cultural analysis of racism has been the development of post-colonial and colonial discourse theories. Central to this enterprise, though not always explicit, is what Said calls 'contrapuntal reading'. This is defined as follows:

> As we look back at the cultural archive, we begin to reread it not univocally but *contrapuntally*, with a simultaneous awareness both of the metropolitan history that is narrated and of those other histories against which (and together with which) the dominating discourse acts. In the counterpoint of Western classical music, various themes play off one another, with only a provisional privilege being given to any particular one; yet in the resulting polyphony there is concert and order, and organised interplay that derives from the themes, not from a rigorous melodic or formal principle outside the work. In the same way, I believe, we can read and interpret English novels, for example, whose engagement (usually suppressed for the most part) with the West Indies or India, say, is shaped and perhaps even determined by the specific history of colonisation, resistance, and finally native nationalism. At this point alternative or new narratives emerge, and they become institutionalised or discursively stable entities.
>
> (1994: 59–60)

This 'reading back' of the 'colonial discourse' is the method of postcolonial theory: through this contrapuntal reading, it is possible to study the discourse and history (or, rather, discourses and histories) of colonialism. So, the history of colonialism is seen in terms of a discourse – which Said (1995) calls Orientalism – that postulates an inherent (or essentialised) difference between the metropolitan West and the colonised Other, the latter represented as homogeneous, unchanging, and essentially inferior. This discourse is promoted through a number of channels: the academic study of the colonised Other, their culture, language, etc. (which were in reality Western constructions); the system of colonial institutions; and a popular, everyday discourse for representing the colonised Other that spread across the whole of European culture. It is a discourse rather than an ideology, but it contributes to the ideology of racism by attributing to European civilisation, and therefore to 'white' people, a superficial notion of responsibility (the 'white man's burden') that veiled the noumenal ideology of racism, including the belief in 'racial' typology and hierarchy.

Much can be learned about the ideology of racism by this theory and method but its conscious distancing of relations of production and of the interaction of political and economic relations results in silence about other aspects of domination and exploitation. The analysis of narratives of novels cannot reveal all that we need to know about colonial relations of domination.

European colonialism assumed a number of different cultural and developmental patterns. What they all had in common from the mid-seventeenth century until the early twentieth century was a process whereby Europeans occupied and settled on land in other parts of the world, subsequently organising the production of commodities for exchange on the world market. Thus, from the mid-seventeenth century onwards, European representations of the Other were generated and reproduced in the course of a history of contact between different populations enmeshed in specific relations of production and expressing distinct cultural values. These representations actively structured the transformation and repro-duction of either modified, extant modes of production, or the new modes of production created as a result of colonialism. In the latter case, modes of production rarely took the form emergent in Europe, based on commodity production and the commodification of labour power. Rather, they were characterised to a greater or lesser degree by forms of direct physical and legal-political compulsion, that is, unfree labour (cf. Miles 1987a; Kolchin 1987). Where some mineral or agricultural item could be obtained or produced and become a commodity for sale on the world market, access to land and the provision of labour had to be organised. The latter entailed the identification of people who would provide labour power, the creation of conditions under which they would make labour power available, and the suppression of resistance to such attempts.

The organisation of production in colonial Kenya, for example, was a material process sustained and effected by racialisation and the articu-lation of racism. The European colonisers and the African indigenous populations met each other as human beings already organised into classes and, as far as the former were concerned, against the background of a long history of 'knowing' the African through a variety of written and oral sources, and, in some cases, previous experience of meeting and living among Africans. They came to Africa, therefore, with a representation of the African as Other that was logically related to the articulated rationale of civilising people at a less advanced stage of development (Thornton 1965: 158). It was on this basis that the process of primary accumulation was carried through. As a result, the economic relations of production had a particular ideological content.

British colonisers arrived in Kenya with a discourse of 'race'. This was a ranking that placed the African at the bottom of a scale of 'civilisation' and gave the European colonisers a specific responsibility. For those who also believed in social Darwinism, 'civilising the natives' was considered to have dire consequences which they accepted without equivocation. Sir Charles Elliot, who was one of the early Commissioners of the East African Protectorate, wrote in a memorandum to the Foreign Office in London, in April 1904:

> Your Lordship has opened this Protectorate to white immigration and colonisation, and I think it well that in confidential correspondence at least, we should face the undoubted issue – viz., that the white mates black in a very few moves. . . . There can be no doubt that the Masai and many other tribes must go under. It is a prospect which I view with equanimity and a clear conscience. . . . [Masaidom] is a beastly, bloody system founded on raiding and immorality.
>
> (Bennett 1965: 270–1)

Others believed that the 'civilising' process was less a process of genocide, and more a matter of patient acceptance of slow change. An official government memorandum on 'native policy' stated:

> In dealing with African savage tribes we are dealing with a people at the genesis of things . . . and we cannot expect to lift them in a few years from this present state to that of a highly civilised people. . . . The evolution of races must necessarily take centuries to accomplish satisfactorily.
>
> (Cited in Sorrenson 1968: 227)

Others were less patient. A settler protest against the proposal for a common electoral roll and an equal franchise stated that the theory of waiting 'till the backward races (whom the Report itself describes as twenty centuries behind the Europeans) have reached their standard is an impossible proposition that no virile and governing race could be expected to acquiesce in' (cited in Bennett 1965: 310).

The idea of 'race' as a biological reality was given legal status in treaties and legislation. The agreement that removed the Masai from the Rift Valley in the East African Protectorate and established the Masai reserve required their representatives to confirm that they were 'fully satisfied that the proposals for our removal to definite and final reserves are for the undoubted good of our race' (Sorrenson 1968: 195) while the 1915 Crown Lands Ordinance defined 'race' as 'persons of European, Asiatic or African origin as the case may be' (1968: 174). The settlers therefore racialised the African populations that they came to 'civilise' and they necessarily racialised themselves as the agents of 'civilisation'. This was a universal process insofar as the population of the whole world was racialised, and racism created a hierarchy of 'racial' suitability.

Thus, when the Colonial Secretary in London suggested that the infant colony be opened to Jewish refugees from Eastern Europe, the arguments of the early settlers opposing this were openly racist (Mungeam 1966: 104; Sorrenson 1968: 38–9). The more pressing practical issue for the settlers was the manner in which the 'civilisation' of the savage and backward African 'race' might be achieved. The settlers' primary solution was that the African should provide labour power for the European who had gained access to the land but who had little or no intention to labour on it. In the view of one settler who spoke for the majority, the 'white man' was 'the master race and . . . the black men must forever remain cheap labour and slaves' (cited in Sorrenson 1968: 238). This racism was a class ideology. It was a representation of a group of people who had accessed the means of production with the objective of making others work for them.

This discourse invented a biological hierarchy of the world's population that fitted certain groups for certain positions in the relations of production. Thus, the 'white race' was destined not only to rule politically, but also to organise and direct production. The African 'race' was destined to provide it with labour power to realise a surplus from agricultural commodity production. Thus, racism was not simply a legitimation of class exploitation. It represented the social world in a way that identified a specific population as a labouring class. The remaining problem was to organise the social world in such a way that forced that population into its 'natural' class position: in other words, reality had to be created in accordance with that representation in order to ensure the material objective of production.

At the time of European settlement, and with the exception of the coastal strip, East Africa was occupied by a number of spatially and culturally distinct populations engaged largely in nomadic subsistence production (Sorrenson 1968: 28; Brett 1973: 168; Tignor 1976: 3–4, 14). The British colonisers of the late nineteenth century therefore had to convince or force these populations to give up land to permit their own settlement, and to provide them with labour power when they were already well able to satisfy their own material wants. The measures by which these objectives were achieved established a form of commodity production, based on unfree labour, alongside subsistence production.

Gaining access to land was one of the first problems confronted by the European colonisers, and one that required the use of force in order to establish initial settlement (Low 1965: 31; Tignor 1976: 15). Once residence had been established, the settlers had then to gain control over sufficient land to permit the development of agricultural commodity production. This led to a conflict of interests with the African populations who used the land for subsistence production as well as the population of Indian origin which had long been present in East Africa as merchants and traders. The central strategy employed by the settlers, and effected by the colonial state, was to establish exclusive European access to land in areas considered suitable climatically for European occupation and agricultural production (the 'White Highlands', as they became known), to dispossess the Africans resident in these areas, and to create African reserves where the indigenous populations could reproduce themselves in areas adjacent to those occupied by European landowners (Tignor 1976: 30–2). Indians, too, were excluded from owning or renting land in the Highlands and were subject to restrictions on where they might live in the towns (Sorrenson 1965: 680–2, 1968: 159–75). These conflicting interests ensured an ongoing process of resistance and accommodation on the part of the African and Indian populations to European colonisation.

The creation of reserves was not originally intended by the settlers (Sorrenson 1965: 683) and was achieved somewhat haphazardly by two means, both of which were facilitated by the creation of African chiefs by the dominant colonial class. Few African populations in Kenya had individual chiefs but it did not prove difficult to find individuals willing to fulfil this role when it enabled them to accumulate land and livestock (Mungeam 1966: 129–30; Tignor 1976: 42, 49; Sender and Smith 1986: 42–3). Land that was considered by the settlers to be unoccupied and unexploited by Africans was defined as 'waste' land and was then sold or leased to European settlers, thereby establishing private property relations (Sorrenson 1965: 675–7, 682; Wrigley 1965: 227–8). From the point of view of the African populations, this entailed setting limits on their previous nomadic patterns. In other words, what for the European settlers was 'waste' land had been, for the nomadic Africans, available for temporary production and residence.

The second means was to 'negotiate' with African populations in order to define the boundaries within which they would live. In the special case of the Masai, this required their removal to other locations under the terms of a treaty to free the land for European occupation (Sorrenson 1968: 182–9, 210–25). This process began in the very early years of the twentieth century (Mungeam 1966: 202–4), but it was not until 1915 that the Governor of the colony was given the power to proclaim the creation of reserves, and so most were not formally constituted until 1926 (Sorrenson 1965: 683; Tignor 1976: 32). Moreover, their boundaries were subject to subsequent revision in order to release more land for European settlement and it was only after 1932 that the boundaries were finally established (Wrigley 1965: 259–60; Sorrenson 1965: 687–9).

For the European settlers, the establishment of reserves by the colonial state was central to establishing control over land, but by itself this did not permit the constitution of agricultural commodity production. Although initial settler plots were relatively small (Wrigley 1965: 219), they came to exceed 5,000 acres in some cases and these were too large to be farmed by a single family (Low 1965: 51). Thus, not only was land necessary but so were human beings to provide labour power. The creation of reserves did not by themselves force the 'natives' to work for European settlers because they permitted the 'natives' to maintain their 'traditional' mode of life (Stichter 1982: 44–5).

Various strategies were employed to procure African labour power as cheaply as possible. All depended upon the intervention of the colonial state. Hence, the 'natural' role of the African 'race' to provide cheap labour power could only be achieved by human intervention. One method was the use of direct or indirect compulsion. This was widely used by the colonial state to construct the infrastructure of colonisation and to establish the conditions for agricultural commodity production. Forced labour was a development of African communal (unpaid) labour that was intended to produce collective benefits for the population from which the labourers were drawn and that was used for path-making and bush-clearing. The colonial state at district level modified this system, using the new 'chiefs' as intermediaries, to provide labourers for local road-building, the construction of 'public' buildings and for porterage. It also directed some communal labour on to farms (Tignor 1976: 43). After 1920, this compulsion became dominant and explicit. The colonial state would demand of a local chief that a specified number of fit men be recruited for a certain period to construct roads, railways and docks away from the men's place of residence, and in return for a small cash wage which was lower than that paid to voluntary labourers. Those nominated by the chief faced a variety of sanctions if they refused. Often, those recruited were required to work for private employers engaged in contracted tasks from the colonial state (Wrigley 1965: 231, 237; Clayton and Savage 1974: xvi–xvii, 29, 44, 134–9).

A second strategy was the 'squatter system'. This encouraged African communities to live on European-owned land where they were expected to provide a certain amount of labour power during a year, in return for which they received the right to use a certain area of land to produce their means of subsistence (see Wrigley 1965: 231–2; Bennett 1965: 277). By the 1920s, this was the relationship by which landowners obtained the largest proportion of labourers (Clayton and Savage 1974: 128). Under a variant of this system, employers could hire labourers on an annual contract, as a result of which they were required to work for the employer for a minimum of 180 days, in return for which they received free of rent an acre of land per head and a small wage (Sorrenson 1968: 150; Brett 1973: 171–2; Clayton and Savage 1974: 32, 128–31). This relation of production approximated serfdom but as agricultural production expanded, it became increasingly problematic for the landowner by virtue of the quantity of land occupied by Africans, and by the end of the 1920s it was in decline and being replaced by a system of wage labour (Wrigley 1965: 257).

The third strategy was to 'induce' Africans 'voluntarily' to enter the emergent labour market where they would sell their labour power for a wage. 'Inducement' took two main forms. The first was taxation which became a central force in the early 1920s (Tignor 1976: 183). By requiring Africans to pay a tax in cash to the colonial state, sections of the African population were thereby required to seek a cash income that was at least sufficient to pay the tax (Low 1965: 23; Sorrenson 1968: 151, 155; Brett 1973: 188; Clayton and Savage 1974: 143–6). The second was the state's 'encouragement' of Africans to make their labour power available to landowners. This inducement was often direct but was usually mediated by the 'chiefs' who served in effect as colonial officials (Tignor 1976: 53, 105, 182). But when evidence of such 'encouragement' became public during the first decade of the twentieth century, there was conflict with the Colonial Office in London (Wrigley 1965: 231). The same sequence of events occurred after the First World War. In 1919 and 1920 the colonial state published circulars that stated that Africans should provide labour power and that instructed its District Officers to use all lawful means to encourage this, and to press local chiefs and elders to do the same. In response to widespread criticism, these circulars were initially legitimated by Parliament in London as being in the 'real interests' of Africans because they were intended to eliminate 'idleness and vice' from the African way of life. This legitimation reconciled the imperial, paternalistic mission of civilising the 'inferior races' with the task of providing a labour force for the 'superior, master race' (Brett 1973: 188–9; Clayton and Savage 1974: 32–41, 110–17; Tignor 1976: 173).

In combination with the establishment of the reserves, these two forms of inducement led to the creation of a migrant labour system within Kenya (Stichter 1982). And the 1920s was the decade that witnessed the major expansion of agricultural commodity production (of coffee, sisal, maize, and later tea), organised by European landowners, for exchange on the world market (Wrigley 1965: 235; Brett 1973: 176; Tignor 1976: 145). Throughout this decade, there was an increase in labour migration that coincided with a decline in forms of compulsory recruitment and African peasant production. The latter was actively discouraged by the colonial state, through legislative means, because of the implications of successful cash crop production for the labour supply (Tignor 1976: 292). Consequently, the reserves were incapable of producing sufficient for subsistence, becoming less locations for the reproduction of the 'traditional' African way of life and more reservoirs of labour from which the European landowners could recruit when necessary. The decline in African peasant production was therefore a major factor in creating a migrant labour force because it meant that some other means of earning a cash income had to be found in order to pay taxes. Thus, the 'voluntary' search by an increasing proportion of African men for a purchaser for their labour power in the 'White Highlands' was grounded in socially constituted conditions of economic compulsion. In the 1920s, the spatially limited reserves began to be unable to produce enough to sustain the increasing African population (Stichter 1982: 30–89).

We have described here the forms of social intervention of a colonising class, supported by the state, intended to establish commodity production in a spatial location where the existing population reproduced itself in the absence of commodity production and money as a medium of exchange. The creation of this new mode of production entailed the reorganisation and subordination of that subsistence mode of production. This process of relieving a section of the population of the means of production in order to compel the sale of labour power for a wage (that is, the process of creating a proletariat which is a central dimension of 'primary accumulation') is a universal feature of the transition to a capitalist mode of production, and necessarily depends on compulsion. But, as Marx (1976: 86) pointed out, it always takes a historically specific form.

The process of primary accumulation is often analysed primarily as a transformation of economic relations, effected by the state. However, this transformation in Kenya was effected not only by the actions of colonial state, but was also shaped decisively by racialisation and racism. The economic transformation was represented by the European invaders as an interaction between 'races', and the process of transition was effected by means of the racialisation of the emergent land-owning class and the partially dispossessed African. Hence, the people who were identified as the source of expoiltable labour power were ideologically constructed as an inferior 'race'. The process of class formation was racialised: the creation of the partially dispossessed labouring class was not only motivated by racism but was effected through the institutionalisation of that racism in a system of racialised segregation, by which the different 'races' were allocated not only to different economic roles but also to different spatial locations. Economic and political relations were thereby socially constructed in accordance with the ideology of racism.

The ideology of racism was used not only to select people to fill certain positions in the structure of class relations but class relations were themselves structured in a particular manner to create a large proportion of Africans as suppliers of cheap labour power. What became the proletarian, or semi-proletarian, class position of the African was articulated as the appropriate position for a population at a different stage of human development, for a different (and inferior) kind of human being. To conclude, in this historically specific instance of primary accumulation, the labouring class was created by a dialectic between a process of material (but partial) dispossession of the means of production and a process of racialisation. Consequently, racism became a relation of production because it was an ideology that shaped decisively the formation and reproduction of the relation between exploiter and exploited: it was one of those representational elements which became historically conducive to the constitution and reproduction of a system of commodity production. Once more, racism as ideology and racism as a relation of production were complementary and inseparable.

CAPITALISM AND CLASS RELATIONS

An essential aspect of the reproduction of the capitalist mode of production is the processes by which people are distributed to various sites in the hierarchy of economic relations, because the accumulation process can be obstructed if, for example, there are insufficient numbers of people available to function as wage labourers. In a world economy dominated by the capitalist mode of production, this structures the temporary and permanent migration of people from one nation state to another to fill the increased number of manual, administrative and, sometimes, skilled positions. Moreover, capitalists as well as capital have been mobile across national boundaries. However, with the onset of a major crisis in the accumulation process in the early 1970s, international migration into Western Europe was much reduced and the size of the relative surplus population within Western Europe fluctuated considerably as people were expelled from the labour force and brought into it again. In this broad structural cycle of accumulation, there has occurred a complex dialectical process of inclusion and exclusion of people in and from the different sites of class relations as the size of these sites has expanded and contracted.

A variety of criteria are used to effect this process. Among them, in conjunction with migration, has been the signification of phenotypical difference, which has been central to the inclusion and exclusion of people in and from wage labour, and to the allocation of people to the range of different sites in the hierarchy of wage labour. We explore this theme with reference to the example of Britain.

The British economy, like other Western European economies, experienced significant labour shortages in the 1940s and 1950s in the context of the reorganisation of the labour market after the Second World War. The vast majority of migrants who entered Britain to fill these vacant positions came either from colonies and ex-colonies and were British subjects who were not initially subject to immigration control, or were citizens of the Republic of Ireland who were given privileged access to the British labour market. Consequently, unlike some other Western European nation states, there was no extensive use of a migrant labour system based on the issue of work and residence permits by the state (Castles *et al.* 1984: 20–8). This migration proceeded by largely informal means, but regulated by the condition of the labour market (Peach 1968). This relationship broke down with the imposition of immigration controls on British subjects born in the Commonwealth in 1962 and 1965 (although citizens of the Irish Republic were excluded from these controls). Thereafter, migrants from the Caribbean and Indian subcontinent were mainly dependants of those who had arrived during the 1950s in order to find paid work, although in the late 1960s and again in the early 1970s, they were joined by migrants from East Africa who were, in effect, political refugees (e.g. Twaddle 1975).

The vast majority of the migrants of the 1950s arrived with little or no capital and therefore had no choice but to sell their labour power for a wage, even where their intentions were to accumulate capital. Because only a small proportion were specifically recruited before migration, most filled positions found for them by family, friends or themselves. There were exceptions: a small minority of migrants, mainly from the Asian subcontinent, arrived with some capital and the intention of extending their existing capitalist interests (Nowikowski 1984); another small minority of migrants arrived to fill professional positions, notably within the National Health Service (Unit for Manpower Studies 1977: 58–61). These exceptions apart, we are left to explain the reasons why so many migrants from the Asian subcontinent and the Caribbean filled semi- and unskilled positions in manual wage labour.

A key part of the explanation lies in the fact that these positions were vacant as a result of the movement of indigenous labour into 'new jobs', characterised by higher rates of pay and better conditions of work. In the course of post-war economic restructuring, the expansion of light engineering, consumer durable industries and the service sector entailed the creation of new areas of wage labour employment, while older sectors of production (such as textile production and metal manufacture) faced increasing international competition and worsening conditions of work (e.g. Fevre 1984: 17–54; Duffield 1985: 144–52). Consequently, certain economic sectors faced acute shortages of labour, and in conditions of full employment, these positions could not be filled from the population within Britain. Thus, structural circumstances defined a demand for labour in certain sectors of the economy, and it was these positions that African Caribbean and Asian migrants filled.

However, unlike migrant labour recruited by a contract system (whereby a contract locates the migrant in a specific position in the hierarchy of wage labour and confines the migrant to that position for a specific period of time), African Caribbean and Asian migrants were theoretically free to sell their labour power to whoever they wished. They were therefore free to compete with indigenous labour for access to the

ber of new, higher paid jobs with better conditions. Thus,
ost African Caribbean and Asian workers were employed
or unskilled manual work (placing them in an inferior
n the ranks of manual wage labour) requires additional
We find this in the fact that labour recruitment depends,
at least in part, on an employer's conception of the abilities and skills
required for the job to be effectively carried out, and of the abilities and
skills of the people who offer their labour power for sale. The employer
tries to match the perceived qualities of the applicants to the perceived
requirements of the job. The employer's evaluation of these qualities and
requirements therefore functions as criteria of inclusion and exclusion in
that they serve to differentiate those who seek jobs.

Consequently, employers rank people present in the labour market.
Where the resulting hierarchy is constructed in such a way that the qualities
of individuals are perceived as representative of a wider collectivity,
and where the individual is deemed to possess the criteria that designate membership of that collectivity, the question of suitability may be
determined by reference to the perceived qualities of the collectivity rather
than to those of the individual applicant. In such circumstances, the
processes of inclusion and exclusion are effected by signification and group
categorisation. Where such a process is effected by reference to phenotypical
characteristics, the recruitment of labour is racialised. That is, the labour
market is perceived to include members of different 'races', each of which
is seen to possess a range of different skills and abilities which distinguish
that group as a supposed 'race'.

Since the 1950s, the British labour market has been racialised in this
way. Employers have signified certain physical and cultural characteristics
(notably skin colour, and hence the designation 'coloured labour' or
'coloured workers') of African Caribbean and Asian migrants and their
British-born children, and this signification has structured recruitment
processes. Employers believed or assumed that the labour market consisted
of a number of different 'races', and that these 'races' had different characteristics that influenced their employability. During the 1950s and early
1960s, this process of racialisation was accompanied by the exclusion
of these migrants in two ways (Wright 1968: 212). First, many employers
refused to employ any 'coloured' workers, and most would only do so
where there was no other source of labour power available. In other words,
in a racialised labour market, British employers consistently excluded
Asian and African Caribbean workers while 'white' labour was available.

Second, where African Caribbean and Asian migrants were employed, they were nevertheless excluded from certain sorts of job, or their numbers in the workforce were often limited to a predetermined quota.

Part of the explanation for this exclusionary practice lies in the fact that the majority of migrants, including those who considered themselves skilled in the context of relations of production in the Caribbean and the Asian subcontinent, had few skills relevant to an industrial capitalist economy (Wright 1968: 30–40). On this criterion, they were likely to be excluded from any form of skilled manual or non-manual employment. Additionally, racism was a determining factor. Some employers explained their exclusionary practices by reference to the anticipated or real opposition of their existing workforce to working with 'coloureds', opposition that they endorsed by acting in this manner. Others negatively stereotyped Asians as 'slow to learn', or African Caribbean people as lazy, unresponsive to discipline and truculent, or 'coloured people' generally as prone to accidents or requiring more supervision than 'white' workers (Wright 1968: 89–144). In all these instances, migrants were signified by skin colour and attributed collectively with negatively evaluated characteristics. Not all employers in Wright's survey articulated such racist views, so unanimity should not be assumed. Nevertheless, the interrelationship between the racialisation of migrants, racism and exclusionary practice limited the parameters of the labour market open to migrants from the Caribbean and Asian subcontinent. Thus, while there existed a demand for an increase in the size of the British working class – which thereby stimulated migration – racism and associated exclusionary practices placed those migrants in, and largely restricted them to, semi- and unskilled manual working-class positions.

This interrelationship between racialisation, racism and exclusionary practice continued to constitute a structural constraint for people of Asian and African Caribbean origin seeking wage labour, thereby maintaining a hierarchy of concordance and setting ideological limits to the operation of the labour market. This was particularly significant during the period of high unemployment in Britain in the 1980s. Since the 1960s, however, major studies on the nature and extent of exclusionary practice (e.g. Daniel 1968; Smith 1977; Brown 1984; Modood *et al.* 1997) have shown that acts of exclusion of Asian and African Caribbean people when searching for work are widespread, although they became more covert after they were made illegal in 1968 (Modood *et al.* 1997: 83).

More specifically, Jenkins (1986) demonstrated that there was wide scope for racialisation and racism to structure the decisions of managers in the course of recruiting workers, and therefore to determine their position in the labour market. From the theoretical perspective adopted here, the study is problematic because it utilised an inflated concept of racism (1986: 5) and presupposed the nature of the common-sense categories employed by managers (1986: 80). Nevertheless, Jenkins showed that a majority of managers made decisions about labour recruitment with a set of racist stereotypes and more general negative beliefs about African Caribbean and Asian workers that were similar to the common themes of contemporary racism in Britain (1986: 83–4, 107–9). Thus, they tended to regard 'immigration' as a 'bad thing', to define workers of African Caribbean and Asian origin as 'not-British', and to believe that there were 'too many of them' in Britain. In addition, managers commonly believed that the employment of Asian and African Caribbean workers created problems for them or their organisation (1986: 95–105). Finally, Jenkins demonstrated that several criteria of acceptability sought by managers when recruiting workers led to the systematic exclusion of applicants of African Caribbean and Asian origin (1986: 79). Moreover, these criteria, beliefs and assumptions were held in a context where the predominant methods of identifying job applicants were to conduct a search within the organisation or by 'word of mouth', procedures which provided considerable scope for racism to sustain exclusionary practices (1986: 134–5).

At the beginning of the twenty-first century, it is more difficult for employers to recruit labour in such an informal manner, partly because 'indirect discrimination' is also illegal, but there is still scope for racialisation and racism to influence the structuring of the labour market covertly. However, periods of high unemployment, such as the 1980s, tell us more about the relationship between capitalism and racism than periods of low unemployment (such as the present time), because studying these periods enable us to investigate the racialisation of the relative surplus population. During the 1980s, people of Asian and African Caribbean origin were represented across all the main economic sites of capitalist production in Britain (Field *et al*. 1981; Miles 1982: 167–88), including the small petite bourgeoisie and bourgeoisie (Anon. 1983: 429; Wilson 1983; Nowikowski 1984; Werbner 1984: 181; Barber 1985: 475; Anon. 1987: 22), though, of course, position in economic relations does not constitute the totality of class position. The majority of Asian and African Caribbean people of working age were economically active and in paid employment, occupying a proletarian economic position. However, more men were economically active than women (though the opposite was true of African Caribbean men and women), and more likely to be in manual jobs, and there were significant differences according to national origin – for example, East African men had a far higher proportion in employment than Pakistani and Bangladeshi men and women (see, for example, Brown 1984: 305; Barber 1985: 469–70; Anon. 1987: 19–20). By the late 1990s, Chinese men had a higher proportion in employment than African Asian men, and the gap between men and women of African Caribbean origin had effectively disappeared (Modood *et al*. 1997: 84–111). Overall, however, there was a 'more or less constant "ethnic penalty" paid by non-white people measured in terms of the jobs than similarly qualified people achieve' (Modood *et al*. 1997: 84; see also Heath and MacMahon 1995).

In spite of the proletarian position of Asian and African Caribbean people, and in spite of the variation by gender and national origin, it is clear that they constituted a significant part of the relative surplus population, and that this was a racialised constitution rather than a consequence of a skills shortage among migrants: in 1984, of Asian and African Caribbean people aged 16 years and over, 21.3 per cent of men and 19.1 per cent of women were unemployed, a figure which rose to 34 per cent for Pakistani and Bangladeshi men, and 40 per cent for Pakistani and Bangladeshi women; furthermore, people of Asian and African Caribbean origin aged between 16 and 34 years and born in Britain were *more* likely to be unemployed than those born outside Britain (Barber 1985: 473–4; Anon. 1983: 428). In the period of relatively low unemployment in the mid-1990s, however, this was not unambiguously the case (with the exception of African Caribbean men without formal qualifications), suggesting that this relative surplus population was being drawn into employment at this time (see Modood *et al*. 1997: 91–2).

The view that Asian and African Caribbean people in Britain collectively constitute a 'black' underclass, a collectivity homogenous in its poverty and economic disadvantage relative to 'white' people as a result of racism and systematic exclusionary practices, is therefore mistaken (see Rex and Tomlinson 1979: 1–35; Sivanandan 1982: 11, 123), even during the high unemployment of the 1980s. It is mistaken on both counts: the characterisation of the population of African Caribbean and Asian origin in Britain in the 1980s as occupying a unitary class position; and the explanation of the economic positions of this population as solely a consequence of racism and exclusionary practice. This can be further demonstrated by considering the reasons for the increasing proportion of Asian people who occupy a petit-bourgeois class position in Britain.

In common with many economically induced migrations, Asian migration to Britain has been motivated in part by a desire not only for economic advancement but also for entry into the petite bourgeoisie. For example, a large proportion of the Patidars who originate from Gujarat in India arrived in Britain, from India and from East Africa, with a merchant ideology. Thus, although the vast majority of these migrants entered British economic relations as sellers of labour power, they retained the intention of self-employment in some form of trading activity. Not all, and perhaps only a minority, have managed to effect this transition, but for those who have, it is a transition that is shaped in part by the intentions and objectives that originally motivated the migration (Tambs-Lyche 1980: 57, 60, 125). The implications of this motivation for movement into the petite bourgoisie on the part of Asian migrants and their children have been reinforced for some by the experience of racism and exclusionary practice, the belief being that self-employment will serve to insulate them from such experiences within the labour market (Forester 1978: 420–3; Anwar 1979: 125; Nowikowski 1984: 158, 164).

Some have not had this option, however, and, on several dimensions, the economic position occupied by a large proportion of Asian and African Caribbean people has been and remains inferior to that of the indigenous population. Of those who occupy a proletarian economic position, African Caribbean and Asian men have been much less likely than indigenous men to be employed in non-manual jobs, and within manual employment they have been much more likely to be engaged in semi- and unskilled jobs (Brown 1984: 157–65). Concerning the relative surplus population, official data, for all its limitations, shows that, during periods of high unemployment, unemployment rates for people of Asian and African Caribbean origin collectively have been significantly higher than for the indigenous population (Newnham 1986: 9–12), while the gap has been smaller, though still appreciable, during periods of low unemployment (see Modood et al. 1997: 83–4). This implies, although it does not demonstrate, that racism and related exclusionary practices are significant factors in the determination of the class position of people of Asian and African Caribbean origin in Britain. Hence, the analytical task is to assess the manner in which racialisation and racism interact with other processes in the allocation of persons to particular positions in the hierarchy of class relations.

CONCLUSION

We have suggested that a major analytical task is the historical (as opposed to abstract theoretical) investigation of the interpolation of racialisation and racism in political and economic relations, and such relations in concrete social formations. Although racism as a relation of production interacts so strongly with racism as ideology as to be inseparable (we could say that each is instrumental in the reproduction of the other), one should presuppose that racism is a necessarily contradictory phenomenon rather than that it is functional to the mode of production. Such an analysis highlights both the specificity and the generality of the historical development of the capitalist mode of production. Among the generalities, we have highlighted class as a dimension that interacts with racism in the production of inequalities. It has been argued that processes of (voluntary and forced) international migration have been instrumental in the formation of a relative surplus population, and that this has tended to concentrate racialised migrant labour within the proletariat of Western capitalist economies.

Thus, we can conclude that there is a dialectical relationship between migration and racism. The victims of racism are often people who have, or whose ancestors have, a specific migration history. Almost all people of Asian and African Caribbean origin in Britain are either themselves migrant labourers, or (in the majority of cases) the close relatives or descendants of migrant labourers, and they are frequently victims of a racism that is articulated on the pretext that they 'don't belong here'. The same is true of the Irish experience in Britain, and of the experiences of migrants from a plurality of former colonies to the metropoles of Western Europe. In Australia, the Aboriginal and Torres Strait Islander people have a specific status vis-à-vis the history of migration. In this case, neither they nor their ancestors have migrated to Australia. They became victims of racism as a result of a colonial migration of British settlers who defined the colony as *terra nullus* (a vacant land) and the people they found there as non-persons. Furthermore, racism can act as a push factor in migration, impelling people to escape from violence (Zolberg *et al.* 1989), as with recent refugee migrations of Romani people from Slovakia and the Czech Republic, have been greeted with racist hostility by sections of the British media and political society. As this example and the longer history of the Romani people illustrate (see, for example, Fraser 1995; Fonseca 1996; Moreau 1996), in the longer term, racism begets migration, which begets racism, which begets migration, and so on.

One social-scientific term that is frequently heard, inside and outside the academy, is 'globalisation'. While this is commonly believed to be a unique feature of the post-Cold War 'new world order', it is a process that has been occurring for some time, and was observed by Marx and Engels in the mid-nineteenth century (1967: 84). Nevertheless, it has gradually accelerated since that time, and, no doubt, has moved up a gear since the break up of the Soviet Union and its sphere of influence in international relations and the world economy. While specific capitalist and proletarian classes have an existence grounded in a particular nation state (as a result of which they always have a certain cultural character and profile), the movements of capital and labour have become increasingly international, with the result that the existence of national boundaries potentially constitute obstacles to their circulation. The process of circulation is dictated by the central dynamic of the capitalist mode of production, the accumulation of capital (Marx 1976: 762–801). The competitive nature of capitalist production results in ongoing processes of capital centralisation and concentration in particular, but also changing spatial locations, processes that in turn have implications for the size of the working population in those various locations. This process occurs within and (increasingly) across national boundaries, with the result that labour (along with capital) must be permitted to circulate within and (increasingly) across those national boundaries in order to fill particular economic sites.

The international circulation of labour power is, unlike the circulation of capital, simultaneously a spatial mobility of human beings: labour power is a capacity of human beings and cannot be divorced from their physical presence. However, in a world of nation states, human beings express a totality of cultural attributes (e.g. language, dress, diet) that are in part signs of their being constituted originally within a specific nation state, and possess a legal status and identity as citizens. Nationality may be compared with membership of a club that permits exclusive access to its facilities and services but simultaneously bars, at least formally, the holder from access to the facilities and services of all other clubs. Thus, access to any other club requires the permission of the officials. In a world of nation states, nationality is potentially a factor of international immobilisation, and mobility therefore becomes conditional on states permitting the entry of 'aliens', or members of other clubs. Even where entry is granted, their distinct cultural profile has the potential to be signified as a measure of their membership of another.

A contradiction has arisen from this set of historically constituted circumstances. Where the process of capital accumulation is obstructed by a shortage of labour power within the nation state, the state is faced with the possibility of permitting or organising the recruitment of labour from outside the nation state in order to effect its central role as the guarantor of the conditions for the reproduction of the capitalist mode of production. This requires the establishment of the legal conditions for the permanent or temporary entry of citizens of other nation states to fill vacant sites in the hierarchy of class relations. In many Western European nation states, from the late 1940s until the early 1970s, the state established a contract migrant worker system (Castles *et al*. 1984: 11–39) to resolve the problem of labour shortage by permitting the temporary entry of foreign nationals. However, because of conjunctural contradictions (Miles 1986), many of these temporary entrants became effectively permanent settlers (though less often citizens), as did ex-colonial migrants who, by way of contrast, entered Western Europe as citizens of the colonial nation state. Both groups have been joined by migrants who have entered Western European nation states as political refugees (e.g. Paludan 1981).

So, the relationship between migration and racism is not simply an economic matter, as recent hostility towards 'asylum seekers' has shown. Indeed, the migrant presence has been the object of political debate for some time, though this political development has been uneven, that is, it has occurred at different times in different places: in Britain and Switzerland in the mid-1960s, in France, Germany and the Netherlands in the 1970s. A further measure of the unevenness of this political development may be found in a comparative analysis of the rise of neo-Fascist political parties (Husbands 1982): in Britain, the National Front achieved political prominence and limited success during the 1970s (see Walker 1977; Fielding 1981; Taylor 1982), while in France the *Front National* became a significant political force in the 1980s (see Ogden 1987).

The totality of this historical variation and specificity remind us that there is no simple correlation between representational and political processes, on the one hand, and economic processes, on the other, for it demonstrates that the migrant presence was problematised within the political arena in some nation states before the economic crisis of capitalism in the early 1970s. Thus, when seeking an explanation for the signification of the migrant presence, it cannot be explained simply or solely as an attempt by the ruling classes of Western Europe to recreate a sense of imagined community by defining an Other as an illegitimate presence in a period of crisis which, *inter alia*, has led to mass unemployment. The working class has the power to shape the political agenda outside periods of generalised crisis and in response to its own material circumstances and ideological conceptualisation as they have been perceived to have been influenced by the migrant presence. Thus, in certain European societies, the state has been forced to respond to demands 'from below', although often refracted through elected politicians, for the halting of immigration and the reduction in the size of the population of migrant origin (see DeLey 1983; Wihtol de Wenden 1987).

Identifying and explaining the ideological content of the process of signification is an equally complex task. Another measure of difference between the European nation states lies in the content of the representation of the nature of the 'problem', both officially and in everyday, common-sense terms (see Hammar 1985; Grillo 1985). While such representations may change over time, it is legitimate to compare the Dutch reference to *ethnische minderheden* with the French terms *immigrés* and *étrangers*, the German category of *Gastarbeiter* and the (German-speaking) Swiss *Fremdarbeiter* or *Fremdarbeitskrafte*, the British reference to *immigrants* and the perceived problem of *race relations*, and the Swedish term *invanderer*. Thus, it is evident that the ideological content of the process of problema-tisation has varied from one social formation to another. It is therefore important to identify empirically the differences that are signified as important. It is certainly the case that the migrant presence permits a re-evaluation of Self on the part of sections of the indigenous population by their identification of the migrant as Other, but whether this is effected through the signification of cultural or biological characteristics, or some combination of both, cannot be determined in advance.

In the case of Britain, it is now clear that the problematisation of the migrant presence occurred through the signification of both biological and cultural characteristics, and that the working class played an active role in a process of racialisation. This process, and the related articulation of racism, was a significant political force before the onset of major economic crisis and it was a form of partially autonomous resistance from below in that it derived from experience of competition for scarce resources and localised economic decline (see Phizacklea and Miles 1980: 167–76). However, as we have seen, the British state has also been an active agent of racialisation by, *inter alia*, passing exclusionary immigration legislation which has institutionalised racism and identifying young people of African Caribbean origin as a threat to 'law and order'. In so doing, the economic and political consequences of the crisis of capital accumulation have been expressed in part through the idea of 'race', objectifying the population of African Caribbean and Asian origin, who have become an internal Other, represented in law, policing practices, politicians' speeches, media reporting, and everyday discourses, as a problematic and undesirable presence, not only a symptom but also a cause of crisis (Hall 1978; CCCS 1982: 9–46).

This all being said, migration is neither a necessary nor an inevitable correlate of racism. There are several examples of long-settled populations becoming the object of racism and exclusionary processes. The most obvious and well-known is that of Jewish people in Germany during the 1920s and 1930s, a population that had German citizenship and that was sufficiently 'invisible' within German culture and society to require the Fascist state to find a way to mark them as a distinct minority. Hence, the state established complex procedures to identify Jewish 'ancestry' and required Jewish people to mark themselves by wearing a sign in the form of a yellow star. A second, and more immediate, example is the racism and exclusionary practice of Balkan states towards ethnicised populations that had previously been nationalised by means of the creation of the state of Yugoslavia after the Second World War. We address this example in the next chapter.

6

RACISM, THE NATION STATE AND GLOBALISATION

INTRODUCTION

The contextualisation of racism requires consideration of not only class relations but also of the nation state in order for us to examine in more detail the relationship between racism and political and ideological relations. The relationship between the rise of capitalism and the nation state has been a central theme in many of the social sciences and certainly preoccupied the 'founding fathers' of sociology. Of course, states (in the sense of a set of institutions dedicated to the exercise of political power within a particular territorial space) existed prior to capitalism and various writers have therefore sought to develop typologies of different kinds of state (e.g. the nation state, the colonial state and so on). As we shall explore in this chapter, what distinguishes the nation state is the claim that the world's population is 'naturally' divided into distinct nations, each of which has the right to distinct and separate political organisation and representation by means of a state.

Two themes therefore dominate this chapter. First, we explore how the rise of the nation state was accompanied by the ideology of nationalism, an ideology that (like racism) was premised on a distinction between Self and Other. This paves the way for a discussion about the relationship between racism and nationalism. Second, we consider some of the forces that are undermining the reproduction of the nation state and assisting in the creation of supra-national political structures in a world economy increasingly dominated by international corporations. This process is accompanied by a reorganisation of the dialectic of Self and Other, and of the interplay of nationalism and racism.

CAPITALISM AND THE NATION STATE

The process of racialisation and the articulation of racism have become central to another dimension of the reproduction of the capitalist mode of production: the role of the nation state in maintaining the conditions for that reproduction. One aspect of that role is the generation and reconstruction of a sense of the 'imagined community' of nation.

The development of capitalism in Europe has been synonymous with the development of the nation state. Indeed, the spatial division of the world, and the formation of some form of centralised political authority claiming sovereignty within each space by reference to an alleged 'natural' community, was the context for the emergence of the capitalist mode of production and not a product of it (see Corrigan and Sayer 1986). Thus, capitalism did not suddenly emerge everywhere but, rather, England, a territorial unit consolidated by the activity of a feudal state and ruling class, gradually became the first thoroughgoing capitalist state. It is for this reason that the debate about the transition from feudalism to capitalism (e.g. Hilton *et al.* 1978; Holton 1985) was, in part, about why capitalism developed first in England.

The state has been, and remains, central to the creation and reproduction of the capitalist mode of production and the nation. Indeed, these processes presuppose the existence of the state. The processes of dispossessing those who have access to land and concentrating wealth in the hands of a small section of the population within a nation state have usually been effected by some combination of legal procedure and physical force while the expansion of the boundaries of the nation state to incorporate other populations has usually also required compulsion. Moreover, once capitalism has been established, antagonistic class interests give rise to conflict that must be mediated, contained and suppressed. Furthermore, the existence of one nation state may be threatened by the economic and political interests of the ruling class of another. Hence, the state implements strategies to protect and advance the interests of those who own capital within its boundaries, and to maintain its territorial space against physical invasion. The mediation of class conflict and protection of the boundaries of the nation are tasks carried out by the state which therefore include among its institutions a legal system, armed forces and police.

Yet the nation state has never fully contained within its spatial boundaries either the capital or the population that are thought to be expressions of a distinct and separate nation. The history of European colonialism is a history of capital accumulation beyond the boundaries of the European nation states (and therefore also a history of conflict between competing European capitalisms) and of territorial expansion and settlement in continents beyond Europe. As we have seen, this expansion and settlement has been associated intimately with the process of racialisation and the articulation of the ideology of racism. This particular kind of expansion was largely brought to an end in the aftermath of the Second World War as a result of a combination of strategic de-colonisation and national liberation struggle, but it has been replaced by two other developments that have special significance for the nature and scope of the nation state.

The first development concerns the creation and growth of the trans-national corporation. A proportion of private companies (including companies in manufacturing as well as in the service sector) have extended their economic activities beyond the national boundaries of their origin and/or formal site of registration, growing in size dramatically and operating in an increasing number of nation states. This has been facilitated by trans-national mergers and other forms of consolidation of ownership. Many of these trans-national corporations have grown to the point where their value exceeds the gross domestic product of many nation states. Formally, such companies remain the subject of state regulation in each nation state in which they operate, but their ability to locate and relocate investment within the capitalist world system gives them a real economic power that exceeds that of the nation state.

The second development concerns the creation of supra-nation-state institutions such as the European Union as well as regional alliances of nation states committed to some degree of economic coordination or collaboration. In different ways and to different degrees, these initiatives set limits and constraints to the power and autonomy of the nation state. Clearly, the most advanced form of this development is the European Union, which has established a supra-state administrative authority (the European Commission) and a supra-state political structure (the European Parliament), as well as, more recently, a European currency. There is considerable debate about the extent to which these developments entail the dissolution of the nation state, but few would disagree that the nation state is transformed by them.

In this final chapter, we explore some examples of the many ways in which changing political and ideological relations associated with the rise, reproduction and transformation of the nation state interact with racialisation and the ideology of racism. As with the previous chapter, it is our intention to contextualise the reproduction of racism and to demonstrate its multiple forms and transformations.

RACISM, THE NATION STATE AND THE RISE OF CAPITALISM

Anderson (1983) has traced the connections between the rise of capitalism and the expression of nationalism as a representational form that purported to identify culturally and historically distinct populations, each with a 'natural right' to govern itself. The nationalist political project was therefore coupled with a representational project of constructing a history and an emotional sense of shared distinctiveness that would, in turn, create a collective sense of Self defined dialectically by the presence of the Other. In this way, Britain (for example) was defined in part by an opposition with France. For Anderson, the crucial determinant in this project was the coincidence of the development of print-languages and the generalisation of commodity production, one instance of which was the book, which created the possibility of imagining a nation as a linguistic community (1983: 41–9).

Language was simultaneously medium and message: not only was a difference of language used to create an imagined community of readers and speakers, but it also permitted the generation of explanations for differences of language which could legitimate an idea of a distinct nation. Historical writing attempted to identify the unique 'spirit' and characteristics of a nation, each instance of which was constructed as a real thing in itself, a living entity. This process of reification was accompanied by a search for the origin of each nation (Barzun 1965: 27–8). During the nineteenth century, when the process of capitalist development and a conscious strategy of nation state formation within Europe was at its most vigorous, many advocates of nationalism drew upon scientific racism to identify these supposedly distinct, natural collectivities. Racism was especially appropriate to this task because it suggested that natural differences between 'nations' were grounded in biology, constituting a solid defence of the idea of historical inevitability that is central to the nationalist doctrine (Miles 1987b: 41; see also Mosse 1978: 50, 94).

However, a classification of 'races' that identified Caucasian, Negroid and Mongoloid as the main categories – while distancing Europeans, represented collectively as Caucasians, from so-called Negroid and Mongoloid 'races' – did not distinguish between different populations within Europe. This tripartite classification of 'races' was not the only classification available. When attention turned specifically to Europe, divisions were hypothesised between, for example, Nordic (or Teutonic), Roman, Gallic (or Celtic) and Anglo-Saxon 'races', and between Aryan and Semitic 'races' (Barzun 1965: 12–33, 97–114).

In many of these classifications, language was identified not only as the central signifier and therefore unifier of the imagined community, but also as the expression of 'race' (Barzun 1965: 98; Mosse 1978: 38–41). Language was represented as a difference in itself but, for some nationalists, it was also a sign of a more fundamental, biological differentiation between European populations. Even when nations were represented as composite populations, containing different 'racial' mixtures, it was also concluded that the proportion of superior and inferior 'races' determined the position of the 'nation' on the scale of superiority and inferiority. Indeed, for Gobineau, the mixing of inferior and superior 'races' led to 'degeneration' and therefore determined the course of historical development (see Mosse 1978: 51–5). This idea of 'degeneration' played a central role in the rise of the eugenics movement and in asserting Aryan superiority and Jewish inferiority in Germany (Mosse 1978: 82–8; Günther 1970: 197–8, 267).

The Europeans engaged in the creation and mobilisation of nationalist sentiment in order to create nation states in the nineteenth century were largely members of the rising bourgeoisie, and drew on the ideas of an intelligensia (Nairn 1981: 96–103, 153–4). Nationalism was a means to overthrow monarchic and aristocratic political domination (Kedourie 1993: 4–5) and to secure political control within a territorial unit that would permit the accumulation of capital on a scale to allow competition with units of capital located in extant nation states. In this sense, nationalism was rooted in the uneven development of capitalism, and was therefore an ideology of unification (Hobsbawm 1977: 5), in the senses of creating a sense of community and of establishing spatial boundaries within which the processes of capital accumulation and proletarianisation could occur. In pursuit of these interests, the bourgeoisie had to mobilise politically people who would subsequently be subject to its economic and political domination, and it could only do so by creating a sense of imagined community and common interests. It had to represent its own interests as the collective interests of the nation, and this was achieved by emphasising whatever 'differentiae' (Nairn 1981: 340) were available.

The available differentiae were sometimes grounded in the discourse of 'race'. Where such grounding occurred, the ideas of 'nation' and 'race' were not so much identical (Mosse 1978: 45) as mutual reflections, each highlighting and magnifying the other in the manner of an image in opposite, facing mirrors. Hence, racism was (and remains) an ideology that can simultaneously define positive qualities in Self as well as negative qualities in the Other, and therefore, in such circumstances, it 'thinks in terms of historical destinies' in exactly the same manner as nationalism (cf. Anderson 1983: 136; Gilroy 1987: 44–5).

Seton-Watson puzzles over whether the French nationalism of the late nineteenth century can really be defined as such because it did not constitute a component part of a movement for political independence (1977: 449). The problem originates in limiting a definition of nationalism in this way. Nation state formation has often also involved the use of force, as well as negotiation, to include culturally distinct populations within an expanding territorial boundary and the active creation of myths of historical origin and tradition to justify their inclusion (e.g. Hobsbawm 1983). This latter process is more recent than the former and was only *justified* by an ideology of nationalism from the late eighteenth century (Kedourie 1993: 1–11). In other words, historically, a number of nation states were constituted in the absence of nationalism (Seton-Watson 1977: 6). Furthermore, once a nation state exists, and with capitalist interests intertwined politically in its constitution, the nationalist objective inevitably shifts from nation state formation to that of guaranteeing the economic and political conditions that sustain the reproduction of the nation state. Thus, if the main nationalist project in Europe of the nineteenth century was the creation of a sense of imagined community, during the twentieth century it has increasingly become one of reproducing the sense of imagined community in a rapidly changing economic and political context, a context that demonstrates that the relationship between the capitalist mode of production and the nation state is becoming increasingly contradictory.

Where the ideology of nationalism has existed, either before or after the nation state, it has asserted the existence of a *natural* division within the world's population between collectivities each with a distinct cultural profile and therefore a distinct capacity for constituting a self-governing nation state within a given geographical space. Because each 'nation' is defined as a unit capable of reproducing itself over time, it presumes, without always specifically identifying, a presence of women and men. Consequently, there is a basis for interaction between nationalism and sexism (as well as homophobia and the fear of 'miscegenation').

In order to demonstrate the close correspondence between the ideologies of nationalism and racism, Miles applied Anderson's (1983: 15–16) suggestion that the 'nation' constitutes an imagined community:

> Like 'nations', 'races' too are imagined, in the dual sense that they have no real biological foundation and that all those included by the signification can never know each other, and are imagined as communities in the sense of a common feeling of fellowship. Moreover, they are also imagined as limited in the sense that a boundary is perceived, beyond which lie other 'races'.
>
> (Miles 1987b: 26–7)

Consequently, 'nations', like 'races', are the product of human invention (Hobsbawm 1983: 13–14). In Anderson's terms, the central difference between nationalism and racism lies in the former's additional claim that the 'nation' can only express itself historically where it occupies exclusively a given territory wherein the 'people' can govern themselves. No similar political project is explicit in the ideology of racism.

The ideas of 'race' and 'nation' are therefore supra-class and supra-gender forms of categorisation with considerable potential for interaction. That potential was reinforced by the development of scientific racism from the eighteenth century. In its most extreme form, it argued that 'race' determined cultural capacity and historical development, and therefore that each 'nation' was the expression of a particular biological capacity. This was an articulation in which 'race' and 'nation' were identical, rather than interacting. Such an articulation was clearly expressed in the writings of Gobineau (1970: 164), a key figure in the development of scientific racism in nineteenth-century Europe.

These ideologies – nationalism and racism – are not independent and autonomous forces but are generated and reproduced within a complex interplay of historically constituted economic and political relations. The interaction between nationalism and racism is therefore historically specific and contingent. Miles (1987b: 32–40) has demonstrated the interaction between racism and nationalism in the case of England where, by the early nineteenth century, an earlier myth of Anglo-Saxon origin had been subsumed under an idea of 'race'. Consequently, it was widely believed that the English were largely an Anglo-Saxon 'race' characterised by an inherent capacity for freedom and an ability to create democratic institutions, capacities which they could express in other parts of the world in which they settled (Horsman 1976, 1981: 9–77; MacDougall 1982).

In England, the speeches of the politician Enoch Powell during the late 1960s were widely (and correctly) condemned as expressing racism, but their ideological content was as much nationalist as racist. Powell was seeking to reconstruct a sense of Englishness in the context of economic decline and the exposure of the failures of Labourism as a political alternative to the Conservative Party. As Nairn has expressed it:

> It was more than a case of locating a new scapegoat: this scapegoat was to have the honour of restoring a popular content to English national self-consciousness, of stirring the English 'corporate imagination' into life once more, by providing a concrete way of focussing its vague but powerful sense of superiority.

> (Nairn 1981: 274)

As Miles (1988) has suggested, Powell's discourse asserted that the coherence of the 'nation' (which he conceived as a homogenous cultural unit with a distinctive history) was subverted by the presence of a population of migrant origin that was actively reproducing its cultural and 'racial' distinctiveness. Consequently, the 'English people' were the true victims of migration and, as England was 'their' country, the only logical solution was to 'repatriate' the Other in order to restore historical and cultural unity (Powell 1969: 281–314, 1972: 189–212). For Powell, the issue was not whether or not people of Asian and African Caribbean origin were inferior 'races', but one of reconstructing a positive sense of Englishness that, he believed, combined with free market economics, would restore England's position in the world economy.

Such discourse seems almost mainstream in contemporary British political and media discourses. Its representational content is classically nationalist, but sustained by racism. This sustenance depends in part on a simultaneous signification of cultural differentiae and somatic features: the Other is differentiated by skin colour as well as by clothing, diet, language, religion, and so on. The presence of the Other is represented as problematic by virtue of, for example, its supposed use of the resources and facilities of 'our own people', its propensity to violence, or its stimulation of the 'natural prejudice' of 'our own people' against those whose 'natural home' (or 'nation') is elsewhere. The negation of the negation is represented as the catharsis of 'repatriation' (Miles and Phizacklea 1984; Miles 1988).

It is an ideological specificity of the British case that, although the language of 'inferior races' may have disappeared from the House of Commons (if not always from the propaganda of extreme right-wing and Fascist groups), the problematisation of the migrant presence has been consistently expressed in the discourse of 'race' and 'race relations'. This distinguishes the British situation from most other Western European countries. Nevertheless, although specific discourses differ, throughout Western Europe the migrant presence is signified as problematic and has been used to highlight the existence of a boundary between Self and Other. Insofar as that boundary is measured by reference to cultural differentiation alone, it is an expression of nationalism. Whether or not it interacts with racism is a matter for comparative ethnography, discourse analysis and quantitative research. However, in post-1945 Western Europe, nation states have admitted culturally distinct populations to resolve problems of labour shortage, then cited their presence as a disintegration of the imagined community, and articulated an exclusionary nationalism to sustain that sense of imagined community. The fact that racism has also been articulated to the same end leads to the conclusion that theories of racism that seek explanation solely by reference to colonial strategies and experience have limited analytical power.

RACISM, THE NATION STATE AND SETTLER CAPITALISM

Yet colonialism was a specific context for nation formation where European settlers sought to establish a state that was at least partially, or not wholly, autonomous from the 'mother country'. Each case is, of course, historically specific but one might expect racism to play a significant role with respect to nation state formation given (as we have seen) its role in establishing and justifying colonial settlement and the development of commodity production for the world market.

Here, we consider the example of the British settler colonies of Australia. During the second half of the nineteenth century, a capitalist mode of production was introduced in those colonies, supported by an ideology of nationalism to which the ideology of racism was central (Denoon 1983). There was, in other words, an interdependence between nationalism and racism such that the parameters of each ideology overlapped to determine the criteria for membership of the emergent nation state. The criteria included the white 'races' as acceptable members of the Australian 'nation' and simultaneously excluded people of Asian and Pacific origin. *Inter alia*, it was argued that people of the Anglo-Saxon 'race' had a special capacity for self-government by constitutional means. Thus, the idea of the Anglo-Saxon 'race' sustained a sense of superiority of both 'race' and 'nation' (Huttenback 1976: 15–17), one that resulted in the creation of a settler capitalist society that excluded 'inferior races'.

This interdependence developed in the course of a transition from a convict settlement (with few, if any, commercial interests) to the formation of a number of distinct colonies, each dominated by merchant and commodity producing interests. It was most pronounced in the political debate leading up to the formation of the Commonwealth of Australia in 1901, the outcome of which was an exclusionary practice that ensured that the imagined community of Australia would consist exclusively of members of the 'white races'. The 'White Australia' policy, formally established in 1901, was not the outcome of a particular set of representations, but derived from a complex economic and political struggle between different fractions of capital and labour over migration flows into the Australian colonies, flows that were intimately connected with various initiatives to sustain and increase the supply of labour power as commodity production increased after the 1830s (McQueen 1970: 43–7; de Lepervanche 1984: 54). The consequence was a racialisation of migration flows and of immigration policy.

The Australian continent was sparsely populated prior to European settlement and the Aboriginal population proved resistant to incorporation into the emergent capitalist relations of production, with the consequence that continuing migration was necessary to sustain the formation of proletarian and petit-bourgeois classes. Migration flows from Europe did not consistently meet the demand, and those seeking labour were regularly involved in initiatives to recruit labour from elsewhere in the world, often under relations of indenture (see Miles 1987a). In the context of the struggle to create a labour force 'willing' to provide labour power, we can locate the interaction between nationalism and racism.

During the early period of European settlement, the local state and many settlers anticipated that the Aboriginal population would serve as manual labourers within the economic relations that they were establishing (Reynolds 1972: 109). However, the nature of Aboriginal production and social relations militated against any simple form of incorporation and the eventual consequence was widespread conflict and, after the successful assertion of European military technology and sheer numbers, the extensive disintegration of those economic and social relations (Rowley 1970). This process was readily comprehensible in terms of the Darwinian notion of the survival of the fittest, and the Aboriginal population became widely regarded among European settlers as a 'doomed race' (Evans *et al.* 1975: 85–90). Subsequently, the prevalent image of the Aborigine among the European population remained a racist one. A combination of marginalisation and extermination placed the vast bulk of the Aboriginal population both materially and conceptually beyond the social relations accompanying commodity production. Thus, the debate about the nature of the imagined community of Australia rarely considered the original inhabitants of the continent.

A different process operated with respect to the Asian populations and the Pacific islanders who entered the Australian colonies in the nineteenth century. From the 1820s, the rise of pastoralism, initially in New South Wales, was accompanied by a recurring shortage of labour as convict labour and free migration from Europe proved unable to meet demand, and various private initiatives were made to recruit indentured shepherd labour from India and China (Willard 1967; de Lepervanche 1984: 37–42). The discovery of gold led to a significant increase in the migration of male labourers from China to work in the goldfields in the 1850s and again in the 1870s. This presence aroused considerable opposition, following which legislation restricting the entry of Chinese people was passed (Crawford 1923: 56–75; Willard 1967: 21, 24, 32–3). Willard suggests that economic and ideological considerations were interdependent:

> The heterogeneous mass of humanity on the Australian goldfields had objected to the presence of an exclusive and, in their opinion, an inferior Asiatic race – especially an 'inferior' people that proved able to mine so successfully as the Chinese.
>
> (1967: 35)

With the development of cotton and sugar production in Queensland in the 1860s, there was another initiative to recruit indentured labour from India, but this source was by-passed when landowners found they could indenture labour from the Pacific Islands. Consequently, Pacific islanders were the main source of manual labour for the Queensland sugar industry in the late nineteenth century (Saunders 1982). There was considerable hostility towards these indentured migrant labourers who, like the Chinese, were regarded as an economic threat by other sections of the working class and were signified as an 'inferior race'. Additionally, their recruitment under terms of indenture (unfreedom) was perceived as threatening the development of democratic processes. One consequence of hostile agitation was legislation confining Pacific islanders to employment in tropical agriculture (Evans *et al.* 1975: 178–80).

With various examples of exclusionary legislation operating in the separate colonies, there was growing political awareness of the need for an immigration policy (a euphemism for exclusionary practice) that would apply throughout the continent. Some Chinese migrants had entered one colony from another overland after legislation was passed restricting entry through the ports. By the mid-1890s, the various colonial governments agreed to restrict entry of 'coloured races' into the colonies (Willard 1967: 108–10).

The underlying racist agitation which sustained, and was legitimated by, this move increased the pressure on the political leadership of the separate colonies to move towards federation (Palfreeman 1972: 136). The Attorney-General of the first Federal Government later commented:

> No motive power operated more universally on this Continent, or in the beautiful island of Tasmania, and certainly no motive power operated more powerfully in dissolving the technical and arbitrary divisions which previously separated us than the desire that we should be one people, and remain one people, without the admixture of other races.
>
> (Cited in Willard 1967: 119)

The demand to keep out 'coloured inferior races' was dialectically linked with an emerging sense of imagined community of Australians, a collectivity that signified 'whiteness' as a sign of superiority and inclusion.

This move towards an explicit ban on the entry into Australia of 'all coloured races' was, as far as the London government was concerned, sympathetically received in private and, because it was formally committed to a liberal policy of equality of peoples, a source of embarrassment in public. A Colonial Office memorandum commenting on the Conference expressed sympathy with the desire of the Australian colonies to avoid the 'permanent presence of a considerable element of an inferior race' (cited in Yarwood 1962: 263). However, to maintain a 'liberal' public image, the British government disallowed the planned legislation. Nonetheless, it offered an alternative mechanism of exclusion that had the same effect although it was achieved by less explicit means. The model was Natal where, in 1897, entry into the colony was made dependent on English-language ability (Huttenback 1976: 139–41; Palfreeman 1972: 137). The so-called 'Natal formula' was formally adopted and implemented in Australia in the 1901 Immigration Restriction Act which institutionalised racism in Australian immigration law and established an exclusionary practice effected by the state.

The significance for the racialisation of the Chinese, Asian and Pacific Island migrants, and hence the characterisation of the 'White Australia' policy, has been a matter of some considerable debate. Willard argued in 1923 that 'the validity and the morality of Australia's policy seems to depend on the validity and the morality of the principle of nationalism' (Willard 1967: 206) and that the fundamental reason for the 'White Australia' policy was the 'preservation of British-Australian nationality' (1967: 189). The denial that racism was a fundamental motive behind the 'White Australia' policy was echoed by writers in the 1950s who argued that it resulted from either an accurate and justifiable resistance by the emergent working class to the use of cheap labour by employers (Dallas 1955: 52), or from the expression of patriotism (Nairn 1956: 18–19).

The central weakness of this debate has been the presentation of the issue in simplistic 'either/or' terms. Attempts to represent the process of determination as one in which either the economic or the ideological factor was the sole 'cause' are mistaken because they fail to appreciate the complex totality of economic, political and ideological relations which led to the 1901 Immigration Restriction Act. However, the development of commodity production and formation of a working class in the various Australian colonies *sustained* the articulation and reproduction of the ideology of racism; this had its own determinant effects in association with the ideology of nationalism in the subsequent political debates about the form that the Commonwealth of Australia should take.

The interdependent articulation of nationalism and racism is inadvertently demonstrated in Willard's defence of the 'White Australia' policy as an exclusive and legitimate expression of nationalism. Willard appeared to argue that equality of treatment and cultural homogeneity were essential to the successful formation of a democratic nation state and that this was guaranteed by the 'White Australia' policy. An appeal was thereby made to an ideology (of nationalism) that had positive connotations and was widely expressed in Europe. Consequently, the issue was presented as a legitimate desire by an imagined (homogeneous) community to express its unique character in the formation of a democratic, formally egalitarian nation state. Yet Willard's advocacy of this principle of nationalism simultaneously expressed a belief in the existence of different, discrete 'races', each with a distinct set of characteristics and capacity for incorporation into a democratic nation state.

The primary theme of the argument was that 'racial unity is essential to national unity' (Willard 1967: 189, 207), a claim premised on the belief that Asian and Pacific Island migrants were different 'races'. Willard claimed that these migrants were 'unfitted to exercise political rights, and incompetent to fulfil political duties' (1967: 193), and, specifically, that Asians had abilities which made them 'dangerous competitors' (1967: 197–8). Moreover, compared with the European 'race', these 'races' were not only different but also inferior, an argument justified, for example, by the continued use of Pacific islanders as a source of labour under relations of indenture, which 'could be nothing else but the deliberate commercial exploitation of an inferior by a superior race' (1967: 197).

Moreover, Willard hypothesised that the permanent residence of such 'races' or 'alien people' in Australia 'would have a bad social effect on the community' (1967: 9). She argued, referring to Australians: 'The well-marked social and political evil inevitably connected with the co-existence of distinct races in one country, constantly recurred to their minds, and influenced them to take the first steps in the development of the policy' (1967: 192). The main example cited by Willard was that these 'alien peoples' were a source of cheap labour which caused competition, and this in turn:

> . . . would be a sure cause for racial strife, for it would arouse a primary instinct to fight for the right to existence such as Australians conceived it. It would acutely sharpen and intensify the political and social differences resulting from racial division.
>
> (1967: 200)

In order to sustain the claim that this was a universal and inevitable response, reference was made to 'world experience', the examples of the United States, Natal and Transvaal being cited (1967: 208–9). Thus, the hostile reaction of Australians was interpreted not as racism but as an inherent preference of the Australian (or 'white') 'race' to ensure its survival. Allowing members of different 'races' to live in Australia would therefore stimulate the expression of this 'primary instinct': the presence of the racialised Other was represented as the problem; the solution, logically, was to prevent their settlement. Hence, Willard argued that, because it is 'natural' that people belonging to supposedly different 'races' will wish to sustain their distinct and separate communities, the boundary of inclusion/exclusion that defined the imagined community of Australia was necessarily drawn by reference to 'race'. This argument advanced in the 1920s is very similar to that articulated in Britain in the 1980s, suggesting once again that the 'new racism' has a longer pedigree than the concept suggests.

It is certainly the case that sections of the Australian working class believed their income would be reduced by an increasing number of Asian workers who entered 'unfree' relations of production and who worked for lower wages (Dallas 1955: 49, 52). There was justification for this interpretation where employers legitimated their recruitment by arguing that it cost less than European labour (e.g. de Lepervanche 1984: 38). However, the arguments against the Asian and Pacific Island presence in the Australian colonies were also political. In the case of agitation against indentured Pacific Island labour in Queensland, liberal-minded politicians made common cause with working-class opposition, claiming that the use of such a source of labour facilitated the development of large landed estates and absenteeism, created contempt for certain kinds of manual labour and obstructed the development of democratic institutions (Willard 1967: 161; Connell and Irving 1980: 122). Thus, the fact that Pacific Island labourers were enmeshed in unfree relations of production was used as a means of formulating a sense of common community by defining them as Other for economic and political reasons.

The significance of economic and political relations cannot be divorced from the ideological context in which the demand for exclusion was articulated. The European (predominantly British) settlers of the nineteenth century brought with them a discourse of 'race' and the agitation against the recruitment and employment of Indians, Chinese and Pacific islanders took a racist form insofar as these populations were signified as distinct and inferior 'races' with undesirable secondary characteristics (see Davison 1985). The Labour movement was as much a leading force in the expression of this racism as sections of the emergent bourgeoisie (McQueen 1970: 50–5). Moreover, although the openly racist provisions of the legislation as originally drafted were dropped, the debate on the 1901 Act revealed that racism was a determinant motive in the formulation of the legislation. In the course of the debates, the alleged biological inferiority of the 'coloured races' was cited as a reason for their exclusion from Australia (Palfreeman 1972: 137). Yarwood (1964: 24) comments: 'Men in 1901 had seen little reason to doubt that the white races enjoyed an inherent superiority, which appeared to have been amply demonstrated by their conquests in Africa and Asia in the previous twenty years'. The use of racism as a form of representation was therefore an independent determinant, but, paradoxically, depended on the existence of material conflicts which required interpretation and negotiation.

Thus, in late nineteenth-century Australia, a sense of imagined community was formulated in the light of the experience of European settlers in dealing with, *inter alia*, Aboriginal resistance to their presence and conflicts provoked by recruiting labour from the South Pacific and parts of Asia. The boundary that was to determine membership of the imagined community was drawn using the idea of 'race' as a criterion of inclusion/ exclusion. On the basis of this racialisation of the potential imagined community, additional criteria were employed to establish a hierarchy of 'races', with the consequence that the parameters of Australian nationalism and the criteria of admission to the Australian nation state were shaped in part by racism. Hence, 'inferior races' were excluded in the interests of sustaining a supra-class entity with the potential to sustain a sense of common identity grounded in a specific form of cultural and biological homogeneity. By these means, those groups whose labour power had been appropriated under relations of unfreedom to sustain economic development were subsequently excluded from membership of the imagined community of a 'White Australia'. Racism as an unfree relation of production and racism as ideology were inseparable phenomena, shaping in turn the early imagined community of the Australian nation. Racism was instrumental in the formation of the Australian nation, but the same has been true of European nation states, as we saw previously.

RACISM, SEXISM AND THE NATION STATE

Historically, the formation and reproduction of the nation state has been and is intimately interrelated with sexism. Sexism denotes a process whereby real biological characteristics are identified as absolute differences, and are associated in a deterministic manner with a number of additional (real and attributed) biological and cultural characteristics in order to identify two essentially different categories of human being: men and women. Thus, femininity and masculinity are represented as essentially different qualities inherent in women and men, from which conclusions are drawn about their respective, differential participation in economic and political relations. Sexist arguments additionally claim that these supposed differences explain and justify the differential and inferior treatment of women.

In so far as the nation state is self-consciously a political community of citizens, sexism has played a major role in the formation of nation states by justifying the exclusion of women from full and active citizenship. Many observers have charted this by, for example, analysing the struggle by women to vote. The date of the introduction of universal adult suffrage can therefore serve as a comparative measure of nation state formation. Similarly, sexism has played a central role in legitimating the structuring of the labour market within capitalist societies. In certain historical conjunctures, women have been actively encouraged to enter wage labour and in others they have been actively discouraged (see Bland *et al*. 1978). Moreover, this instance of signification has served to allocate women to specific positions within the hierarchy of wage labour, for example, to exclude them from positions of skill and heavy manual labour and from positions which receive relatively high wages (Oakley 1981: 150–62).

The reproduction of the nation state refers to a number of distinct activities and processes. One of these concerns the biological reproduction of the population that is conceived as constituting the citizens of the nation over which the state exercises authority and it is here that one finds very specific articulations of racism and sexism that take as their starting point the biological capacity of women to bear children. The signification of this capacity, and the subsequent confinement of the task of child-rearing to women, has served to exclude women from a wide range of economic and political activities in a large number of historical contexts. One consequence of this exclusion has been to represent women as, and ensure that they function as, breeding machines, a representation and confinement that links in a most significant way with the process of racialisation, on the grounds that biological reproduction is central to the task of reproducing 'races'. Within European nation states during the period of colonial expansion, the confinement of women to the domestic sphere was often justified in terms of producing a 'fit and able race' capable of realising its imperial mission. And, in British settler colonies such as Australia and Canada, much effort was expended in certain periods on ensuring that a proportion of the migrating settlers were women 'of good stock' who would provide 'suitable' marriage partners for male settlers and who would therefore allow the reproduction, and maintain the purity, of the British 'race'. Not surprisingly in such circumstances, much emphasis was placed upon increasing the birth rate (see MacKenzie 1984: 160). It is therefore not surprising that, in nineteenth-century Australia (de Lepervanche 1987), the impetus for colonisation was represented as a masculine project: 'Physically proficient men, white and preferably British, were regarded as the best colonisers whose forceful nature, competitiveness and even occasional resort to brutality against inferiors were regarded as virtues to be applauded' (Evans 1975: 10). In these ways, women have been signified as breeding machines to reproduce the 'race' and the nation. In such circumstances, sexism has been intrinsic to nationalism.

In situations where migration, and populations of migrant origin, have been racialised, there have been parallel concerns about 'diluting the purity of the race'. This has often been expressed in the language of 'racial degeneration' or 'miscegenation'. For example, during the large-scale migrations to Western Europe in the 1950s and 1960s, racist reactions often focussed on the possibility that 'our women' might be 'stolen' and that 'mixed race' children would weaken the homogeneity of the nation. In some circumstances, and where migrants have been recruited to fill a temporary shortage of labour, single men have been recruited on a contract basis and women have been excluded absolutely in an attempt to prevent the settlement and reproduction of an 'inferior race'. In addition, in situations of colonial settlement, considerable concern has been expressed about the potential for the wives of colonial settlers to be 'seduced' by sexually virile 'natives'. This has had major consequences for social control in the colonial situation, with both the European women and the colonised men often being subject to strict observation and, in the case of the latter, extreme forms of punishment, especially where putatively 'inter-racial' sexual relationships have been illegal.

The extensive literature on the articulation of racism and sexism deals with many themes in addition to this very specific subject of the reproduction of the nation state. Much of this body of work is concerned with the analysis of specific historical and contemporary circumstances, including a significant literature on the relationship between gender and migration (e.g. Phizacklea 1983; Potts 1990: 213–21). This literature demonstrates that sexism is refracted through the norms, including traditional gender roles, of a community, and that these in turn are reinforced through the processes of migration and racialisation (e.g. Parmar 1982; Afshar 1989; Anthias 1992). There is also a considerable collection of writing on the interaction of class, gender and ethnicity (e.g. Carby 1982;

Collins 1991; Anthias and Yuval-Davis 1993). It is clear that much of this literature arises out of the cultural studies tradition (cf. hooks 1982; Lorde 1984, 1996; Mirza 1997), though it is less clear to what extent it has an origin in the American 'race relations' paradigm. Conceptually, given our conscious 'distancing' from the former tradition, and rejection of the latter paradigm, we have chosen not to engage with them here, although it is acknowledged that these historical and contemporary studies have produced evidence and analysis that can nevertheless be analysed within the framework of a study of the articulation of racism and sexism as ideologies and their respective associations with exclusionary practices. In the context of the present discussion, however, what is especially significant is the centrality of sexism in the reproduction of the nation state.

GLOBALISATION AND THE NATION STATE

Seton-Watson's puzzlement over the characterisation of French nationalism in the nineteenth century highlights another issue of current relevance, that is the disjuncture between nationalism and the nation state. If, historically, it was possible for nationalism to exist in the absence of a nation state, and vice versa, this suggests that a decline of the nation state would not necessarily be accompanied by a decline of nationalism. In this chapter, we have identified two phenomena that have been instrumental in the transformation of nation state power, and even (in some analyses) the decline of the nation state, namely the wealth and power of transnational corporations, and the development of supra-nation-state institutions (the European Union, NAFTA, etc.).

Even if such developments have contributed to the decline or dissolution of the nation state, in the post-Cold War world this has not been accompanied by a decline in nationalism. If anything, the new world order that has evolved since the early 1990s has seen an intensification of nationalism, most significantly (though not exclusively) in Eastern and Central Europe. In most cases, however, the combination of economic globalisation, the establishment of supra-national institutions and the decentralisation of power in many nation states has removed the nation state, qua a sovereign set of institutions within a given territory, as a point of reference for nationalism. Some 'sovereigntist' groups (e.g. the UK Independence Party on the British right, or the Mouvement des Citoyens on the French centre-left) appeal to this idea, but their nationalism is not based on an actual manifestation of this idea.

So, if the nation state as a concrete manifestation of the idea of sovereignty has become an anachronistic point of reference for nationalism, where are nationalist groups to find an alternative point of reference, and how do their political projects interact with racism? There are diverse possibilities here, but there are three that are particularly germane to this discussion, and to current international politics: refugee migration, supra-national 'civilisations' and religion.

We analyse refugee migrations as follows. The collapse of Eastern European state communism in the late 1980s and early 1990s, the power of trans-national corporations and the development of supra-state institutions are processes that have transformed the nation state in a contradictory manner. The increasing anachronism of the concept of nation state sovereignty has not coincided with a disappearance of conflict over the 'nature' and 'role' of the nation state, or over its boundaries. In some cases, conflict continues to occur over the geographical borders of nation state territory (e.g. Israel and Palestine, India and Pakistan, Britain and Ireland), but, more important to the present argument, there is continuing and even intensified conflict over the question of who 'belongs' to the nation. Boundaries have been established which exclude Kurds from membership of the Turkish nation, Romani people from membership of the Czech nation, Albanian Muslims from membership of the Serbian nation, and so on.

In the case of Yugoslavia, and the break-up of Yugoslavia, these boundaries were established through a process of ethnicisation, which had deep historical roots. Ethnic boundaries were established historically through conflict with and colonisation by the Ottoman Empire, and the establishment of a *millat* system in the late fourteenth century which distinguished religious communities and allowed them to partially govern themselves according to their own cultural-legal codes. Importantly, however, 'Muslim' later came to be an ethnicised category (e.g. Gellner 1983: 72), and Muslims were represented as those who had collaborated with Ottoman rule, or even as the former oppressors.

Political boundaries were established in the aftermath of the First World War, when the state of Yugoslavia was created, and of the Second World War, when Marshal Tito drew the internal boundaries of the Yugoslav federal state. During the communist period, ethnic conflict was largely superseded by a process of nation-building that was effected ideologically by a very specific interplay of nationalism and socialism, in part in opposition to the state communism of the Soviet Union. Following the death of Tito, and with the collapse of Eastern European state communism, this very specific project of nation-building was undermined by a plurality of ethnicised nationalist political projects. What this triggered was not exactly a *catharsis* manifest in ethnic conflict (as nations cannot so easily be psychoanalysed), but a new process of nation-building: initially in Croatia and Slovenia, later in Serbia, and, in a contested or ambivalent way which remains largely unresolved, in Bosnia and Herzegovina, Macedonia, Montenegro and Kosovo. This process excluded the ethnicised Other, who became a victim of discrimination, violence and genocide, and who consequently became a refugee.

In general terms, such exclusion, particularly where it is manifest in violence and 'ethnic cleansing', is a common cause of refugee migration. Thus, refugee migration is rooted in the world economy, international politics and ideologies of the post-Cold War era. This disproves the claims made by politicians and sections of the media that, because claims for political asylum have increased since labour migration was 'stopped', they are the (bogus) culmination of free economic migration, not forced refugee migration. Labour migration is not necessarily free (unless escaping extreme poverty and even starvation is seen as a free choice), and there is no simple distinction between economic and political (or free and unfree) migration (e.g. Zolberg 1983; Zolberg *et al.* 1989; Kay and Miles 1992: 4–8, 179–93).

Despite the wrongs of such representations, refugee migration has provided an Other for nationalist groups to juxtapose with their own concept of Self. In other words, it has established a specific Self–Other dialectic which constitutes an alternative (to the nation state) point of reference for nationalist groups. The Other may be perceived as 'not really belonging' to the nation, establishing a cause of his or her transformation into a refugee, or the Other may have already migrated and claimed refugee status, but be greeted with hostility. The refugee has become another new Other, though there are continuities from the labour migration of the 1950s, 1960s and 1970s. In other words, there is a different origin and impetus for migration, but the 'same' anti-immigrant discourse.

Ironically, much of this anti-immigrant discourse is articulated by nationalist groups who hark back to nation state sovereignty as a necessary means to control immigration, while it is supra-nation-state institutions (such as the European Union) that increasingly regulate migration flows. Some such institutions maintain or aspire to an approximate contiguity with the second alternative point of reference for nationalist groups which we identified, the supra-national 'civilisation'. Following the hijacking and crashing of four aeroplanes in the United States on 11 September 2001, the Prime Minister of Italy, Silvio Berlusconi, made an intervention in which he appealed to the 'superiority' of Western Christian 'civilisation' over Islam. Other movements ranging from pan-Africanism and Arab nationalism to the Islamic resurgence (often known as Islamic funda-mentalism) have made comparable claims for the superiority of a culture, religion or even 'race', claims which can be supported, at least partially, by appeal to Samuel Huntington's identification, reification and analysis of seven or eight meta-'civilisations', namely Sinic, Japanese, Hindu, Islamic, Orthodox, Western, Latin American and, 'possibly', African (1998: 45–7), some of which are destined to 'clash' in the twenty-first century, especially Islam and the West (1993: 35, 1998: 209–18). Significantly, this analysis has been extremely influential in the formation of recent American foreign policy, and may turn out (if it has not already) to be a self-fulfilling prophecy.

The third point of reference is the religious tradition and identity of a people, which may or may not be accompanied by a commitment to any religious practice, belief system or theology, but which excludes the Other. Even in the case of conversion, the national Other is still excluded because of the emphasis on tradition. Through this process, then, even in the context of nation state transformation or decline, an Other is identified and excluded. Where the Other is Muslim, civilisation and religion as points of reference for nationalism are united, because the Muslim is identified as representing both a different civilisation and an alien religion. Such representations have been made, for example, of post-war migrants from the Pakistani Punjab and Kashmir to Britain, and from Algeria to France – they are not always about the Middle East, nor are they only recent. They have given rise to what has come to be called Islamophobia, a phenomenon which interacts significantly with racism, and which is of increasing sociological (see Halliday 1999; Brown 2000) and political importance.

As far as the identification and exclusion of a religious Other is concerned, this may be an extreme case. It is true that many, perhaps all, religious institutions and world-views have greater legitimacy when they are ethnicised, because then someone's religion can be seen as an inevitable consequence of his or her birth and/or socialisation. When they are seen as representing a racialised Other, however, there is a stigma attached to one of 'Us' who is a member of the religion in question, and the interaction with racism is at least a potential experience for the representative of the religious and racialised Other. This may not be a historical constant, but it is a feature of the *longue durée* of Western history.

However, there is something unique about Islamophobia. When Muslims become a racialised group, an amalgam of nationality ('Arab' or 'Pakistani', for example), religion (Islam) and politics (extremism, fundamentalism, terrorism) is frequently produced in Orientalist, Islamophobic and racist discourses. In contrast, most religions are not represented in an amalgam with terrorism, or even ethnic or national distinctiveness. In the 1990s, as we have seen, the ethnicisation of Bosnian Muslims became a pretext for 'ethnic cleansing' – it was claimed that this was necessary to defend Europe from 'Islamic fundamentalism' and 'terrorism', as the Ottomans had been stopped at Vienna. However, like other religious Others, the alleged distinctiveness of the Muslim is not usually regarded as biological or somatic, so Islamophobia is not to be regarded as an instance of racism. However, it does interact with racism, and, as we saw in Chapter 1, there was an anachronistic quasi-racialisation of the Muslim (as 'Saracen', 'Turk' or 'Moor') in the Middle Ages.

According to the Runnymede Trust, Islamophobia is articulated in terms of a 'closed view of Islam'. In systematic terms, this means that Islamophobia is present when some of the following conditions are satisfied:

1. Islam seen as a single monolithic bloc, static and unresponsive to new realities.
2. Islam seen as separate and other – (a) not having any aims or values in common with other cultures (b) not affected by them (c) not influencing them.
3. Islam seen as inferior to the West – barbaric, irrational, primitive, sexist.
4. Islam seen as violent, aggressive, threatening, supportive of terrorism, engaged in a 'clash of civilisations'.
5. Islam seen as a political ideology, used for political or military advantage.
6. Criticisms made by Islam of 'the West' rejected out of hand.
7. Hostility towards Islam used to justify discriminatory practices towards Muslims and exclusion of Muslims from mainstream society.
8. Anti-Muslim hostility accepted as natural and 'normal'.

(Commission on British Muslims and Islamophobia 1997: 5)

As Brown (2000: 80–1; cf. Al-Azmeh 1996: 104; Halliday 1999: 893, 896–7) points out, 'neo-Afghanism', an Islamic tendency which is concerned with a 'pure' and 'authentic' Islam, also possesses some of these characteristics and, as such, articulates a 'closed view of Islam', but this would not normally be classed as an instance of Islamophobia. More significant for our purposes, however, is identifying where a closed view of Islam, articulated in *opposition* to Islam, or in an attempt to *denigrate* Islam, interacts with racism. Such an interaction is most clearly visible in the consequences of this interaction: exclusionary practices, exclusionary discourses and hostility. When there is an interaction between the articulation of racism and Islamophobia, Muslims (qua a racialised group as well as a religious Other) are variously characterised as inferior and backward (but with a 'noble savage' quality), as incompatible with Westerners, or even as direct threat to the West (Brown 2000: 84). In all of these cases, in parallel with Orientalist discourses and with the ideology of racism, Islam is represented as, *stricto sensu*, *essentially* different from the West, and as homogeneous or even inferior.

The formulation of the concept of Islamophobia has been criticised by Halliday (1999) for four reasons: the homogeneous view of Islam, like the 'neo-Afghanism' mentioned earlier; the 'perennialist' implication that current Western anti-Muslim discourses are the same as those articulated historically, for example during the Crusades; the associated homogenisation of anti-Muslim discourses in different national and pan-national contexts; and the confusion, as Halliday sees it, between attacks on Islam and attacks on Muslims. On the first three points, Halliday juxtaposes his own modernist perspective, arguing that Islamism in the Muslim world is a 'variant of radical Western discourse' (1999: 894), which is nation state specific, and that: 'On the European side . . . there are significant differences of emphasis, prejudice, engagement depending on the colonial histories, the geographical location, the composition of the immigrant community' (1999: 896). On these points, Halliday is entirely correct, but the existence of different 'Islamophobias' does not invalidate the concept of Islamophobia any more than the existence of different racisms invalidates the concept of racism.

Pursuing the fourth point, Halliday argues that: '"Islam" as a religion *was* the enemy in the past: in the crusades or the *reconquista*. It is not the enemy now. . . . The attack now is not against *Islam* as a faith but Muslims as a people. . . . Hence the more accurate term is not "Islamophobia" but "anti-Muslimism"' (1999: 898). Aside from the methodological argument preferring 'ordinary language' to neologism (cf. Brown 2000: 83) – and the term 'Islamophobia' is now widely used by *inter alia* Muslims themselves – neither Muslims nor Islam exist without the other, so it is not really possible to separate hatred of Muslims from a hatred of Islam. Islamophobia is often based on stereotypes about the religion (e.g. terrorism and misogyny), which are 'channelled' into attacks on Muslims. Hence, Islamophobia can be defined '*primarily* as a hostility towards Islam, rather than Muslims, though it must manifest itself (secondarily) as hostility towards Muslims' (Brown 2000: 87). When the hatred of the theology is not present, we are more likely to be seeing anti-immigrant sentiment, racism or xenophobia than Islamophobia.

Importantly, then, many of the stereotypes and misinformation that contribute to the articulation of Islamophobia are rooted in a particular perception of Islam. In the aftermath of the hijacking and crashing of four planes in the United States on 11 September 2001, American sales of the Qur'an increased significantly, apparently because people wanted to find out what had motivated these actions. Of course, the readers will have been disappointed, because terrorism is not prescribed in the Qur'an, but rather the image of the Muslim as terrorist is one that has been constructed through a history of Western representations of the Muslim Other (including those described in Chapter 1). Indeed, pacifism is not an unknown concept in Muslim thought (e.g. Esack 1997; Harris 1998; Berndt 2000: 54–72) although, admittedly, it is not a mainstream concept either.

However, the significance of Islamophobia and representations of Islam in international politics is not delineated by the sociological reality or theological framework of Islam, but by significations and perceptions. Thus, the attacks of 11 September 2001 were associated with Islam, while other attacks, such as the Oklahoma City bombing, have not been associated with 'white' people, or with Christianity, or anything else that represents the mainstream of Western societies. In contrast, the deracialisation of the Muslim as terrorist sits uneasily, or in a contradictory manner, alongside the racialisation of Muslims, which is central to a range of exclusionary practices within Western nation states.

So the example of Islamophobia illustrates the process we have been discussing, that is the identification of new points of reference for nationalism, for the relationship between nationalism and racism, and the consequent identification and exclusion of an Other. The Muslim is *identified* as Other on the basis of religious differences and of a particular conception of civilisation. On religious differences, the Muslim, if he or she is a practising Muslim, practises a religion that is unfamiliar to many in the West, that historically has been identified as antipathetic to the West or to Christendom, and that appears central to everyday life in a way that is sometimes regarded as deviant in the West – thus, the Muslim will always be regarded as practising irrespective of whether or not this is the case for any individual. As the representative of a different civilisation, the Muslim will be regarded as having a fundamentally different mindset, or even engaged in a clash of civilisations, in other words, an enemy within. This is significant at the micro-social level, where Islamic dress codes, for example, are often seen as a matter for concern, and in the international political arena, as Huntington's self-fulfilling prophecy and our discussion in this section indicate.

Subsequently, the Muslim is *excluded* in at least three different ways. First, he or she is subject to exclusionary practices, so may find it difficult to secure suitable employment, housing or health care, for example. This is particularly relevant for Muslims living in Western nation states. Second (again, particularly in the West), the Muslim is excluded from the nation, not necessarily in the sense of being excluded from citizenship of the nation state (though such exclusion may occur), but in the sense of not being regarded as 'really belonging'. Such an exclusion is premised on a belief in cultural incompatibility and an emphasis on national 'roots', implying either a blood theory of nationality combined with a racialisation of the Muslim, or an expectation that a member of the nation will have a 'tradition' of association with and commitment to the nation that has been handed down from generation to generation, combined with an assumption that Islam is a new feature of the West. This assumption is incorrect (see, for example, Nielsen 1995: 4–6, 39–42; Mattar 1998). Third, the Muslim is excluded from the civilisation, because he or she is regarded as the representative of another civilisation.

For Muslims living in the West, particularly where they have also been racialised, this may make them an object of *inter alia* curiosity, distrust, animosity, violence and other exclusionary practices. In international politics, the Muslim is represented as the personification of an enemy civilisation, a representation that legitimates the Middle East and South Central Asian policies of Western nation states (although these policies are not the object of unanimous agreement between, or even within, Western governments), the representation of Palestinian victims of Israeli military activities as 'unworthy victims' (cf. Herman and Chomsky 1994: 37ff.), the support for repressive 'secular' regimes in some nation states with a Muslim majority, and direct military action against the governments and peoples of some Muslim states. The centrality of such phenomena to current, post-Cold War, international politics is clear. It is also a consequence of the relationship between racism, nationalism, the nation state and globalisation.

CONCLUSION

The example of Islamophobia illustrates many of the themes of this book: there are racisms, they interact with other ideologies and phenomena, and they are rooted in actual events. Furthermore, methodologically, the best way of identifying different racisms is in terms of the different phenomena with which they interact, and the events in which they are rooted. In this chapter, we have considered capitalism, nationalism, sexism, globalisation and Islamophobia as phenomena that interact with racism, and the end of the Cold War, the break-up of Yugoslavia, and the aftermath of the attacks on 11 September 2001, as events in which the contemporary transformations of racism may be rooted. This is by no means an exhaustive list. In all cases, however, a process of racialisation has occurred, resulting in the inclusion and exclusion of certain racialised populations.

CONCLUSION

A central objective of this book has been to justify the retention of racism as a key concept within the social sciences. Having established theoretically a concept of racism as an ideology which is not restricted by being grounded in a single empirical instance, and having linked that concept with that of racialisation, we believe that it is possible to facilitate the study of racism in a comparative perspective and to explore the multiplicity of its determinants. It therefore becomes possible to further encourage the analysis of many different racisms in a wider context.

A simple description of the different forms that racism has taken historically has use primarily as a catalogue for the history of certain ideas. Such a catalogue does, however, prepare the ground for the more important and difficult analytical task of explaining the historically specific articulations of racialisation and racism within political and economic relations. Thus, the real challenge is to place the concepts of racialisation and racism at the centre of a historical, as well as a contemporary, sociology which is concerned with the origin and development of, as well as the current structure and process of, the capitalist mode of production globally (a development which involves a continuing interaction with non-capitalist modes of production).

In conducting that analysis, and in light of the arguments of this book, there should be a sensitivity to three aspects of the nature of the expression of racism. First, as an ideology, it is necessary to delineate the complexity of its reproduction. This means, in particular, avoiding any assumption of simple, historical duplication. Ideologies are never only received but are also constructed and reconstructed by people responding to their material and cultural circumstances in order to comprehend, represent and act in relation to those circumstances. Ideological reproduction is therefore a consequence of a transaction between historical legacy and individual and collective attempts to make sense of the world.

There are important consequences. The specific content of racism should be expected to change temporally and contextually. A discourse 'inherited' from the past is likely to be reconstituted if it is to be used to make sense of the world in a new context, while new circumstances can be expected to stimulate the formation of new representations. Moreover, the expression of racism should be distinguished analytically from the reception of racism. Studies of the discourse of racism articulated by journalists, editors, writers, scientists, priests and politicians are common, as is demonstrated by the relatively numerous studies of the development of scientific racism and of the manner in which racism is articulated in newspapers. It should not be assumed that the *expression* of racism is synonymous with the communication of racism, nor that the audience necessarily comprehends and accepts the ideology that has been identified as present (van Dijk 1993: 242). It does not automatically follow that the expression of racism in a newspaper will result in all its readers articulating a racist message. That this is a mistaken assumption is demonstrated by the existence of researchers who are able to identify and question this ideology. Moreover, if it were true, there would be little or no scope for anti-racist intervention. Indeed, in recent decades, the anti-racist movement has been extremely active and has had a significant impact on both public consciousness and the determination of public policy. Consequently, considerably more attention should be devoted to identifying and explaining the active construction and reproduction of racism among people in different class locations, and the reception and rejection of racism by the audiences of the mass media and politicians, etc.

The second aspect is that the effects of its expression always interact with the extant economic and political relations and with other ideologies. Thus, although there may be formal (or political) reasons to attempt to assess the independent impact of the expression of racism, it should always be remembered that those who articulate it and those who are its object are located in a wider, complex web of social relations. Consequently, the expression of racism may be the result of an attempt to secure other interests and outcomes and its effects may be contextualised by other facets of people's economic and political circumstances. Moreover, where those who are its object do share in other respects a structural position with others who are not similarly affected, or differ in other respects from those who are similarly affected, it is necessary to demonstrate that the outcome attributed to the effects of racism has not been partially or wholly determined by some aspect of the shared structural position or by the other differences between them. It should be emphasised once more that to argue this is not to deny but rather to contextualise the effectivity of racism.

There is an important implication. Racism and related exclusionary practices have their own specificity and give rise to particular, exclusive experiences. But the material consequence or outcome, the fact of exclusion, may be shared with others. For example, we have shown that racism has played an important role in excluding a significant minority of people of Caribbean and Asian origin from skilled manual and non-manual work, and indeed from the labour market in Britain. But these are not the only people excluded from skilled manual and non-manual work or from the labour market. In a context of fluctuating and relative scarcity, where the total number of jobs within a nation state is less than the total population seeking paid work and where the number of skilled manual and non-manual positions is even less, exclusionary practices are structurally required, but may be effected by means of, for example, some combination of sexism, racism and nationalism as well as the formal possession of acquired skills. Similarly, in capitalist societies which are unable to provide sufficient and adequate housing for their populations, some mechanism of inclusion/exclusion is necessary to allocate people to housing of poor quality and racism is one amongst a number of such mechanisms. By seeking to contextualise the impact of racism within class relations, one can begin to contextualise the specificity of the experience of racism, not in order to deny it, but rather in order simultaneously to highlight and generalise it by means of demonstrating the linkages with other means of exclusion.

Third, formal theoretical generalisations about the nature and conse-quences of the expression of racism should be able to account for their 'multidimensionality' and their 'historical specificity'. We have emphasised that the articulation of racism always has a number of economic, political and representational consequences, some of which can be contradictory. Moreover, the nature of those consequences changes historically, partly in accordance with different class interests and strategies, different strategies of resistance, and different material and cultural contexts. Definitions of racism which attribute the ideology with an ontologically and exclusively functional, economic and colonial character systematically obscure its multidimensionality and specificity. Simplistic analysis, not surprisingly, gives rise to simple solutions, and the continuing articulation of racism, when seen against the background of its long historical genesis, is sufficient testimony to the limitations of such analyses.

FURTHER READING

SOCIOLOGICAL CONCEPTS OF RACISM

Barot, R. (2001) 'Racialisation: The Genealogy and Critique of a Concept', *Ethnic and Racial Studies*, 24 (4): 601–18.

Bulmer, M. and Solomos, J. (1999) *Racism*, Oxford: Oxford Paperbacks.

Goldberg, D.T. (1993) *Racist Culture: Philosophy and the Politics of Meaning*, Oxford: Blackwell.

Miles, R. (1993) *Racism After 'Race Relations'*, London: Routledge.

Omi, M. and Winant, H. (1994) *Racial Formation in the United States: From the 1960s to the 1990s* (second edition), New York: Routledge.

Solomos, J. (1993) *Race and Racism in Britain*, Cambridge: Cambridge University Press.

Wieviorka, M. (1995) *The Arena of Racism*, London: Sage.

CULTURAL ANALYSES OF RACISM

Gilroy, P. (1993) *The Black Atlantic*, London: Verso.

—— (2000) *Between Camps: Nations, Cultures and the Allure of Race*, London: Penguin.

Mac an Ghaill, M. (1999) *Contemporary Racisms and Ethnicities*, Buckingham: Open University Press.

van Dijk, T. (1993) *Elite Discourse and Racism*, London: Sage.

Wetherell, M. and Potter, J. (1992) *Mapping the Language of Racism: Discourse and the Legitimation of Exploitation*, New York: Colombia University Press.

HISTORICALLY SPECIFIC RACISMS

Banton, M. (1987) *Racial Theories*, Cambridge: Cambridge University Press.

Cohen, P. (1988), 'The Perversions of Inheritance', in P. Cohen and H.S. Bains (eds) *Multi-Racist Britain*, Basingstoke: Macmillan (pp.9–118).

Fryer, P. (1984) *Staying Power: The History of Black People in Britain*, London: Pluto Press.

Said, E.W. (1995) *Orientalism: Western Conceptions of the Orient*, London: Penguin.

Verkuyten, M. and ter Wal, J. (eds) (2000) *Comparative Perspectives on Racism*, Aldershot: Ashgate.

ANTI-RACISM

Bonnett, A. (2000), *Anti-Racism*, London: Routledge.
Lloyd, C. (1998) *Discourses of Anti-Racism in France*, Aldershot: Ashgate.
Taguieff, P.-A. (1995) *Les Fins de l'Antiracisme*, Paris: Michalon.
—— (2001) *The Force of Prejudice*, Minneapolis: University of Minnesota Press.

POLITICAL ECONOMY OF MIGRATION

Castles, S. and Miller, M.J. (1998) *The Age of Migration*, London: Macmillan.
Joly, D. (1996) *Haven or Hell? Asylum Policies and Refugees in Europe*, Basingstoke: Macmillan.
Miles, R. (1987) *Capitalism and Unfree Labour: Anomaly or Necessity?*, London: Tavistock.
Sassen, S. (2001) *The Global City*, Princeton: Princeton University Press.
Zolberg, A., Sergio, A. and Astri, S. (1989) *Escape from Violence*, New York: Oxford University Press.

RACISM AND SEXISM

Anthias, F. and Yuval-Davis, N. (1993) *Racialised Boundaries: Race, Nation, Gender, Colour and Class and the Anti-Racist Struggle*, London: Routledge.
Carby, H. (1982) 'White Woman Listen! Black Feminism and the Boundaries of Sisterhood', in CCCS, *The Empire Strikes Back: Race and Racism in 70s Britain*, London: Hutchinson.
Collins, P.H. (1991) *Black Feminist Thought*, New York: Routledge.
Guillaumin, C. (1995) *Racism, Sexism, Power and Ideology*, London: Routledge.
Mirza, H.S. (ed.) (1997) *Black British Feminism: A Reader*, London: Routledge.
Potts, L. (1990) *The World Labour Market: A History of Migration*, London: Zed Books.

RACISM AND NATIONALISM

Anderson B. (1991) *Imagined Communities: Reflections on the Origin and Spread of Nationalism*, London: Verso.
Balibar, E. and Wallerstein, I. (1991) *Race, Nation, Class: Ambiguous Identities*, London: Verso.
Nairn, T. (1975) 'The Modern Janus', *New Left Review*, 94: 3–29.
—— (1997) *Faces of Nationalism*, London: Verso.

EXTREME-RIGHT POLITICS

Balibar, E. (1991) 'Es Gibt Keinen Staat in Europa: Racism and Politics in Europe Today', *New Left Review*, 186: 5–19.

Cheles, L., Ferguson, R. and Vaughan, M. (eds) (1991) *Neo-Fascism in Europe*, London: Longman.

Ezekiel, R. (1995) *The Racist Mind: Portraits of American Neo-Nazis and Klansmen*, London: Viking.

Husbands, C.T. (1988) 'Extreme Right-Wing Politics in Great Britain: The Recent Marginalisation of the National Front', *West European Politics*, 11 (2): 65–79.

Wieviorka, M. et al (1993) *La France Raciste*, Paris: Editions du Seuil.

BIBLIOGRAPHY

Afshar, H. (1989) 'Gender Roles and the "Moral Economy of Kin" among Pakistani Women in West Yorkshire', *New Community*, 15 (2): 211–25.

Al-Azmeh, A. (1996) *Islams and Modernities*, London: Verso.

ALTARF (All London Teachers Against Racism and Fascism) (1984) *Challenging Racism*, London: ALTARF.

Anderson, B. (1983) *Imagined Communities: Reflections on the Origin and Spread of Nationalism*, London: Verso.

Anon. (1983) 'Ethnic Origin and Economic Status', *Employment Gazette*, 91: 424–30.

—— (1987) 'Ethnic Origin and Economic Status', *Employment Gazette*, 95: 18–29.

Anthias, F. (1983) 'Sexual Divisions and Ethnic Adaptation: The Case of Greek-Cypriot Women', in A. Phizacklea (ed.) *One-Way Ticket*, London: Routledge and Kegan Paul.

—— (1992) *Ethnicity, Class and Migration: Greek Cypriots in Britain*, Aldershot: Gower.

—— and Yuval-Davis, N. (1993) *Racialised Boundaries: Race, Nation, Gender, Colour and Class and the Anti-Racist Struggle*, London: Routledge.

Anwar, M. (1979) *The Myth of Return: Pakistanis in Britain*, London: Heinemann.

Arens, W. (1979) *The Man-Eating Myth: Anthropology and Anthropophagy*, New York: Oxford University Press.

Augstein, H.F. (ed.) (1996) *Race: the Origins of an Idea*, Bristol: Thoemmes Press.

Babbitt, S.E. and Campbell, S. (eds) (1999) *Racism and Philosophy*, Ithaca and London: Cornell University Press.

Baldry, H.C. (1965) *The Unity of Mankind in Greek Thought*, Cambridge: Cambridge University Press.

Balibar, E. (1991) 'Racism and Nationalism', in E. Balibar and I. Wallerstein, *Race, Nation, Class: Ambiguous Identities*, London: Verso (pp. 37–67).

Banton, M. (1970) 'The Concept of Racism', in S. Zubaida (ed.) *Race and Racialism*, London: Tavistock.

—— (1977) *The Idea of Race*, London: Tavistock.

—— (1980) 'The Idiom of Race: A Critique of Presentism', *Research in Race and Ethnic Relations*, 2: 21–42.

—— (1987) *Racial Theories*, Cambridge: Cambridge University Press.

—— (1991) 'The Race Relations Problematic', *British Journal of Sociology*, 42 (1): 115–30.

—— (1996a) *International Action Against Racial Discrimination*, Oxford: Clarendon Press.

—— (1996b) 'The Racism Problematic', in R. Barot (ed.) *The Racism Problematic: Contemporary Sociological Debates on Race and Ethnicity*, Lampeter: Edwin Mellen (pp. 20–43).

—— (2001) 'Progress in Ethnic and Racial Studies', *Ethnic and Racial Studies*, 24 (2): 173–94.

Barber, A. (1985) 'Ethnic Origin and Economic Status', *Employment Gazette*, 93: 467–77.

Barker, A.J. (1978) *The African Link: British Attitudes to the Negro in the Era of the Atlantic Slave Trade, 1550–1807*, London: Frank Cass.

Barker, M. (1981) *The New Racism*, London: Junction Books.

Barot, R. (2001) 'Racialisation: The Genealogy and Critique of a Concept', *Ethnic and Racial Studies*, 24 (4): 601–18.

Barth, F. (1969) *Ethnic Group and Boundaries*, Boston: Little, Brown and Co.

Barzun, J. (1938) *Race: A Study in Modern Superstition*, London: Methuen.

—— (1965) *Race: A Study in Superstition*, New York: Harper and Row.

Bastide, R. (1968) 'Color, Racism, and Christianity', in J.H. Franklin (ed.) *Color and Race*, Boston: Houghton Mifflin Company.

Baudet, H. (1976) *Paradise on Earth: Some Thoughts on European Images of Non-European Man*, Westport: Greenwood Press.

Bauman, Z. (1989) *Modernity and the Holocaust*, Cambridge: Polity Press.

Bearce, G.D. (1982) *British Attitudes Towards India, 1784–1858*, Westport: Greenwood Press.

Beddoe, J. (1885) *The Races of Britain: A Contribution to the Anthropology of Western Europe*, Bristol: J.W. Arrowsmith.

Benedict, R. (1983) *Race and Racism*, London: Routledge and Kegan Paul.

Bennett, G. (1965) 'Settlers and Politics in Kenya', in V. Harlow and E.M. Chiver (eds) *History of East Africa* (vol. II), Oxford: Clarendon Press.

Berndt, H. (2000) *Non-Violence in the World Religions*, London: SCM Press.

Biddiss, M. (1975) 'Myths of the Blood: European Racist Ideology 1850–1945', *Patterns of Prejudice*, 9 (5): 11–19.

Billig, M. (1976) *Social Psychology and Intergroup Relations*, London: Academic Press.

Bland, L., Brunsdon, C., Hobson, D., and Winship, J. (1978) 'Women "Inside and Outside" the Relations of Production', in Women's Studies Group *Women Take Issue: Aspects of Women's Subordination*, London: Hutchinson.

Blauner, R. (1972) *Racial Oppression in America*, New York: Harper and Row.

Blum, L. (1999) 'Moral Asymmetries in Racism', in S.E. Babbitt and S. Campbell (eds) *Racism and Philosophy*, Ithaca and London: Cornell University Press.

Boas, F. (1940) *Race, Culture and Language*, New York: Free Press.

Bodmer, W.F. (1972) 'Race and IQ: the genetic background', in K. Richardson, D. Spears and M. Richards (eds) *Race, Culture and Intelligence*, Harmondsworth: Penguin.

Bodmer, W.F. and Cavalli-Sforza, L.L. (1976) *Genetics, Evolution, and Man*, San Francisco: W.H. Freeman.

Bolt, C. (1971) *Victorian Attitudes to Race*, London: Routledge and Kegan Paul.

Bonnett, A. (2000), *Anti-Racism*, London: Routledge.

Boyd, W.C. (1950) *Genetics and the Races of Man: An Introduction to Modern Physical Anthropology*, Oxford: Basil Blackwell.

Braudel, F. (1984) *Civilisation and Capitalism: 15th to 18th Century: Volume III, The Perspective of the World*, London: Collins.

Brett, E.A. (1973) *Colonialism and Underdevelopment in East Africa: The Politics of Economic Change, 1919–1939*, London: Heinemann.

Brink, A. (1983) *A Chain of Voices*, London: Fontana.

Brown, C. (1984) *Black and White Britain: The Third PSI Study*, London: Heinemann.

Brown, M.D. (2000) 'Conceptualising Racism and Islamophobia', in J. ter Wal and M. Verkuyten (eds) *Comparative Perspectives on Racism*, Aldershot: Ashgate.

Carby, H. (1982) 'White Woman Listen! Black Feminism and the Boundaries of Sisterhood', in CCCS, *The Empire Strikes Back: Race and Racism in 70s Britain*, London: Hutchinson.

Carmichael, S. and Hamilton, C.V. (1968) *Black Power: The Politics of Liberation in America*, London: Jonathan Cape.

Carter, B, Harris, C., and Joshi, S. (1987) 'The 1951–55 Conservative Government and the Racialisation of Black Immigration', *Immigrants and Minorities*, 6: 335–47.

Cartwright, J. (2000) *Evolution and Human Behaviour: Darwinian Perspectives on Human Nature*, Basingstoke: Macmillan.

Castles, S., Booth, H., and Wallace, T. (1984) *Here for Good: Western Europe's New Ethnic Minorities*, London: Pluto Press.

Cavalli-Sforza, L.L. (2001) *Genes, Peoples and Languages*, London: Penguin.

Cavalli-Sforza, L.L., Menozzi, P. and Piazza, A. (1994) *The History and Geography of Human Genes*, Princeton, N.J.: Princeton University Press.

CCCS (Centre for Contemporary Cultural Studies) (1982) *The Empire Strikes Back: Race and Racism in 70s Britain*, London: Hutchinson.

Chachage, C.S.L. (1988) 'British Rule and African Civilisation in Tanganyika', *Journal of Historical Sociology*.

Clark, L.L. (1984) *Social Darwinism in France*, Birmingham: University of Alabama Press.

—— (1988) 'Le Darwinisme Social en France', *La Recherche*, 19: 192–200.

Clayton, A. and Savage, D.C. (1974) *Government and Labour in Kenya, 1895–1963*, London: Frank Cass.

Cohen, P. (1988), 'The Perversions of Inheritance', in P. Cohen and H.S. Bains (eds) *Multi-Racist Britain*, Basingstoke: Macmillan (pp. 9–118).

—— (1992) '"It's Racism What Dunnit": Hidden Narratives in Theories of Racism', in J. Donald and A. Rattansi (eds) *'Race', Culture and Difference*, London: Sage (pp. 62–103).

Cole, R.G. (1972) 'Sixteenth Century Travel Books as a Source of European Attitudes Toward Non-White and Non-Western Culture', *Proceedings of the American Philosophical Society*, 116: 59–67.

Collins, P.H. (1991) *Black Feminist Thought*, New York: Routledge.

Comas, J. (1961) '"Scientific" Racism Again?', *Current Anthropology*, 2: 303–40.

Combe, G. (1830) *System of Phrenology*, Edinburgh: John Anderson.

Commission on British Muslims and Islamophobia (1997) *Islamophobia: A Challenge For Us All*, London: Runnymede Trust.

Connell, R.W. and Irving, T.H. (1980) *Class Structure in Australian History*, Melbourne: Longman Cheshire.

Corrigan, P. and Sayer, D. (1986) *The Great Arch: English State Formation as Cultural Revolution*, Oxford: Basil Blackwell.

Crawford, P.C. (1923) *Chinese Coolie Emigration to Countries Within the British Empire*, London: P.S. King and Son.

Curtin, P.D. (1961) '"White Man's Grave": Image and Reality, 1780–1850', *Journal of British Studies*, 1: 94–110.

—— (1965) *The Image of Africa: British Ideas and Action, 1780–1850*, London: Macmillan.

Curtis, L.P. (1968) *Anglo-Saxons and Celts*, Connecticut: University of Bridgeport Press.

—— (1971) *Apes and Angels: the Irishman in Victorian Caricature*, Washington: Smithsonian Institution Press.

Dallas, K.M. (1955) 'The Origins of "White Australia"', *Australian Quarterly*, 27: 43–52.

Daniel, N. (1960) *Islam and the West: The Making of an Image*, Edinburgh: Edinburgh University Press.

—— (1966) *Islam, Europe and Empire*, Edinburgh: Edinburgh University Press.

—— (1975) *The Arabs and Medieval Europe*, London: Longman.

Daniel, W.W. (1968) *Racial Discrimination in England*, Harmondsworth: Penguin.

Davis, D.B. (1984) *Slavery and Human Progress*, New York: Oxford University Press.

Davison, G. (1985) 'Unemployment, Race and Public Opinion: Reflections on the Asian Immigration Controversy of 1888', in A. Markus and M.C. Ricklefs (eds) *Surrender Australia? Essays in the Study and Uses of History*, Sydney: Allen and Unwin.

Dawidowicz, L. (1977) *The War Against the Jews, 1933–45*, Harmondsworth: Penguin.

de Lepervanche, M. (1984) *Indians in a White Australia*, Sydney: Allen and Unwin.

—— (1987) 'Racism and Sexism in Australian National Identity', Mimeo paper read in Department of Sociology, University of Glasgow.

DeLey, M. (1983) 'French Immigration Policy Since May 1981', *International Migration Review*, 17, 2: 196–211.

Denoon, D. (1983) *Settler Capitalism: The Dynamics of Dependent Development in the Southern Hemisphere*, Oxford: Clarendon Press.

Dickason, O.P. (1984) *The Myth of the Savage and the Beginnings of French Colonialism in the Americas*, Edmonton: University of Alberta Press.

D'Souza, D. (1995) *The End of Racism*, New York: Free Press

Duffield, M. (1985) 'Rationalisation and the Politics of Segregation: Indian Workers in Britain's Foundry Industry, 1945–62', in K. Lunn (ed.) *Race and Labour in Twentieth-Century Britain*, London: Frank Cass.

Durkheim, E. (2002) *Suicide: A Study in Sociology*, London: Routledge Classics.

Erikson, T.H. (1993) *Ethnicity and Nationalism: Anthropological Perspectives*, London: Pluto Press.

Esack, F. (1997) *Qur'an, Liberation and Pluralism*, Oxford: Oneworld.

Essed, P. (1991) *Understanding Everyday Racism: An Interdisciplinary Theory*, London: Sage.

EEC (European Economic Community) (1986) *Report of the Committee of Inquiry into the Rise of Fascism and Racism in Europe*, Brussels: European Economic Community.

Evans, R. (1975) 'Race Relations in a Colonial Setting', in R. Evans, K. Saunders, and K. Cronin *Exclusion, Exploitation and Extermination: Race Relations in Colonial Queensland*, Sydney: Australia and New Zealand Book Company.

Evans, R., Saunders, K., and Cronin, K. (1975) *Exclusion, Exploitation and Extermination: Race Relations in Colonial Queensland*, Sydney: Australia and New Zealand Book Company.

Eze, E.C. (ed.) (1997) *Race and the Enlightenment: A Reader*, Oxford: Blackwell.

Fanon, F. (1967) *The Wretched of the Earth*, Harmondsworth: Penguin.

Febvre, L. and Martin, H-J. (1976) *The Coming of the Book: The Impact of Printing, 1450–1800*, London: New Left Books.

Fevre, R. (1984) *Cheap Labour and Racial Discrimination*, Aldershot: Gower.

Field, S. *et al.* (1981) *Ethnic Minorities in Britain: A Study of Trends in their Position since 1961*, London: HMSO.

Fielding, N. (1981) *The National Front*, London: Routledge and Kegan Paul.

Fleming, G. (1986) *Hitler and the Final Solution*, Oxford: Oxford University Press.

Fonseca, I. (1996) *Bury Me Standing*, London: Vintage.

Forester, T. (1978) 'Asians in Business', *New Society*, 23 February: 420–3.

Fox-Genovese, E. and Genovese, E.D. (1983) *Fruits of Merchant Capital*, New York: Oxford University Press.

Fraser, A. (1995) *The Gypsies*, Oxford and Cambridge, Mass.: Blackwell.

Friedman, J.B. (1981) *The Monstrous Races in Medieval Art and Thought*, Cambridge, Mass.: Harvard University Press.

Fryer, P. (1984) *Staying Power: The History of Black People in Britain*, London: Pluto Press.

Gellner, E. (1983) *Nations and Nationalism*, Oxford: Blackwell.

George, H. (1984) *American Race Relations Theory: A Review of Four Models*, Lanham, Md.: University Press of America.

George, K. (1958) 'The Civilised West Looks at Primitive Africa: 1400–1800', *Isis*, 49: 62–72.

Gergen, K.J. (1968) 'The Significance of Skin Color in Human Relations', in J.H. Franklin (ed.) *Color and Race*, Boston: Houghton Mifflin Company.

Giddens, A. (1991) *Modernity and Self-Identity*, Cambridge: Polity.

Gilroy, P. (1987) *There Ain't No Black in the Union Jack*, London: Hutchinson.

—— (2000) *Between Camps: Nations, Cultures and the Allure of Race*, London: Penguin.

Gobineau, A. de (1970) 'Essay on the Inequality of the Human Races', in M. Biddiss (ed.) *Gobineau: Selected Political Writings*, London: Cape.

Gordon, P. and Reilly, D. (1986) 'Guestworkers of the Sea: Racism in British Shipping', *Race and Class*, 28 (2): 73–82.

Goldberg, D.T. (1990) 'The Social Formation of Racist Discourse', in D.T. Goldberg (ed.) *Anatomy of Racism*, Minneapolis: University of Minnesota Press.

—— (1993) *Racist Culture: Philosophy and the Politics of Meaning*, Oxford: Blackwell.

Gossett, T.F. (1965) *Race: The History of an Idea in America*, New York: Schocken Books.

Gould, S.J. (1984) *The Mismeasure of Man*, Harmondsworth: Penguin.

Gramsci, A. (1971) *Selections from the Prison Notebooks*, London: Lawrence and Wishart.

Grillo, R.D. (1985) *Ideologies and Institutions in Urban France: The Representation of Immigrants*, Cambridge: Cambridge University Press.

Guillaumin, C. (1980) 'The Idea of Race and its Elevation to Autonomous Scientific and Legal Status', in UNESCO *Sociological Theories: Race and Colonialism*, Paris: UNESCO.

—— (1995) *Racism, Sexism, Power and Ideology*, London: Routledge.

Günther, H.F.K. (1970) *The Racial Elements of European History*, New York: Kennikat Press.

Gurnah, A. (1984) 'The Politics of Racism Awareness Training', *Critical Social Policy*, 11: 6–20.

Hakluyt, R. (1972) *Voyages and Discoveries*, Harmondsworth: Penguin.

Hall, S. (1978) 'Racism and Reaction', in Commission for Racial Equality *Five Views of Multi-Racial Britain*, London: Commission for Racial Equality.

—— (1980) 'Race, Articulation and Societies Structured in Dominance', in UNESCO *Sociological Theories: Race and Colonialism*, Paris: UNESCO.

Haller, J.S. (1971) *Outcasts from Evolution: Scientific Attitudes of Racial Inferiority, 1859–1900*, Urbana: University of Illinois Press.

Halliday, F. (1996) *Islam and the Myth of Confrontation*, London: I.B. Tauris.

—— (1999) '"Islamophobia" Reconsidered', *Ethnic and Racial Studies*, 22 (5): 892–902.

Hammar, T. (ed.) (1985) *European Immigration Policy: A Comparative Study*, Cambridge: Cambridge University Press.

Harbsmeier, M. (1985) 'Early Travels to Europe: Some Remarks on the Magic of Writing', in F. Baker (ed.) *Europe and its Others*, Vol. 1, Colchester: Essex University Press.

Harding, J. (2000) *The Uninvited: Refugees at the Rich Man's Gate*, London: Profile Books.

Hare, R.M. (1986) 'What is Wrong with Slavery?', in P. Singer (ed.) *Applied Ethics*, Oxford: Oxford University Press.

Hargreaves, A.G. (1995) *Immigration, 'Race' and Ethnicity in Contemporary France*, London: Routledge.

Harris, C. (1987) 'British Capitalism, Migration and Relative Surplus Population', *Migration*, 1: 147–90.

Harris, R.T. (1998) 'Nonviolence in Islam: The Alternative Community Tradition', in D.L. Smith-Christopher (ed.) *Subverting Hatred: The*

Challenge of Nonviolence in Religious Traditions, New York: Orbis (pp. 95–113).

Heath, A. and MacMahon, D. (1995) *Education and Occupational Attainments: the Impact of Ethnic Origins*, Paper 34, Centre for Research into Elections and Social Trends.

Henriques, J. (1984) 'Social Psychology and the Politics of Racism', in J. Henriques, W. Hollway, C. Urwin, C. Venn, and V. Walkerdine, *Changing the Subject: Psychology, Social Regulation and Subjectivity*, London: Methuen.

Herman, E.S. and Chomsky, N. (1994) *Manufacturing Consent*, London and New York: Vintage.

Herrnstein, R.J. and Murray, C. (1994) *The Bell Curve*, New York: Simon and Schuster

Hertz, F. (1928) *Race and Civilisation*, London: Kegan Paul, Trench, Trubner and Co.

Hibbert, C. (1984) *Africa Explored: Europeans in the Dark Continent*, Harmondsworth: Penguin.

Hilton, R. *et al.* (1978) *The Transition from Feudalism to Capitalism*, London: Verso.

Hirschfeld, M. (1938) *Racism*, London: Gollancz.

Historikerstreit (1987), *Die Dokumentation der Kontroverse um die Einzigartigkeit der nationalsozialistischen Judenvernichtung*, München/Zürich: Piper.

Hobsbawm, E. (1962) *The Age of Revolution*, London: Weidenfeld and Nicolson.

—— (1977) 'Some Reflections on "The Break-up of Britain"', *New Left Review*, 105: 3–23.

—— (1983) 'Introduction: Inventing Traditions', in E. Hobsbawm and T. Ranger (eds) *The Invention of Tradition*, Cambridge: Cambridge University Press.

—— (1990) *Nations and Nationalism since 1780*, Cambridge: Cambridge University Press.

Hoel, B. (1982) 'Contemporary Clothing "Sweatshops": Asian Female Labour and Collective Organisation', in J. West (ed.) *Work, Women and the Labour Market*, London: Routledge and Kegan Paul.

Holton, R.J. (1985) *The Transition from Feudalism to Capitalism*, London: Macmillan.

hooks, b. (1982) *Ain't I a Woman? Black Women and Feminism*, London: Pluto Press.

Hooton, E.A. (1947) *Up From the Ape*, New York: Macmillan.

Horsman, R. (1976) 'Origins of Racial Anglo-Saxonism in Great Britain Before 1850', *Journal of the History of Ideas*, 37 (3): 387–410.

—— (1981) *Race and Manifest Destiny: The Origins of American Racial Anglo-Saxonism*, Cambridge, Mass.: Harvard University Press.

Huntington, S.P. (1993) 'The Clash of Civilisations?', *Foreign Affairs*, 72 (3): 22–49.

—— (1998) *The Clash of Civilisations and the Remaking of World Order*, London: Touchstone.

Husband, C. (1982) 'Introduction: "Race", the Continuity of a Concept', in C. Husband (ed.) *'Race' in Britain: Continuity and Change*, London: Hutchinson.

Husbands, C. (1982) 'Contemporary Right-wing Extremism in Western European Democracies: A Review Article', *European Journal of Political Research*, 9: 75–99.

Huttenback, R.A. (1976) *Racism and Empire: White Settlers and Coloured Immigrants in the British Self-Governing Colonies 1830–1910*, Ithaca, N.Y.: Cornell University Press.

Huxley, J. and Haddon, A.C. (1935) *We Europeans: A Survey of Racial Problems*, London: Cape.

Index on Censorship (2000) Special issue on 'The New Slavery', 29 (1).

Jencks, C. and Phillips, M. (eds) (1998) *The Black–White Test Score Gap*, Washington, D.C.: Brookings Institution.

Jenkins, R. (1986) *Racism and Recruitment: Managers, Organisations and Equal Opportunity in the Labour Market*, Cambridge: Cambridge University Press.

Joly, D. (1996) *Haven or Hell? Asylum Policies and Refugees in Europe*, Basingstoke: Macmillan.

Jones, G. (1980) *Social Darwinism in English Thought: The Interaction Between Biological and Social Theory*, Brighton: Harvester Press.

Jones, J.S. (1981) 'How Different are Human Races?', *Nature*, 293: 188–90.

Jones, T. and Ereira, A. (1996) *Crusades*, London: Penguin.

Jordan, W.J. (1968) *White Over Black: American Attitudes Toward the Negro, 1550–1812*, Chapel Hill: University of North Carolina Press.

Joshi, S. and Carter, B. (1984) 'The Role of Britain in the Creation of a Racist Britain', *Race and Class*, 25, 3: 53–70.

Kabbani, R. (1986) *Europe's Myth of Orient: Devise and Rule*, London: Macmillan.

Kamin, L.J. (1977) *The Science and Politics of I.Q.*, Harmondsworth: Penguin.

—— (1999) 'Behind the Curve', in A. Montagu (ed.) *Race and IQ* (expanded edition), New York: Oxford University Press (pp. 397–407).

Katz, J.H. (1978) *White Awareness: Handbook for Anti-Racism Training*, Norman: University of Oklahoma Press.

Kay, D. and Miles, R. (1992) *Refugees or Migrant Workers? The Recruitment of Displaced Persons for British Industry 1946–1951*, London: Routledge.

Kedourie, E. (1993) *Nationalism*, London: Hutchinson.

Kiernan, V. (1972) *The Lords of Human Kind: European Attitudes to the Outside World in the Imperial Age*, Harmondsworth: Penguin.

King, M.L. (2000), *Why We Can't Wait*, New York: Signet Classic.

Kitano, H.H.L. and Daniels, R. (2001) *Asian Americans: Emerging Minorities*, Upper Saddle River, N.J.: Prentice Hall.

Knowles, L.L. and Prewitt, K. (1969) *Institutional Racism in America*, Englewood Cliffs: Prentice-Hall.

Kolchin, P. (1987) *Unfree Labour: American Slavery and Russian Serfdom*, London: Harvard University Press.

Krausnick, H., Buchheim, H., Broszat, M., and Jacobsen, H.A. (1968) *Anatomy of the SS State*, London: Collins.

Küng, H. (1978) *On Being a Christian*, Glasgow: Collins.

Lambert, H. (1995) *Seeking Asylum: Comparative Law and Practice in Selected European Countries*, Dordrecht and Boston: M. Nijhoff.

Leech, K. (1986) '"Diverse Reports" and the Meaning of "Racism"', *Race and Class*, 28 (2): 82–8.

Lewis, B. (1982) *The Muslim Discovery of Europe*, London: Weidenfeld and Nicolson.

Lloyd, C. (1998) *Discourses of Anti-Racism in France*, Aldershot: Ashgate.

Lorde, A. (1984) *Sister Outsider: Essays and Speeches*, Freedom, Cl.: The Crossing Press.

—— (1996) *Zami: A New Spelling of my Name*, London: Pandora.

Low, D.A. (1965) 'British East Africa: The Establishment of British Rule', in V. Harlow and E.M. Chiver (eds) *History of East Africa*, Vol. II, Oxford: Clarendon Press.

Lynn, R. (1991) 'Race Differences in Intelligence: A Global Perspective', *Mankind Quarterly*, 31: 255–96.

Mac an Ghaill, M. (1999) *Contemporary Racisms and Ethnicities*, Buckingham: Open University Press.

McBride, J. (1998) *The Color of Water*, London: Bloomsbury.

Macdonald, I.A. (1983) *Immigration Law and Practice in the United Kingdom*, London: Butterworths.

MacDougall, H.A. (1982) *Racial Myth in English History: Trojans, Teutons and Anglo-Saxons*, Montreal: Harvest House.

MacKenzie, J.M. (1984) *Propaganda and Empire: The Manipulation of British Public Opinion, 1880–1960*, Manchester: Manchester University Press.

Macpherson, W. (1999) *The Stephen Lawrence Inquiry: Report of an Inquiry by Sir William Macpherson of Cluny*, London: Stationery Office.

McQueen, H. (1970) *A New Britannia: An Argument Concerning the Social Origins of Australian Radicalism and Nationalism*, Victoria: Penguin.

Marx, K. (1976) *Capital, Volume 1*, Harmondsworth: Penguin.

Marx, K. and Engels, F. (1967) *The Communist Manifesto*, London: Penguin.

Maser, W. (1970) *Hitler's Mein Kampf: An Analysis*, London: Faber and Faber.

Mason, D. (1982) 'After Scarman: A Note on the Concept of Institutional Racism', *New Community*, 10 (1): 38–45.

Massey, D.S. (1986) 'The Social Organisation of Mexican Immigration to the United States', *Annals of the American Academy of Political and Social Science*, 487: 102–13.

Mattar, N.I. (1998) *Islam in Britain 1558–1685*, Cambridge: Cambridge University Press.

Miles, R. (1982) *Racism and Migrant Labour: A Critical Text*, London: Routledge and Kegan Paul.

—— (1984a) 'Marxism Versus the "Sociology of Race Relations"?', *Ethnic and Racial Studies*, 7 (2): 217–37.

—— (1984b) 'The Riots of 1958: The Ideological Construction of "Race Relations" as a Political Issue in Britain', *Immigrants and Minorities*, 3 (3): 252–75.

—— (1986) 'Labour Migration, Racism and Capital Accumulation in Western Europe Since 1945', *Capital and Class*, 28: 49–86.

—— (1987a) *Capitalism and Unfree Labour: Anomaly or Necessity?*, London: Tavistock.

—— (1987b) 'Recent Marxist Theories of Nationalism and the Issue of Racism', *British Journal of Sociology*, 38 (1): 24–43.

—— (1988) 'Beyond the "Race" Concept: The Reproduction of Racism in England', in M. de Lepervanche and G. Bottomley (eds) *The Cultural Construction of Race*, Sydney: University of Sydney Press.

—— (1992) 'Le racisme européen dans son contexte historique: réflexions sur l'articulation du racisme et du nationalisme', *Genèses*, 8: 108–31.

—— (1993) *Racism After 'Race Relations'*, London: Routledge.

Miles, R. and Dunlop, A. (1986) 'The Racialisation of Politics in Britain: Why Scotland is Different', *Patterns of Prejudice*, 20 (1): 23–32.

—— (1987) 'Racism in Britain: the Scottish Dimension', in P. Jackson (ed.) *Race and Racism*, London: George Allen and Unwin.

Miles, R. and Muirhead, L. (1986) 'Racism in Scotland: A Matter for Further Investigation', in D. McCrone (ed.) *Scottish Government Yearbook: 1986*, Edinburgh: Edinburgh University Press.

Miles, R. and Phizacklea, A. (1981) 'Racism and Capitalist Decline', in M. Harloe (ed.) *New Perspectives in Urban Change and Conflict*, London: Heinemann.

Miles, R. and Phizacklea, A. (1984) *White Man's Country: Racism in British Politics*, London: Pluto Press.

Miles, R. and Torres, R.D. (1999) 'Does "Race" Matter? Transatlantic Perspectives on Racism after "Race Relations"', in R.D. Torres, L.F. Mirón and J.X. Inda (eds) *Race, Identity and Citizenship: A Reader*, Malden, Mass. and Oxford: Blackwell (pp. 19–38).

Mirza, H.S. (ed.) (1997) *Black British Feminism: A Reader*, London: Routledge.

Mitter, S. (1986) 'Industrial Restructuring and Manufacturing Homework: Immigrant Women in the UK Clothing Industry', *Capital and Class*, 27: 37–80.

Modood, T. *et al.* (1997) *Ethnic Minorities in Britain*, London: Policy Studies Institute.

Montagu, A. (ed.) (1964) *The Concept of Race*, New York: Free Press.

—— (1972) *Statement on Race*, London: Oxford University Press.

—— (1974) *Man's Most Dangerous Myth: The Fallacy of Race*, New York: Oxford University Press.

—— (ed.) (1999) *Race and IQ* (expanded edition), New York: Oxford University Press.

Moody-Adams, M.M. (1994) 'Culture, Responsibility, and Affected Ignorance', *Ethics*, 104: 291–309.

—— (1997) *Fieldwork in Familiar Places: Morality, Culture and Philosophy*, Cambridge, Mass. and London: Harvard University Press.

Moreau, R. (1996) *The Rom: Walking the Path of the Gypsies*, Toronto: Key Porter Books.

Moscovici, S. (1981) 'On Social Representation', in J.P. Forgas (ed.) *Social Cognition: Perspectives on Everyday Understanding*, London: Academic Press.

—— (1982) 'The Coming Era of Representations', in J-P. Codol and J-P. Leyens (eds) *Cognitive Analysis of Social Behavior*, The Hague: Martinus Nijhoff.

—— (1984) 'The Phenomenon of Social Representations', in R.M. Farr and S. Moscovici (eds) *Social Representations*, Cambridge: Cambridge University Press.

Mosse, G.L. (1978) *Toward the Final Solution: A History of European Racism*, London: Dent and Sons.

Mungeam, G.H. (1966) *British Rule in Kenya: 1895–1912: The Establishment of Administration in the East Africa Protectorate*, Oxford: Clarendon Press.

Nairn, N.B. (1956) 'A Survey of the History of the White Australia Policy in the Nineteenth Century', *Australian Quarterly*, 28: 16–31.

Nairn, T. (1981) *The Break-Up of Britain*, London: Verso.

Nash, G.B. (1972) 'The Image of the Indian in the Southern Colonial Mind', in E. Dudley and M.E. Novak (eds) *The Wild Man Within: An Image in*

Western Thought from the Renaissance to Romanticism, Pittsburgh: University of Pittsburgh Press.

Newnham, A. (1986) *Employment, Unemployment and Black People*, London: Runnymede Trust.

Nielsen, J.S. (1995) *Muslims in Western Europe*, Edinburgh: Edinburgh University Press.

Novak, M.E. (1972) 'The Wild Man Comes to Tea', in E. Dudley and M.E. Novak (eds) *The Wild Man Within: An Image in Western Thought from the Renaissance to Romanticism*, Pittsburgh: University of Pittsburgh Press.

Nowikowski, S. (1984) 'Snakes and Ladders: Asian Business in Britain', in R. Ward and R. Jenkins (eds) *Ethnic Communities in Business: Strategies for Economic Survival*, Cambridge: Cambridge University Press.

Oakley, A. (1981) *Subject Women*, Oxford: Martin Robertson.

Ogden, P. (1987) 'Immigration, Cities and the Geography of the National Front in France', in G. Glebe and J. O'Loughlin (eds) *Foreign Minorities in Continental European Cities*, Stuttgart: Franz Steiner Verlag Wiesbaden.

Omi, M. and Winant, H. (1986) *Racial Formation in the United States: From the 1960s to the 1980s*, New York: Routledge and Kegan Paul.

—— (1994) *Racial Formation in the United States: From the 1960s to the 1990s* (second edition), New York: Routledge.

Palfreeman, A.C. (1972) 'The White Australia Policy', in F.S. Stevens (ed.) *Racism: The Australian Experience, Vol. 1: Prejudice and Xenophobia*, New York: Taplinger Publishing Co.

Palmer, F. (ed.) (1986) *Anti-Racism – An Assault on Education and Value*, London: Sherwood Press.

Paludan, A. (1981) 'Refugees in Europe', *International Migration Review*, 15 (1/2): 69–73.

Parekh, B. (2000) *The Future of Multi-Ethnic Britain: Report of the Commission on the Future of Multi-Ethnic Britain*, London: Profile Books.

Parmar, P. (1982) 'Gender, Race and Class: Asian Women in Resistance', in CCCS *The Empire Strikes Back: Race and Racism in 70s Britain*, London: Hutchinson.

Peach, C. (1968) *West Indian Migration to Britain*, London: Oxford University Press.

Peukert, D.J.K. (1987) *Inside Nazi Germany: Conformity, Opposition and Racism in Everyday Life*, London: Batsford.

Phillips, D. (1987) 'The Rhetoric of Anti-Racism in Public Housing Allocation', in P. Jackson (ed.) *Race and Racism: Essays in Social Geography*, London: Allen and Unwin.

Phizacklea, A. (ed.) (1983) *One-Way Ticket*, London: Routledge and Kegan Paul.

Phizacklea, A. and Miles, R. (1979) 'Working Class Racist Beliefs in the Inner City', in R. Miles and A. Phizacklea (eds) *Racism and Political Action in Britain*, London: Routledge and Kegan Paul.

—— (1980) *Labour and Racism*, London: Routledge and Kegan Paul.

Poliakov, L. (1974), *The History of Anti-Semitism*, Vol. 1, Oxford: Oxford University Press.

—— (1975) *The History of Anti-Semitism*, Vol. 3, London: Routledge and Kegan Paul.

Popkin, R.H. (1974) 'The Philosophical Basis of Modern Racism', in C. Walton and J.P. Anton (eds) *Philosophy and the Civilising Arts*, Athens: Ohio University Press.

Potts, L. (1990) *The World Labour Market: A History of Migration*, London: Zed Books.

Powell, E.J. (1969) *Freedom and Reality*, Kingswood: Paperfronts.

—— (1972) *Still to Decide*, Kingswood: Paperfronts.

Puzzo, D.A. (1964) 'Racism and the Western Tradition', *Journal of the History of Ideas*, 25 (4): 579–86.

Rath, J., Meyer, A. and Sunier, T. (1997) 'The Establishment of Islamic Institutions in a De-Pillarising Society', *Tijdschrift Voor Economische en Sociale Geografie*, 88: 389–95.

Reeves, F. (1983) *British Racial Discourse: A Study of British Political Discourse About Race and Race-Related Matters*, Cambridge: Cambridge University Press.

Rex, J. (1970) *Race Relations in Sociological Theory*, London: Weidenfeld and Nicolson.

—— (1986) *Race and Ethnicity*, Milton Keynes: Open University Press.

Rex, J. and Tomlinson, S. (1979) *Colonial Immigrants in a British City: A Class Analysis*, London: Routledge and Kegan Paul.

Reynolds, H. (1972) *Aborigines and Settlers: The Australian Experience*, Melbourne: Cassell Australia Ltd.

Rich, P.B. (1986) *Race and Empire in British Politics*, Cambridge: Cambridge University Press.

Richards, G. (1997) *'Race', Racism and Psychology: Towards a Reflexive History*, London and New York: Routledge.

Ripley, W.Z. (1900) *The Races of Europe: A Sociological Study*, London: Kegan Paul, Trench, Trubner and Co.

Robe, S.L. (1972) 'Wild Men and Spain's Brave New World', in E. Dudley and M.E. Novak (eds) *The Wild Man Within: An Image in Western Thought from the Renaissance to Romanticism*, Pittsburgh: University of Pittsburgh Press.

Roediger, D. (1994) *Towards the Abolition of Whiteness*, London: Verso.

Rose, S., Kamin, L.J., and Lewontin, R.C. (1984) *Not In Our Genes: Biology, Ideology and Human Nature*, Harmondsworth: Penguin.

Rowley, C.D. (1970) *The Destruction of Aboriginal Society*, Canberra: Australian National University Press.

Runciman, S. (1951) *A History of the Crusades*, Vol. 1, Cambridge: Cambridge University Press.

Rushton, J.P. (1997) *Race, Evolution, and Behavior*, New Brunswick, N.J.: Transaction Publishers.

Ruthven, M. (1997) *Islam: A Very Short Introduction*, Oxford: Oxford University Press.

Said, E.W. (1983) *The World, the Text and the Critic*, Cambridge, Mass.: Harvard University Press.

—— (1994) *Culture and Imperialism*, London: Vintage.

—— (1995) *Orientalism: Western Conceptions of the Orient*, London: Penguin.

—— (1997) *Covering Islam*, London: Vintage.

Sanders, R. (1978) *Lost Tribes and Promised Lands: The Origins of American Racism*, Boston: Little, Brown and Co.

Sartre, J.-P. (1943) *L'Être et le Néant: Essai d'Ontologie Phénoménologique*, Paris: Gallimard.

—— (1960) *Critique de la Raison Dialectique*, Vol. 1, Paris: Gallimard.

Saunders, K. (1982) *Workers in Bondage: The Origins and Bases of Unfree Labour in Queensland, 1824–1916*, St Lucia: University of Queensland Press.

Schoen, D.E. (1977) *Enoch Powell and the Powellites*, London: Macmillan.

Seale, B. (1970) *Seize the Time: The Story of the Black Panther Party*, London: Arrow Books.

Seidel, G. (1986) *The Holocaust Denial: Antisemitism, Racism and the New Right*, Leeds: Beyond the Pale Collective.

Sender, J. and Smith, S. (1986) *The Development of Capitalism in Africa*, London: Methuen.

Seton-Watson, H. (1977) *Nations and States: An Enquiry into the Origins of Nations and the Politics of Nationalism*, London: Methuen.

Sivanandan, A. (1973) 'Race, Class and Power: An Outline for Study', *Race*, 14 (4): 383–91.

—— (1982) *A Different Hunger: Writings on Black Resistance*, London: Pluto Press.

—— (1983) 'Challenging Racism: Strategies for the '80s', *Race and Class*, 25 (2): 1–12.

—— (1985) 'RAT and the Degradation of the Black Struggle', *Race and Class*, 26 (4): 1–34.

Small, S. (1994) *Racialised Barriers*, London: Routledge.

Smith, D.J. (1977) *Racial Disadvantage in Britain*, Harmondsworth: Penguin.

Smithies, B. and Fiddick, P. (1969) *Enoch Powell on Immigration*, London: Sphere Books.

Snowden, F.M. (1970) *Blacks in Antiquity: Ethiopians in the Greco-Roman Experience*, Cambridge, Mass.: Harvard University Press.

—— (1983) *Before Colour Prejudice: the Ancient View of Blacks*, Cambridge, Mass.: Harvard University Press.

Solomos, J. (1993) *Race and Racism in Britain*, Cambridge: Cambridge University Press.

Sorrenson, M.P.K. (1965) 'Land Policy in Kenya, 1895–1945', in V. Harlow and E.M. Chiver (eds) *History of East Africa*, Vol. II, Oxford: Clarendon Press.

—— (1968) *Origins of European Settlement in Kenya*, Nairobi: Oxford University Press.

Southern, R.W. (1962) *Western Views of Islam in the Middle Ages*, Cambridge, Mass.: Harvard University Press.

—— (1970) *Western Society and the Church in the Middle Ages*, London: Penguin.

Stanton, W. (1960) *The Leopard's Spots: Scientific Attitudes Toward Race in America, 1815–59*, Chicago: University of Chicago Press.

Stepan, N. (1982) *The Idea of Race in Science: Great Britain 1800–1960*, London: Macmillan.

Stichter, S. (1982) *Migrant Labour in Kenya: Capitalism and African Response 1895–1975*, London: Longman.

Stocking, G.W. (1968) *Race, Culture and Evolution*, New York: Free Press.

Symcox, G. (1972) 'The Wild Man's Return: The Enclosed Vision of Rousseau's Discourses', in E. Dudley and M.E. Novak (eds) *The Wild Man Within: An Image in Western Thought from the Renaissance to Romanticism*, Pittsburgh: University of Pittsburgh Press.

Taguieff, P.-A. (1987) *La Force du Préjugé*, Paris: La Découverte.

—— (1990) 'The New Cultural Racism in France', *Telos*, 83: 109–22.

—— (1995) *Les Fins de l'Antiracisme*, Paris: Michalon.

—— (2001) *The Force of Prejudice*, Minneapolis: University of Minnesota Press.

Tambs-Lyche, H. (1980) *London Patidars: A Case Study of Urban Ethnicity*, London: Routledge and Kegan Paul.

Taussig, M. (1987) *Shamanism, Colonialism, and the Wild Man*, Chicago and London: University of Chicago Press.

Taylor, S. (1982) *The National Front in English Politics*, London: Macmillan.

Thornton, A.P. (1965) *Doctrines of Imperialism*, New York: Wiley.

Tignor, R.L. (1976) *The Colonial Transformation of Kenya: The Kambu,*

Kikuyu, and Masai from 1900 to 1939, Princeton: Princeton University Press.

Troyna, B. and Williams, J. (1985) *Racism, Education and the State: The Racialisation of Education Policy*, London: Croom Helm.

Turner, B.S. (1994) *Orientalism, Postmodernism and Globalism*, London: Routledge.

Twaddle, M. (1975) *Expulsion of a Minority: Essays on Ugandan Asians*, London: Athlone Press.

UNHCR (2000) *The State of the World's Refugees 2000*, Oxford: Oxford University Press.

Unit for Manpower Studies (1977) *The Role of Immigrants in the Labour Market*, London: Department of Employment.

Van den Berghe, P.L. (1978) *Race and Racism: A Comparative Perspective*, New York: Wiley.

van Dijk, T. (1993) *Elite Discourse and Racism*, London: Sage.

—— (2000) 'Ideologies, Racism, Discourse: Debates on Immigration and Ethnic Issues', in J. ter Wal and M. Verkuyten (eds) *Comparative Perspectives on Racism*, Aldershot: Ashgate.

Volkenkundig Museum Nusantara (1986) *Met Andere Ogen: 400 Jaar Afbeeldingen van Europeanen Door Verre Volken*, Delft: Volkenkundig Museum Nusantara.

Walker, M. (1977) *The National Front*, London: Fontana.

Wallerstein, I. (1974) *The Modern World System I: Capitalist Agriculture and the Origins of the European World Economy in the Sixteenth Century*, New York: Academic Press.

—— (1995) *Historical Capitalism with Capitalist Civilisation*, London: Verso.

Walvin, J. (1973) *Black and White: The Negro and English Society 1555–1945*, London: Allen Lane.

—— (1986) *England, Slaves and Freedom, 1776–1838*, London: Macmillan.

Wellman, D. (1977) *Portraits of White Racism*, Cambridge: Cambridge University Press.

Werbner, P. (1984) 'Pakistani Entrepreneurship in the Manchester Garment Trade', in R. Ward and R. Jenkins (eds) *Ethnic Communities in Business: Strategies for Survival*, Cambridge: Cambridge University Press.

Wetherell, M. and Potter, J. (1992) *Mapping the Language of Racism: Discourse and the Legitimation of Exploitation*, New York: Columbia University Press.

White, H. (1972) 'The Forms of Wildness: Archaeology of an Idea', in E. Dudley and M.E. Novak (eds) *The Wild Man Within: An Image in Western Thought from the Renaissance to Romanticism*, Pittsburgh: University of Pittsburgh Press.

Wieviorka, M. (1995) *The Arena of Racism*, London: Sage.

Wihtol de Wenden, C. (1987) 'France's Policy on Migration from May 1981 till March 1986: Its Symbolic Dimension, Its Restrictive Aspects and Its Unintended Effects', *International Migration*, 25 (2): 211–19.

Willard, M. (1967) *History of the White Australia Policy to 1920*, Melbourne: Melbourne University Press.

Williams, J. (1985) 'Redefining Institutional Racism', *Ethnic and Racial Studies*, 8 (3): 323–48.

Williams, R.A. (1990) *The American Indian in Western Legal Thought: The Discourses of Conflict*, New York and Oxford: Oxford University Press.

Wilson, D. (1983) 'Asian Entrepreneurs: From High Street to Park Lane', *The Director*, June: 30–2.

Wright, P. (1968) *The Coloured Worker in British Industry*, Oxford: Oxford University Press.

Wrigley, C.C. (1965) 'Kenya: The Pattern of Economic Life, 1902–1945', in V. Harlow and E.M. Chiver (eds) *History of East Africa*, Vol. II, Oxford: Clarendon Press.

Yarwood, A.T. (1962) 'The "White Australia" Policy: A Reinterpretation of its Development in the Late Colonial Period', Historical Studies, 10: 257–69.

—— (1964) *Asian Migration to Australia: The Background to Exclusion 1896–1939*, Melbourne: Melbourne University Press.

Young, K. (1992) 'Approaches to Policy Development in the Field of Equal Opportunities', in P. Braham, A. Rattansi and R. Skellington (eds) *Racism and Antiracism: Inequalities, Opportunities and Policies*, London: Sage (pp. 252–69).

Zolberg, A. (1983) 'Contemporary Transnational Migrations in Historical Perspective: Patterns and Dilemmas', in M.M. Kritz (ed.) *U.S. Immigration and Refugee Policy: Global and Domestic Issues*, Lexington, Mass.: Heath.

Zolberg, A., Sergio, A. and Astri, S. (1989) *Escape from Violence*, New York: Oxford University Press.

INDEX